*The Plant Hunters*

*Also by the same author*

TYLER WHITTLE

# The Plant Hunters

*being an examination of collecting*
*with an account of the careers & the methods*
*of a number of those who have searched*
*the world for wild plants*

*Lyons & Burford, Publishers*

*Library of Congress Cataloging-in-Publication Data*

*Tyler-Whittle, Michael Sidney, 1927–1994*
*The plant hunters: being an examination of collecting, with an*
*account of the careers & the methods of a number of those who have*
*searched the world for wild plants / Tyler Whittle.*
*p. cm.*
*Originally published: Philadelphia: Chilton Book Co., [1970].*
*Includes bibliographical references and index.*
*ISBN 1-55821-592-1 (pbk.)*
*1. Plant collectors—History. 2. Plants—Collection and*
*preservation—History. 3. Botanists—Biography. I. Title.*
*QK15.T95 1997*
*580'.75—dc21 97-15137 CIP*

*Foreword*

LANT hunters are treasure hunters at heart. Having always suspected this, after reading Tyler Whittle's *The Plant Hunters* I know that it's true. How else do you explain the monomania, the mad enthusiasm, the physical bravery, the obliviousness to danger (as well as to rain, snow, unfriendly natives, rock slides, bad cooking, boredom, and all the rest)? You don't have to be crazy to be a plant hunter or to spend a lifetime looking for King Solomon's Mines, but it helps.

Take, for example, the case of Philibert de Commerson, the eighteenth-century French plant hunter and selfconfessed "botanomaniac." In the words of his biographer, "The mere suspicion of a plant unknown to him was an irresistible attraction." He was wont to travel by himself, "taking with him hardly any money or provisions," returning home "sick, scarred with wounds, shaken by falls and accidents of all kinds, as well as utterly worn out by his exertions and by the violence of his own enthusiasm." Nor was Commerson particularly exceptional. "Good God!" wrote the great Swedish botanist Linnaeus, "When I consider the melancholy fate of so many of [botany's] votaries I am tempted to ask whether men are in their right minds who so desperately risk life and everything else through their love of collecting plants."

Linnaeus's gloomy reflections might serve as an epigraph to *The Plant Hunters*, except for one thing: As any gardener knows, or should know, the frantic exertions of men like Philibert de Commerson actually paid off. They found their treasures, and passed them on for our delight. Our gardens would be infinitely poorer and more boring places today had they not scoured the far reaches of the earth for rare and unknown plants, and made them our beautiful commonplaces.

There have been many books about plant hunters, notleast because the hunters themselves—if they survived—seem to have enjoyed writing about their adventures. Some of these books still make good reading, though not all; a man capable of fording an icy river and clambering a vertical two-mile-high cliff face in a search of an elusive pulsatilla is not necessarily a fluent writer. Some who have tried have distinctly failed; Joseph Rock, a distinguished plant hunter who spent most of his life exploring and botanizing in western China, was the despair of editors at the *National Geographic* who had to make sense out of his articles. "He can do more to confuse readers," one fumed, "than any contributor whose work has ever come to my attention anywhere. [He] complains that we 'change his meaning.' If this ever occurred, it was because no one could tell what he meant."

All the more reason, therefore, to welcome Tyler Whittle's crisp account of plant hunting through the ages, the attempt, as he puts it, "of an arm-chair plant hunter to share his own pleasure in the chase." Erudite, appreciative, and funny, it does splendid justice to the travails and achievements of such men as Joseph Hooker, E. H. "Chinese" Wilson, William Dampier (who combined botany with piracy), David Douglas, and dozens of others.

Michael Sidney Tyler-Whittle, to give him his actual full name, was in some ways more elusive than his subjects. Born in Norfolk in 1927, the son of an archdeacon, he read English literature at Cambridge University and for a time intended to become a barrister. From 1944 to 1947 he was in the Royal Marines, returning to Cambridge to teach English; while there, he decided to enter the church and took orders as an Anglican priest. A short spell as a college chaplain led to appointment as rector of a parish church in

Norfolk, but the climate defeated him—he suffered from asthma—and he beat a retreat to a farm called Aquabona near Ravello in Italy, to which he would return regularly during the rest of his life. (One of his favorite hobbies was smuggling Italian plants back to England for trial, and vice versa.)

Whittle was a wonderful storyteller, and all his books—novels, children's books, histories, gardening and botanical books—show his taste for a good yarn. Writing apparently came easily to him, and he usually had a couple of books underway. In later years, after he married and returned from Italy to take up parishes in Staffordshire and Kent, he made a practice of setting aside two days a week to settle down at a table in the library of the Athenaeum club in London to research and write. Doubtful about how his parishioners would regard this activity, he made a point of employing an array of obfuscatory pen names. For the same reason, he flatly refused to take part in any promotion activities for his books.

A bit of a throwback to an eighteenth-century "squarson," Whittle was fond of most outdoor sports, from fox-hunting (later given up) to fishing, walking, sailing, and horse racing. In the fifties he achieved some note with a regular BBC radio program on country matters. In spite of his scholarly bent he was intensely sociable (the American writer Gore Vidal, whom he first met in Italy, became a lifelong friend and correspondent), and proudly admitted keeping every letter he ever received.

Among his many interests, however, botany probably ranked highest. Whittle always enjoyed collecting plants. In his book *Common or Garden* he describes how, starting as a schoolboy, he made a collection of European orchids, and took particular delight in learning a method for preserving their colors before drying (it involved smoking the blooms with a sulfur candle). Self-trained in plant science, he was nevertheless able to range with surprising authority into the technical aspects of the subject. When he died in 1994 he was midway through the compilation of a large work, *The Genus Rosa*, for Oxford University Press.

But for those ordinary readers like me, it is Whittle's fascination with what he calls "the truly astounding exploits of the great plantsmen of the past" that make books such as *The Plant Hunters* precious. Such exploits they were! Thanks to Whittle I can now picture David Douglas (of Douglas fir fame) setting off on an extended journey into a complete wilderness carrying nothing—even a change of clothes—but 102 pounds of paper for drying and packing the plants he expected to find. Or if that's too heroic, consider the vision of Joseph Hooker solving the problem of extricating a hopelessly frozen lichen from a rock on a Patagonian mountainside. He sat on it until it thawed.

—Charles Elliott
London, 1997

*Acknowledgments*

NDEBTEDNESS for the gift or loan of photocopies and for the generously given permission for their reproduction as illustrations is hereby acknowledged to Mr. A. R. Waterston, Keeper of the Department of Natural History in the Royal Scottish Museum, for No. 10, to the Honble. Mrs. Clive Pearson of Parham for No. 14, and to Dr. H. R. Fletcher, Regius Keeper of the Royal Botanic Garden, Edinburgh for No's. 28, 29 and 30; and, for permitting the reproduction of their copyright material at no charge, he is indebted to the Council of the Linnean Society of London for No's. 7 and 9, to the Director, the Arnold Arboretum of Harvard University for No's. 23, 24, 25, 26 and 27, and to the Controller of Her Majesty's Stationery Office and the Director of the Royal Botanic Gardens, Kew for No's. 2, 11, 20 and 21. For advice and help in finding material for illustrations he is grateful to Miss Mea Allen, whose books *The Tradescants* and *The Hookers of Kew* were stores of information, to Mr. R. Desmond, Librarian at the Royal Botanic Gardens, Kew, to Miss Sandra Raphael, formerly Librarian and Archivist to the Linnean Society of London, and to Mr. Ian Lyster of the Department of Natural History in the Royal Scottish Museum.

Formal acknowledgment is also made to the following for license to reproduce copyright photographs: the Radio Times Hulton Picture Library for No's. 1, 18 and 19; the Director, the Royal Botanic Gardens, Kew, for No's. 12, 16, 17 and 22; the Ashmolean, Oxford for No. 3; the National Gallery, London for No's. 4, 5 and 6; the Director, the Rachel McMasters Miller Hunt Botanical Library, Pittsburgh, for No. 8; and the Missouri Botanical Garden (and Claude Johnston) for No. 13.

The author is also much obliged to Mr. Euan Cox of Glencarse in Perthshire, the plant hunter who accompanied Farrer on his last expedition, both for his fascinating history *Plant Hunting in China,* which was an invaluable source of information, and for kindly giving permission to quote from his book *The Plant Introductions of Reginald Farrer;* to Mr. Rolla Rowse of Hasketon in Suffolk for help with particulars about Margary, Forrest and the Chinese province of Yunnan; and to Signor and Signora Pinto Antonio for providing a workroom in their garden at Castiglione di Ravello.

*Author's note*

 COMPREHENSIVE history of botanical exploration has never been attempted, and this
potted study makes no claim to merit the
description. It is, rather, a brief explanation
of why, how and where some plants have
been collected, with an account of a few of
the better known collectors. The size and unwieldiness of
the subject called for such selection and reduction and, as a
matter of convenience, it has been looked at as though
through the wrong end of a telescope: to make the picture
less detailed, much smaller, and yet still clear. It is the
attempt of an armchair plant hunter to share his own
pleasure in the chase.

*To Bridget*

# ❧ The Contents

# ❧ *Introduction*

*On the Powers of Plants*

*The Nature of Plant Collectors and Their Motives for Collecting: the Intrinsic Worth of Plants: Rarity Value: Dahlia and Tulip Lunacy: Botanical Curiosities: Caste Marks and Economic Plants.*

ELL over two hundred years have passed since Linnaeus, Professor of Botany at the Swedish University of Uppsala, took exception to the fact that though deeds of gallantry in his own science were by no means inferior to those of "kings, heroes and emperors," they were denied an equal share of honor and immortality; and with the somber seriousness of his race he inquired: "What labor is more severe, what science more wearisome, than botany?"

This may have been true then. It might still be true of those scientists and enthusiasts who are capable of botanical gallantry. The rest of us—the large number of fringe-botanists—are not required to make such sacrifices. Collecting, sketching, photographing, making herbariums, sowing and planting are continual sources of pleasure; the actual science of botany, a continual source of surprise; the history of our hobby, a continual source of interest.

Being a specialized occupation, botanical collecting has had its professionals; men hired by botanic gardens, horticultural societies, governments interested in economic plants, and syndicates of private gardeners. But the amateurs, mostly with a primary occupation like missionaries, consular officials and supercargos, and others with private means, have also made great contributions to the artificial redistribution of plants.

Among them were many fascinating characters: a few Don Quixotes, some sensation seekers and remittance men;

the good, the brave, the knaves, the bad, the mad; those greedy for fame or cash returns; those who were as restless as Noah's raven going to and fro. And over each of them plants have cast certain spells.

Some have been collected simply because of their intrinsic worth. Lilies, for example, have an obvious attraction; to the Oriental as table delicacies equaling chanterelles in flavor; to the Occidental as undisputed beauties associated from antiquity with virginity and sepulchers, with religious cults and royal dynasties. To find and possess lilies has spurred men to exploits which, depending on one's point of view, could only be described as heroic or utterly foolhardy.

One of the greatest of collectors, Ernest Wilson, almost gave his life for the regal lily which he introduced to the West from a single desolate valley high in the Chinese province of Szechuan. He and his coolies were returning from the valley through wild hill country where the track was narrow and avalanches not uncommon, when a boulder suddenly dropped from the hillside above them and broke his leg in two places. His description is remarkably detached, but we may imagine his unenviable position; suffering greatly from the fractures, still many days' journey from the nearest medical help and attended only by coolies who would have deserted him if they had thought it worth their while. And no sooner had a splint been improvised from his camera tripod than a fresh hazard confronted him in the shape of a mule train traveling in the opposite direction. It was a large train of fifty mules and the track was too narrow for them to be turned. Nor could the train wait while Wilson's party edged its way, one at a time, past each mule in turn because streams of falling pebbles augured another avalanche.

Wilson was rigid with pain but still conscious. It was imperative for him to get to a doctor without delay; moreover, he knew it was impossible to go back. A dangerous solution suggested itself. He told his men to lay him across the narrow track. Then, one by one, the fifty mules stepped over him. Fortunately they were surefooted beasts, but it must have been a nerve-tearing experience.

Wilson's coolies then carried him on a three days' forced march to the nearest missionary post. Every jig and jog must have hurt him. Carried at an energetic speed over rough tracks and paths in an unsprung traveling-chair for seventy-two hours would have been the equivalent of a medieval racking. He lived through it, only to be told by the missionary that gangrene had set in and the leg needed to be amputated. Either heroism—or sheer stubbornness—made him refuse to accept this advice and, though he lived to say "I told you so," the infection atrophied and thereafter one leg was shorter than the other. This gave him what he sometimes called his "Lily limp." Such pain and a minor deformity seem a high price to pay for seven thousand lily bulbs, but so great were the powers of this particular plant that Wilson considered it worthwhile. And lily lovers would agree.

The intrinsic worth of plants at once attracts collectors. If they are rare, as well, they have a second kind of value. The magic of untrodden summits, speed records, possessing the only known specimen of a postage stamp, exercising the *Droit de Seigneur,* all share the attraction of singularity and rarity, but none can have caused such furore as once-rare plants.

The Dahlia's history is strange. Its origin can be traced to Mexico, where the Aztecs called it *Cocoxochitl,* and, in the year of the French Revolution, tubers were sent over to a French priest who was chief gardener at the Escorial. He named it after a leading botanist, Dr. Dahl, but he was less interested in the flowers than in the tubers which he thought might make a tolerable alternative to the potato. The plant, however, became the cause of much envy among those who saw it in bloom in the Escorial gardens. Then, either a gardener was bribed or a plant bandit was unusually successful. A few tubers found their way to Paris where they were sold to the Jardin des Plantes, but, being put in a hothouse, the tubers promptly rotted away. The same thing happened to a number of specimens sent directly from Mexico to England. They were over-cossetted and went into a decline. From seeds or tubers—it is not known which—Napoleon's Josephine managed to grow Dahlias at Malmaison, and she was exceedingly jealous of her collection. Only her hands planted and weeded and generally cared for the imperial Dahlias, until she had so many plants that it was necessary to put a gardener in charge of them. Inevitably, corruption followed. One of her ladies-in-waiting who had asked for a tuber and who had received a curt refusal was determined to outdo her royal mistress' collection. Her lover, a melancholy Polish prince, was ordered to steal sufficient tubers from Malmaison. He did not attempt it himself, but instead bribed the gardener to carry off a hundred roots. When she heard of it the Empress was outraged. She dismissed the gardener and the lady-in-waiting, exiled the melancholy Pole from court, had all her Dahlias chopped up and dug in, and never again would hear the plant named in her presence. It was an expensive gesture because Dahlias were very valuable indeed until, from a third source, that is, from Mexico through Berlin, they were developed and became more common and cheaper. In 1836, a flower bed of growing plants in good condition was bought for 70,000 francs, and a single tuber was exchanged for a diamond. *Cocoxochitl,* the bright Mexican weed, had come far.

The enthusiasm for rare tulips at an earlier period was more manic still, and was a powerful stimulant to plant hunters and gardeners of the day.

The cult had two centers: in the Near East where the tulip was the flower of the royal house of Ozman and the Persian symbol of love, and in the trim flats of the Netherlands. Bulbs were sent from Turkey to Vienna in the equivalent of the diplomatic bag, and in time the Netherlands grasped the heart of the market which to this day Holland has never relaxed.

Plant hunters scoured the Levant for wild species. Hybridizers went to extraordinary lengths to produce novelties and were so successful that abruptly—and, curiously, in the middle of the Thirty Years' War, the most bloody war ever fought—the mania erupted and tulips became articles of general trade. Speculators met to bargain at the house of the Van der Beurse family in Bruges (from which the Bourse had its name), and they even traded in "paper tulips," that is, bulbs that did not yet exist but were promised by a signed certificate. More than ten million "paper tulips" exchanged hands in this way. The real articles were sold in public marts or, in the case of extremely valuable bulbs, by private treaty.

The strangest tales have been told about transactions in the private tulip trade: how one bulb was paid for with a carriage and pair, and yet another with twelve acres of land; how a merchant in Haarlem paid a fortune for a rare bulb and then, discovering that a nearby cobbler had a tulip of precisely the same color, bullied the cobbler into parting with his bulb for fifteen hundred florins, then stamped on it before his eyes. The cobbler, who liked tulips, was dismayed. But it was only when, callously, the merchant told him he had been quite ready to pay ten times as much that the poor man realized the full extent of his loss and went and hanged himself.

There is also a singular story which, because it emanates from many different sources, may well be true. It shows the practical perils of trading in such a perishable and expensive item. One Dutch importer was so delighted to hear that a shipment of tulips had arrived in record time from the Levant that he gave the messenger who brought the news a handsome tip and some red herrings for his supper. The messenger was a seaman, and not overblessed with brains. On his way out of the warehouse he saw what he took to be an onion lying among the costly silks and velvets, and he decided that it would serve as a good relish to the red herrings. It happened to be a *Semper Augustus*, worth about 3,000 guilders, and his supper cost the seaman half a year in jail.

It was with some reason that the English poet Crabbe wrote:

*With all his phlegm it broke a Dutchman's heart*
*At a vast price with one lov'd root to part.*

Like the South Sea bubble, the tulip bubble was bound to burst. On April 27, 1637, a law came into force which obliged tulip contracts in the Low Countries to be fully met like any other civil contract. Confidence in tulips waned. One speculator who had been enjoying an annual income of over sixty thousand florins did not get out in time. Within four years he had lost palaces, carriages, pleasure grounds, and friends. As a beggar in Antwerp he became a living, cautionary tale.

Tulip lunacy subsided for a time, to emerge in an exotic form in eighteenth-century Turkey. There the sultan competed with his grand vizier in the splendor of their tulip *fêtes champêtres*. In one, held at night, the thousands of tulips were embellished by small, colored lamps carried slowly through the beds on the backs of living tortoises. And, to add a further delight, caged birds sang above the tulip beds, eunuch gardeners uttered shrill cries to entertain the guests, and a Turkish band played noisily from behind movable screens of shrubs. Really it is surprising that Schubert did not compose a "Tulip Time"!

By the early nineteenth century American tulip growers began to flood the London market. So many sound bulbs were introduced that their price dropped to within the reach of workingmen. They were added to the sextet of florists' flowers, and "florist" here is not used to describe the shopkeepers and costermongers who simply trade in flowers, but immigrant weavers from the Continent and, after them, English artisans who brightened their otherwise drab lives by growing, developing and specializing in certain flowers—and, later, in gooseberries, parsnips and leeks. Their devotion to the tulip was remarkable. Authentic cases have been recorded of young enthusiasts dying of cold through placing their blankets as a guard against frost over their tulip beds.

By 1849 there was a national tulip show in England and there were three principal sections which must have intrigued as well as mystified nonfanciers.

*Byblomens with bottoms white or nearly so; Bizarres with a yellow ground, broken into a variety of colours; and Roses, with very perfect cups, cherry, and white, and rose bottoms.*

Beyond the clear claim of some plants to captivate collectors with beauty or rarity each plant has a claim to the attention of a botanist. The existence of thousands of withered, flattened collections of pressed flowers testifies to this, as do the herbaria of botanical and science museums. There is living evidence of a kind in all recreated habitats out-of-doors or housed under glass. The *doline* in the Cambridge Botanic Garden illustrates how well it can be done professionally—a keyhole-shaped hole dug in the ground and planted on all sides with plants only found in the Krast country of Jugoslavia. There are plenty of amateurs' gardens of a like character where flower-struck gardeners or science-struck botanists plant their favorite specimens.

To the botanist, a vegetable curiosity is especially worth hunting out. It followed that when the English horticulturalist, John Claudius Loudon, found a specimen of eelgrass in nineteenth-century Venice he was overjoyed and determined to carry it himself all the way back to England. Eelgrass is neither striking in beauty nor particularly rare, but at that time it had not been introduced into England and, as a half-hardy aquatic with a bizarre method of reproducing itself, it had a scientific interest which captivated Loudon. He carried the eelgrass in a tin can over the Alps and on to Paris. There, his hotel bedroom being stuffy and thinking the plant would enjoy a little fresh air, he put the can outside on the window ledge. He roped it down to guard against the awful calamity of it being blown off the ledge and, confident that all was well, he went to bed.

All was not well.

Like southern Italians who casually name the rarest of wild plants *insalata,* Loudon's eelgrass was merely a tasty bit of greenery to the sparrows of Paris. During the night it disappeared, presumably going the way of the Dutch seaman's "onion," and a mourning Loudon carried his empty can back to England as the only trophy of what he thought might have been something of a botanical triumph. However, he was a little consoled to discover that the eelgrass had been introduced to England only a few months before.

Certain plants have another, more disreputable power to attract collectors; that is when society makes them into caste marks. It is for this reason that orchid lovers have always been less numerous than orchid growers and orchid wearers. Since the Industrial Revolution the exotic, tropical orchid has been a status symbol, a fact heavily emphasized by Frederick Boyle who wrote in his book, *About Orchids,* in 1893: "the plant was expressly designed to comfort the elect of human beings in this age."

In order to meet the demand for more and more and more, orchid hunters went to unprecedented lengths, being prepared to travel far through unmapped and dangerous country simply on the hint that a new species or a considerable colony of others might be at the end of their journey; razing thousands of forest trees to the ground in order to collect the epiphytic orchids which lived like birds in their branches; denuding great areas of orchid stocks, in some cases actually removing all trace of a species from its original habitat so that it continued to exist only in captivity; * concealing the whereabouts of colonies by using cabalistic symbols (which meant nothing to anyone else) on their

* In 1847, *Laelia elegans* grew naturally and abundantly on a small island off Brazil. Collectors then said they had never seen such a mass of plants. By 1897, not a single, living specimen remained.

orchid maps and, in some cases, leaving forged maps about in the hope they would be copied secretly and rival collectors sent off on a wild-goose chase.

Side by side with the collecting, hybridizers and breeders worked intensively at home. Propagation was neither easy nor speedy until the recent development of the meristerm system, but nurserymen concentrated on the job of meeting the demand. At the time of the Boer War one English orchid grower had a stock of over ten thousand plants. Another sold his entire stock to an American syndicate for £24,000. † The sale of collections and single specimens was a new excitement in the staid auction rooms of New York, Paris and London. When the long sought-after orchid, *Dendrobium schroederi,* was sold at Protheroe's in London the salesrooms were packed because it was a condition of sale that, in order to pacify the native tribe which had first owned the orchid, the human skull in which it grew had to be bought as well. Such an unusual flowerpot has never been auctioned before or since.

The power to attract hunters of such a remarkable flower as the tropical orchid was very evident. It stood for so much. To some hunters, finding an unknown species was the pinnacle of all their professional ambitions. To the romantic adventurers among their number, orchid hunting was living out a *King Solomon's Mines* existence. To far, far more the orchid was loot. And quite naturally. Meeting a public demand required the expertise of professionals, and marauding adventurers will speedily attach themselves to any profit-making enterprise.

Economic plants have a special importance. They are or can be green treasure to national economics. A firstclass example was Kew's successful smuggling of rubber seeds from Brazil, which, ultimately, was highly profitable to the British government.

The export of such a valuable economic plant as one that produced sap which half-hardened and bounced was

† Roughly equivalent in value to £151,500 ($367,273) today.

prohibited by the Brazilian authorities. There was one way round it. A botanist was sent out from Kew on a "scientific expedition." Among his collections was a large supply of rubber seeds. Speed in transport was essential to keep them viable. The Victorians never, if ever, did things by halves and he promptly chartered a steamer, the *Amazonas,* in the name of the government of India to carry his "botanic collections" directly to London from the Amazon. It was an impressive gesture. The Brazilian customs official noted it. He was charmed, too, to receive a courtesy call from the British consul together with this extravagant charterer of steamers. They invited his assistance in the export of a collection of exotic Brazilian plants for Her Brittanic Majesty's Royal Botanic Gardens at Kew. Queen Victoria, they assured him, would be inexpressibly delighted to see the floral beauties of his country. They left with the necessary clearance papers, and within an hour the *Amazonas* was steaming out of Pará harbor with her precious cargo of seventy thousand rubber seeds.

A few (only about 3,000) germinated at Kew to grow into seedlings. Less than two thousand of these proved robust and healthy enough to be reared and shipped out to Burma and the Malay Archipelago, but there they became the parents of all the rubber trees in the Far East, founders of a great industry and living proof that national dishonesty on a large scale can sometimes pay dividends.

These records of successes should not be taken as an indication that plant hunting invariably has met with such rewards. It has not. Nor should it be thought that the pursuit of plants was ever an easy and comfortable undertaking because, with the exception of the case of Ernest Wilson, the demands it made upon plant hunters, so far, have not been underlined. In the main, they were intrepid, as the following pages will make clear.

# 𝕽 Part One
# Collecting in Pre-Wardian Days
# from 1482 B.C.

### one / Old Civilizations, the Dark and Middle Ages

*Ancient Chinese Gardenmaking: the Putative Age of Certain Plants: an Expedition to the Land of Punt: the gardens of Persia and Media: Trade in Spices and some Flowering Plants: Aristotle-Theophrastus, Dioscorides and Pliny: Roman Excesses: Haphazard and Crude Systematic Botanizing in the Dark and Middle Ages: Albertus Magnus.*

### two / The Renaissance

*The Tyranny and Limitations of the Ancient Greeks: Dr. von Cube's Expedition of 1485: Bock, Brunfels and Fuchs in Germany: von Gesner in Switzerland: Turner in England: Mattioli's successes in Italy: Busbecq at the court of Suleiman the Magnificent: Dodoens, l'Obel and l'Ecluse from the Netherlands.*

### three / English Collectors of the Orangery Era

*Royal Gardeners: Herbalists and Apothecaries: some Distinguished Collectors of Wild Plants: the Infectious Passion for the Orange and 'Choice Greens': John Evelyn's Influence: Patrons and Plant Hunting Parsons: a Bloodthirsty Botanist*

### four / The Golden Age of Botany

*Three representative and illustrious botanical collectors—Linnaeus of Sweden, John Bartram of Philadelphia and Philibert de Commerson from the Dombes*

### five / Kew and Cathay

*Sir Joseph Banks and the Kew Collectors: Masson, Nelson and Caley: Gardening in the Orient: Dutch and English East India Companies: Stringent Restrictions on the activities of Foreign*

*Merchants in China and Japan: Macartney's Mission to Peking:
Kerr and Livingstone: Lord Amherst's Embassy: John Reeves,
Chief Inspector of Tea: the Russian Imperial Ecclesiastical Mis-
sion: some small collecting successes in Japan: and looking West*

## six / David Douglas of Scone

*Learning Gardening and Botany at Scone Palace and Valleyfield:
the Patronage of Sir William Hooker: Douglas' first trip to the
eastern states of North America: with Scouler to the Western
Seaboard: "The Grassman" travels 10,000 miles in two years—
his privations and triumphs: Douglas' return to, and hatred of
London: his third and last Expedition to North America: from
the Colombia Region to California: Don David the Weed-
Gatherer: the end of a Russian Proposal: to the Sandwich Islands and Douglas' death on Hawaii*

REHISTORY often wears a mad "through the looking-glass" aspect. For instance, Europe, in many ways, was the exact opposite of what it is today. The site of Rome and all the great central plain of Italy lay at the bottom of a sea. Where England is now there was once an ice-cold ocean, its surface so thickly packed with floating islands that they jostled one another. The Harz Mountains were islands, too; and what are now the islands of the Greek archipelago were the hills and mountain peaks of a lush plain grazed by the rhinoceros and the hairy mastodon.

What these beasts grazed on is only partially known. There is geological information about certain prehistoric plants, but it is slender. The rose fossils, for example, found in Oregon and Colorado are at least thirty-two million years old. However, the data lies beyond the province of this inquiry for no one can know whether or not there was plant hunting in paleolithic times. Maybe, one day, cave drawings will be discovered which record that among the usual scenes of primitive husbandry, concupiscence and the chase, man had the wisdom to search out economic plants. Until then we may conjecture that he lacked that wisdom.

Even within history some of the earliest known facts are fairly bizarre; few more so than that five thousand years ago the Chinese had fine gardens with pagodas, aviaries, torrents, mist-covered mountains, still lagoons, formalized bridges, and artificial islands of "youth eternal" and "never-ending content." This was long before any sort of civilization had begun to seep into Europe through the keyhole of Crete, and the Chinese Emperor Chin Ming was cultivating roses and other flowers when the Greeks had not even reached Greece.

Such facts, considered however calmly, are still astounding. Equally so is the age—or putative age—of certain living plants. That some of the swamp cypresses seen today in the United States were actually mature when Moses was inundating Egypt with locusts, blood, boils and frogs, gives them a weird aura. Their antiquity is shared by the great redwoods of California which were already hoary with age when Caesar was assassinated on the Ides of March.

Equally difficult to appreciate is that the first recorded plant-hunting expedition took place when Athens, Rome, Paris and London were nonexistent. It was mounted by Hatshepsut, Queen of Egypt,* who wanted frankincense, the gum of a tree now called *Boswellia* after Dr. Johnson's randy biographer. It grew on the shores of East Africa, the Land of Punt, and five ships sailed south to return with quantities of seeds and plants, many *Boswellias* and other living trees. Thirty-one of the trees were successfully established in the queen's temple gardens at Karnak where an official record was carved on the walls to mark the success of the expedition.

It was from the sunbaked land of Sumer at the mouths of the Tigris and Euphrates, and from Egypt on the Nile, that Western civilization drew its origins. It was from these sources, as well, that Westerners drew their love of flowering plants. Persia and Media, in particular, had a profound influence on the gardenmakers of the West. The Persian love of trees, their parks (*paradeios*) where fountains played and carefully bred deer cropped nurtured herbage, their enclosed oasis gardens, and their vast rose gardens

---

* A thousand years before, in 2,500 B.C., a pharaoh named Sankhkere had sent a fleet down the Red Sea to search for supplies of prepared spices, but it could not properly be described as a plant-hunting expedition.

fathered imitations which can be seen today in places as far apart as Hull and Honolulu.

As man grew in sophistication, his need to douse bad smells and flavors was met by merchants who traded in spices over the ancient caravan routes. And certain plants, aromatic or fragrant, or simply decorative also were included in the freight.

Violets were required because they were the basis of Persian sherbet and the main constituent of a sybaritic Roman dish described by Apicius as "violets fried with slices of lemon and orange." They also were used extensively as chaplets all through Greece and Magna Graecia.*

Rose roots were traded, too, between Rome and the rose nurseries of Greece at Cyrene and the far-off nurseries in Persia and Afghanistan. Besides being used as decoration —for carpets and pillow covers—and as cushion stuffing, they were drunk as rose wine, bathed in as rose water, and eaten as rose jelly, rose honey, candied rose petals, and a Roman rose pudding which included among other ingredients, calves' brains, pepper, eight eggs, and oil.

Certainly the peony traveled from East to West. Pliny the Elder called it the oldest of all cultivated flowers and it had been growing in China for centuries before his time. Even today it is still so much an essential part of China that it appears on their postage stamps.

Who first collected the different species of these genera is not known, but it may be taken as a certainty that they were not professionals. In large degree the first plant collectors were amateurs.

In time there was a need for some sort of catalog of plants. China had her ancient, though far from complete *Materia Medica,* but no sort of list had been drawn up in the West.

Then, in the fourth century B.C., Aristotle began his

---

* Pindar's descriptive adjective for Athens was "the violet-crowned" and chaplets of violets were always on sale in the Athenian markets even in the depths of winter.

observations of nature. His two botanical works were lost—
and what were called "Aristotle's Works" were really a
summary of the originals written by one of his pupils, Theophrastus. Moreover, the 450-page summary passed through
other hands and languages; being translated from Greek
into Syrian, from that into Arabic, then into Latin, and
finally (as late as 1350) being translated back into Greek as
"Aristotle's Works."

Four hundred years after Theophrastus, Dioscorides,
physician to Antony and Cleopatra, wrote a descriptive list
of six hundred medicinal plants. It was to have a massive
influence on botany for over a thousand years, as did the
writings of Pliny the Elder who was so passionate a naturalist that scientific curiosity caused him to investigate Vesu-
vius in erruption and, as a result, to be immolated to a
cinder.

Aristotle's pupil, Alexander the Great, demonstrated
that foreign campaigns could be useful to the plantsman.
From his eastern wars Europe gained the double yellow
Persian rose and the Lombardy poplar. And soldiers of all
nationalities, as well as common sailors, merchants and
other travelers, carried plants from place to place either
because they were beautiful, good to eat or useful as medicines or, in the case of imperial legionaries on a tour of duty
abroad, simply because they were reminders of home. In
this way the Madonna Lily spread from Roman camp to
Roman camp right through Europe—as a wound herb for
surgeons' use and as a nostalgic souvenir of home to the
cohorts under their care. In this way, too, among many
other esculents, the cucumber and radish traveled north to
feed and please the Roman administrators who ruled Britain for over five hundred years. Within degree, all these and
many more collectors could be described as "amateur plant
hunters."

A general interest in plants, like scientific curiosity and
many other things, fell into desuetude when the Goths initi-
ated the Dark Ages. By then cultivating herbs had become a
medical affair, the job of monks and apothecaries' assist-

ants, and herbals such as *Bald's Leech Book* were written with more romance than fact between their covers. But the English paid small attention to flowering plants or any sort of gardening from the time Rome withdrew her legions until the Norman Conquest. Then, true to the long-established tradition which allies horticulture and the clergy, priests from Normandy reintroduced gardens and the art of cultivating flowering plants to their fellow-priests in England.

The great Charlemagne was a noted, royal plantsman. Crusaders carried home herbs from the Holy Land to sweeten their dirty castles in Western Europe. Pilgrims, scalds, troubadours, pedlars and other adventurous travelers collected and added to the store of known plants. But more and more it became the province of Churchmen to maintain supplies of plants, to study them systematically and record their observations. One of the most remarkable was Albertus Magnus who lived from 1193 to 1280. He stood out among medieval botanists as a moon against night lights and deserves examination as a worthy representative of prerenaissance plant hunters.

Albertus' long life, if nothing else, marked him as unusual. To live eighty-seven years in a period when very few people reached the age of fifty was in itself an accomplishment. And he was one of those rare beings who juggle their waking time, managing three men's work in a day, and showing proficiency in many arts and skills. Added to all this he was a most uncomplicated, humble man, and he had an ear for anyone.

Precise information was a rare commodity in his day. News traveled slowly and was embroidered on the way. It accounts, perhaps, for the fact that minor contradictions and inconsistencies appear in the recorded events of Albertus' career. But they are small and do not amount to much. On the bare bones of his long and colorful life every authority would agree.

He was very tiny and like that other famous dwarf, Toulouse-Lautrec, he had a title—Count of Bollstädt—but, unlike Lautrec, he was merely little and not at all deformed.

He went to Padua where the university authorities were sufficiently enlightened to produce the first botanic garden in the world and he enjoyed being a student. Formal disputations and informal talk helped to satisfy his natural inquisitiveness and his great thirst for knowledge. The average student applied himself to theology and philosophy and left it at that. Not so Albertus. He mastered the set curriculum and then his inquiring mind took him to investigate other matters—trees, plants, stones, beasts, fishes, the stars and the elements. He believed they deserved close scrutiny as parts of God's creation.

In time he became a Dominican friar, teaching in the schools of Germany and France, and inspiring Thomas Aquinas at the University of Paris. Fortunately for natural history his teaching career was brought to a temporary halt when he was elected a provincial of his order and he had the responsibility of visiting and inspecting each monastery in the province. By a strict application of his vow of poverty, he walked everywhere on foot and, as a result, he botanized over large parts of Northern Europe, his eyes so open for natural history specimens that he became an expert in zoology and mineralogy as well as botany. It was something of a feat of endurance and, in view of the violence of the age, it was a miracle that he managed to survive it at all. To wander, collecting, over tracks and roads infested with cutthroats and live to write seven long volumes on natural history showed that he was particularly blessed.

Albertus' name was soon well known. His wisdom and intellectual brilliance were in demand by his order, by the universities and by contending parties who trusted him as a mediator. Eventually he was offered an attractive post of lecturing in Rome, but no sooner had he established himself than the pope decided he was just the man to send on a delicate mission to Poland. The Poles were early practitioners of euthanasia. Crippled children and the unwanted old were snuffed out, and often eaten. Albertus was charged to make a firm stand against this piece of Baltic barbarism. This he did with great success, and, botanizing his way back to Rome, asked to be allowed to retire to his cell and there contemplate the splendors of God's creation and the certainty of his own speedy end. After all, he was sixty-seven.

The pope was clearly a man of vision. Not only did he refuse Albertus' request, but he made him Bishop of Regensburg.

It was on this famous occasion that the smallness of the new bishop was made evident—for the Holy Father was considerately telling him not to stand and not weary his old knees when suddenly he realized that Albertus was already on his feet and standing upright. It speaks much for both of them that, while cardinals, chaplains and papal officials froze with embarrassment and pretended not to have heard, the pope and the bishop broke the silence simultaneously with loud laughter.

Albertus was too humble a man to realize what he had achieved with his writings on husbandry, and overgenerous in his acknowledgement to Aristotle (that is, to the Latinized version of Theophrastus). He was limited to the extent that he separated all plant life into only two categories,* but he was optimistic enough to attempt a European flora which, because of the large variations in plant habitats, has not been done to this day. He was the first to hunt plants systematically over a large area, and the first to publish accurate descriptions of foliage and the importance of a worked tilth and feeds of manure to successful agriculture. He was precocious, as well, in esthetics, showing an appreciation of water, shorn lawns, and the color and fragrance of flowers in the green pleasure grounds he described, which was far in advance of his time.

If Aristotle may be counted the founder of botany, Albertus Magnus deserves to be remembered as the first systematic plant hunter known to history.

---

* Theophrastus, Dioscorides and Pliny had separated plant life into three categories. The botanists of the Renaissance varied between twenty-five categories (Dodoens) and no category at all (Brunfels).

STIMATING the extent of influence which Dioscorides, Pliny and the Aristotle-Theophrastus interpretation shared between them until the sixteenth century is extraordinarily difficult in an industrial age and from this distance of time. That is, of course, in the Old World. Across the Atlantic, happily ignorant of the old learning and therefore untouched by the new, Mexican gardeners were cultivating a large number of herbs whose curative and prophylactic properties had been known for centuries by the Aztecs. But, in Europe, both gardenmakers and botanists were in thrall to the ancients, and it required progressive, open minds to break free.

One of the first to understand the limitations of the old Greek botanists was von Cube, a rich doctor and amateur botanist from Frankfurt. He had an idea—it was no more —that the flora of Northern Europe differed from that of Southern Europe and beyond. He chose to experiment, and, in 1485, he set out on a plant-hunting expedition accompanied by a botanical painter "of good sense, skilful and cunning." Their itinerary was ambitious—Italy, the Balkans, Crete, Rhodes, Cyprus, the Holy Land, Egypt. And their plant hunting was successful. Doctor von Cube proved that the Greeks of two thousand years before had not written the last word on plant distribution.

His work was consolidated by three fellow countrymen: Hieronymus Bock, Otto Brunfels, and Leonhard Fuchs. They all were from humble homes, all young and antiauthoritarian when Luther posted his Theses, and therefore all were sympathetic to Protestantism. Their work as plant hunters and classifiers was so important that it appeared to alter the science of botany altogether.

To begin with, they loyally tried to cram all the plants they collected into the old Greeks' formula. But reason as well as their age made them rebels. Their new discoveries *were* new. Listing them in herbals, with notes on their description and use, became a lifetime's work.

They had their counterparts in other countries. One of the best botanists, and most unlucky of them all, was the Swiss, Konrad von Gesner. His father, a furrier, was the victim of the bitter religious wars between the Swiss cantons. Gesner himself, though an exceptionally industrious botanical collector and physican, was obliged to take on hackwork, and he never knew what it was to be comfortably off or see his work as a botanical collector in any way commended. Towards the end of his life he was given a university chair of medicine, but it was simply an extra burden bringing him next to no salary. He could barely afford to travel to Vienna when summoned by the Emperor Ferdinand. His one extravagance was to have woodcuts made of fifteen hundred of his own plant drawings. These with a huge portfolio of notes, his own observations of plants and his analysis of them into categories, were to be the foundation of a flora "untouched by Greekery," and, therefore, entirely unique. Misfortune prevented it. Before any of the work had been published he contracted the plague and died. His portfolio, the woodcuts and the drawings were sold for a beggarly 175 guilders, the sum being used to pay the engravers. The purchaser, a botanist named Camerarius (who later was to prove that plants had sexes), used the drawings to illustrate his own writings without any acknowledgement to Gesner. It was not until 1751 that a private enthusiast named Trew, ferreted out two-thirds of von Gesner's woodcuts, and published them under the title of *Gesneri opera botanica*.

The first most considerable botanist in England was William Turner, a clergyman so rooted in Protestantism that he was deprived of the deanery of Wells and obliged to live abroad in less congenial Cologne. There he practiced medicine—having taken a medical degree in Italy—and waited patiently for eight years until the two Protestant burners, Henry VIII and his daughter, Bloody Mary, were safely dead. After two smaller publications, his three-volume *New Herbal* listed about 240 English plants with their localities, and was the first botanical work to be printed in English. This has earned it a position of importance in the Natural Science Museum in London. Turner was essentially a "local" botanist, helped by his family, most of all by his son, Peter, who became a member of Parliament; both of them being painstaking, neat workers and thorough hunters over a small area. Only one introduction is credited to Turner, that vastly useful, exotic, economic plant called lucerne or alfalfa. He died in London, still an absentee dean of Wells, though on this occasion by choice, in the year 1568.

An almost exact contemporary who met with outstanding worldly fortune was the Italian, Pier Mattioli. He had the sort of sunny disposition which conceals roguery and appears to invite success. His commentary, in Italian, on Dioscorides sold thirty thousand copies without any trouble at all. A Latin version hardly could have been expected to have had the same appeal, so Mattioli wisely decided to illustrate it with five hundred woodcuts by the popular artist, Weidnitz. As a result, reprints of both versions were twice ordered. The book was even published in the Near East, in Syria and Persia, and still copies were so highly valued that they were given in dowries and bequeathed in wills.* Understandably, perhaps Mattioli's head was swollen. Less understandably, vanity made him ungenerous, even vindictive to the few who had the scholarship and the courage to point out his mistakes. At his instigation one critic lost his teaching post at Padua University. Another critic found himself being hounded by the Inquisition because Mattioli spitefully drew attention to the fact that he was an orthodox Jew. Because of these flaws in his character

* One copy was bequeathed to Henrietta Maria, Queen of England.

it is difficult to admire Mattioli as a man, and because he
stuck so closely to the profitable last of Dioscorides, it is
difficult to gauge his importance as an innovator. But the
botanists of his day held him in high regard. Having wide
territories of plant life open to him in Italy (which were
denied to others), his contribution to the botanical new
learning and the collecting of dried herbarium specimens
and living plants would have appeared particularly impressive. Certainly he was respected by his contemporaries;
honored with titles and addresses, compensated by a public
subscription when his house was burned to the ground (so
handsomely that he found himself well in pocket after the
rebuilding), and appointed personal physician to the Holy
Roman Emperor, Maximilian II. Mattioli "arrived" in a
sense that no other Renaissance botanical collector was ever
able to match—though one of his friends and an excellent
plant hunter on his own account, came close to enjoying the
same fame.

Augier Ghislain de Busbecq was a Fleming and imperial ambassador at the court of Suleiman the Magnificent at
Constantinople. It gave him great opportunities to hunt out
the plants of Asia Minor which, in the sixteenth century,
was the chief supplier of Europe's bulbs and stocks of flowering plants. In one year alone Busbecq introduced the horse
chesnut, lilac, tulip, mock orange, the Syrian rose mallow,
*Hibiscus syriacus,* and *Hyacinthus orientalis;* and he was
constantly supplying his lucky friend Mattioli with fresh
plants and information.

Of the remaining botanical collectors stimulated by the
Renaissance, three were outstanding. By a coincidence all
were Netherlanders, all were close friends, all came from
comfortable circumstances, and all had a profound influence
on European gardens. Their names were Latinized as Do-
donaeus, Lobelius, and Clusius, but they knew each other as
Rembert Dodoens, Matthias de l'Obel, and Charles de
l'Ecluse.

Dodoens is best remembered as the dupe whose work
was (badly) translated into English by John Gerard,

with barely a pretense at disguising the fact that it was, by far, the larger part of the famous *Gerard's Herball.**

L'Obel is mostly remembered for the flower which has his name. It is forgotten that he earned renown in England where he lived for almost thirty years, marrying an English-woman and being appointed King's Botanist to James I. He was the first to write a detailed description of all the roses cultivated in Europe in Shakespeare's time; that is, of ten species.† He also wrote a history of cereals, discovered the heath rush, both in England and Wales, and was the printer of an exuberant pamphlet entitled, *The Fullest directions for the Brewing of the most agreeable of all German and English cervisia, or Beer.* He managed to quarrel with Gerard. He recognized the Englishman's prowess as a plant hunter and gardener, for Gerard had noted seventy new plants and cultivated more than a thousand flowering plants, but l'Obel also saw that ninety percent of *Gerard's Herball* was the work of his old friend Dodoens, and that even parts of his own notes had been included in a faulty translation from the Latin. It is scarcely surprising (though apparently it surprised Gerard) that after the publication of the *Herball* l'Obel became "a hard man" towards the plagiarist.

Charles de Lécluse was the most enthusiastic plant hunter of the three friends, but this did not confine his interests. On the contrary. Probably more than any other contemporary botanist he was the personification of the Renaissance man; studying law at Louvain, and philosophy at Wittenberg to sit under Melanchthon and Luther, and then in turn at Frankfurt, Strasbourg, Lyons, and Montpellier; being fluent in eight languages; at ease with the distinguished and the great, with Rabelais and with cardinals although he was a passionate Protestant; noted as an histo-

* Equally, very few of the 1,800 illustrations were Gerard's, having been lifted wholesale from a German flora by Jacob Theodore of Bergzabern.

† It is interesting to note that Pliny the Elder had described twelve kinds of rose, but Albertus Magnus only four, and that today it is generally accepted that 120 different species grow in the northern hemisphere.

rian, map maker, mineralogist, zoologist, philosopher, numismatist and, most of all, as a botanical collector. He belonged to the Flemish "Quality," his father being Seigneur de Watènes of Arras, and this gave him the necessary cachet to accompany the Fugger brothers, Johann and Markus, when they traveled through Europe on a grand tour before the days of the "Grand Tour." In Spain alone, l'Ecluse collected two hundred new plants which he wrote about and published under the title of *Rare Spanish Plants*. He traveled, as well, in Turkey, collecting and introducing to Europe, the fritillary, a selection of daffodils, orrice root, *Iris florentina,* and reintroducing the Ranunculus and hyacinth. Later in his career—often through curious roundabout means—he was responsible for the introduction and general distribution of such noted plants as the tuberose (which he received from India, though it is a native of Mexico), the scarlet runner bean from Brazil via Portugal, and the potato from Spain (it had traveled from Peru.) But his plant hunting, as a younger man, in Central Europe was his most remarkable contribution to Renaissance botany.

These were not merely the achievements of a dilettante with infinite resources and plenty of time on his hands. In his up-and-down life l'Ecluse knew poverty and riches in turn, and he wore both with a gentle dignity which won him a large circle of admiring friends. He, also, was caught up in the Low Countries' revolt against Alba. One of his uncles was murdered in the punitive massacre which followed the revolt. His own father lost everything and fled to Antwerp. There l'Ecluse took care of him until he died in 1573. By this time he was in such straitened circumstances that he was grateful to be offered the post of supervisor of the imperial gardens in Vienna. From this low point in his career, he rose to be knighted by the emperor, given a professorial chair at Leyden, and become an established European figure. His most famous work, *Rariorum Plantarum Historia* was published when he was seventy-five. To his friends, he said that no matter how cruel the vicissitudes of life could be, botany and gardening were everlasting solaces.

HERE is a serpentine border of mixed perennials, biennials and annuals in the University Botanic Gardens at Cambridge, not planted according to family or size or color or flowering season or any of the usual reasons, but, ranged in order from north to south, according to the date of their introduction to England. For this reason it has more of an academic interest than anything else; though it is full of surprises for those who associate, say, lamb's ears, coralbells and stocks with Medieval England, and discover they have only been in England for two centuries at the most; and it is equally surprising to those who because of the exotic appearance of bear's-breech and the winter flowering cherry have considered them recent introductions, and find instead that both plants were hoary "natives" long before the Hundred Years' War. The bed makes no claim to be complete. It is merely illustrative, and so it does not show the plant introduction explosions of the seventeenth and nineteenth centuries. The first coincided with the interest shown by a cultivated few in massive orangeries of masonry; the second with a general and less cultivated interest in the huge glasshouse ranges of Victoria's time.

The seventeenth century in England saw its renaissance in botany. Every art and science from sonnet writing to plumbing was revitalized by the new learning, but at a different pace from place to place. When, for example, on the Continent, gardens were altering their character, no longer to be respositories of "rare plants for the contemplation and admiration of nature," these very plants were falling under the notice of English gardenmakers for the first time. French gardeners were interesting themselves in logical progression from vista to vista; in form, shape and texture, in dim grottoes beneath raised terraces, in geometric designs, in parterres of water, colored pebbles and brick dust, in *compartiments de broderie* so exquisite that, as de Serre, the French farming writer, noted, "There really is no need to go to Italy!" The French kings had their "royal embroiderers" to superintend gardens, and the business of flowering plants was really in the province of the *peintre ordinaire de sa majesté pour la miniature* who, more like a floral taxidermist than a plantsman, preserved specimens with paint.

Simultaneously the English were interesting themselves in simples, oranges, and a few "choice and tender greens." Slow to mature, the English did not catch the excitement of botanical collecting until long after everyone else. Having caught it, they applied themselves so vigorously to botany and cultivation that, within a short space of time they had reached a position of excellence which they have yet to lose. And this they did through one of the most turbulent centuries in their political, social and economic history, when Charles I lost his head and his son, James II, lost his throne, when, while "noble reason" stirred men's minds, witches were hunted out and pricked and legally tortured, when religion was often a matter of politics, and vice versa; a century which stretched from *The Tempest* through *Paradise Lost* to *Absalom and Achitophel,* and the pendulum swung to and fro between riotous license and puritanical severity.

It is astounding to think of the English plant hunters working calmly and efficiently in such an age of lace, logic, blood and bigotry.

The Tradescants, father and son, set the pace. There was a third as well, grandson of the first, and all confusingly called John, but Old John and Young John were the great collectors and gardeners.

Old John left his native Suffolk to garden for Queen Elizabeth's secretary, Cecil, Lord Salisbury; having laid out the grounds and supervised the main plantings at Hatfield, he went off to Europe in 1611 to search out "curious greens." Naturally he went to the Low Countries for stocks of bulbs and new varieties, and went on to Paris for further supplies.* But this was simply his job. Private plant hunting out in the field was his first love, a point he proved later by signing on as a gentleman volunteer against the corsairs, at the serious risk of being taken into slavery, so that he would have the opportunity to hunt plants in North Africa. The Algiers Apricocke is one trophy from that harebrained expedition. In fact, Old John hunted in places as far distant as Archangel where he saw many Russian flowers including "*Helebros albus,* enough to load a ship," and as near as South Devon where on a widow's garden rubbish dump he discovered that odd fruit, the Plymouth strawberry, *Fragaria muricata*. It had been rejected as abnormal and, though its descendants are still sometimes seen today, the variety does not appear in commercial fruit lists because the flower petals and sepals combine in the shape of a choirboy's ruff and the bright red fruits have miniature leaves protruding from them in the place of pips.

Old John was a respected friend of Jean Robin,† curator of the *Jardin des Plantes,* after whom the Robinia was named, and they exchanged botanical gossip as well as seeds and vegetative parts. When l'Obel died, Charles I chose Old John as his gardener and after him, Young John, who, well-trained in his father's ways, was at one time a successful hunter in the new colony of Virginia. His introductions from the New World were highly valued and numbered among them lupins, cornflowers, Michaelmas daisies, bergamot, Virginia creeper, swamp cypress, red maple, Canadian

* Included in his treasures was "an exceedingly great cherye"—now listed as Tradescant's Heart or Oxheart.

† Robin also sent over curiosities for Tradescant's Ark, a collection which was to be filched later by a contemporary and sly scientist named Ashmole. He, in turn, bequeathed the loot to Oxford, and gained undeserved immortality as benefactor of the Ashmolean.

colombine, and the spiderwort which botanically bears his name, *Tradescantia.*

Young John remained King's Gardener, working on his catalog of all the Tradescant collections and quietly cultivating his private garden of marvels at Lambeth, right through the English Civil War. He was so detached that he barely seemed to notice the hurly-burly that went on outside his garden walls, not even the beheading of his master, Charles I, which made him, for a time, Parliament's or the Commonwealth's gardener.

That it has been worth a publisher's while to reissue some of the old herbals in recent years, and that out-of-date, unsystematic pharmaceutical treatises are still taken much too seriously by zealous herborists, suggests that Anglo-Saxons, more than any other race, are prone to herb predilection. Its degree would have to be multiplied many times to estimate how much value the seventeenth-century English attached to wound herbs, balms, fever alleviants, anodynes, astringent and antiseptic herbs. A limited number of vegetables and fruits were grown at the time, but to the English "plants" meant "herbs," and it is noteworthy that between three and four hundred medicinal and culinary herbs were listed as the contents of a contemporary English garden, with barely any flowering plants admitted as mere decoration.

Inevitably, then, as the religious houses in England had been shut and looted, and, as gunpowder had made obsolete the defended castle and moated grange, both of which had contained herb gardens, it fell more and more to apothecaries to accept herbalism as their special province. They became the practitioners of botanical knowledge.

It was the botanist's interest to hunt plants and classify them; the gardener's to hunt and cultivate them; the apothecary's to hunt and utilize them.

Doyen of the London apothecaries was John Parkinson of Ludgate Hill, whose book with the punning title *Paridisi in sole Paradisus terrestris,** constituted the first dictionary

* The earthly Park of Park-in-Sun.

of gardening. In the main it listed plants in cultivation, but his description of many wild plants showed that he was also a diligent hunter out in the field. He never traveled very far from London because it was unnecessary. An amazing number of genera with their species were then growing and thriving within sight of the Tower.

Parkinson's careful work over many years was written up in his second book, *Theatre of Plants,* and announced for publication in 1640. Because, clearly, it would be a brand new and important herbal the announcement alarmed the printers of *Gerard's Herball.* They knew they could hold their public only by issuing an up-to-date and revised version of the original, and hired another apothecary, Thomas Johnson, to work over the text and make the necessary amendments. The plethora of mistakes made it a formidable undertaking, and it was made the more difficult for Johnson by the imposed time limit of twelve months. Nevertheless, he managed it and the revised *Herball* was issued before Parkinson's new book came out. No doubt their printers were at loggerheads but no rancor existed between the two apothecaries. This was an unusual feat of good-naturedness, but, then, both men were widely respected for their habitual affability.

Johnson was one of the most attractive personalities in the whole gallery of seventeenth-century plant hunters. He was a Yorkshireman, born in 1600 in the town of Selby, and like many before and since he had the initiative to travel up to London where a wider circle of acquaintances and sharper wits made for a more fulfilled life. He became a member of the Society of Apothecaries. His shop in Snow Hill was to become famous when he exhibited the very first bunch of bananas ever seen in Britain, but he is better remembered for the books he wrote: volume one of the *Botanical Mercury* in 1634, and volume two in 1641. In them he described his plant-hunting expeditions made with other members of the Apothecaries' Society. They called their journeys "simpling trips" and these were as thorough as they were adventuresome.

The first, in 1629, was to Sheppey and the Isle of Grain, and at once they found themselves in trouble. The local people regarded them with the greatest suspicion and persuaded their constable to lock them up for the public safety. The mayor interrogated them with some care before he would let them go. Then, on the Isle of Grain, a sweltering day without any water or food proved that "simpling" was no ordinary country ramble. The results, though, of their four days' journey by ship, horse, and on foot, were very satisfactory: no less than a list of close to 250 discoveries—all early Kentish records.

Johnson's second trip, to the Bay of Margate, was longer, and it yielded over 360 records. His most enterprising piece of "simpling" though was in Wales. He was the first to botanize there and climb mountainous Snowdon in the process, at a time when the most civilized of men still had a real dread of mountains. Even in the following century, his namesake, the illustrious Doctor Johnson, when traveling through the Scottish Highlands insisted on the carriage blinds being drawn to shut out the sight of "horrid crags" without. Apothecary Johnson calmly hired an interpreter and guide—both being necessary in Wales at that time—and, with two companions, scaled Snowdon, rooting up plants as they went.

His motive for hunting plants was ostensibly to find new herbs and learn more about the habitats and growth of others. It was professional, though, being an energetic, adventurious young man, Johnson evidently delighted in the trips he described.

The elm expert, John Goodyer, was a great friend of Johnson's and frequently accompanied him on his expeditions. Being neither an apothecary nor a botanist, he must have been one of the first amateur plant hunters in England. Besides his work on elms it was Goodyer who discovered *Ludwigia* in Britain and the Lungwort peculiar to the New Forest region, *Pulmonaria angustifolia*. His contribution to botany was, in fact, modest; but there was no doubting his enthusiasm for plants. He and Johnson planned to work together on a British flora and make it a comprehensive catalog of plants with descriptions so clear and scientific that it could be used by medical men who needed to be able to identify plants for themselves. It would have freed medicine from the "Mrs. Gamps" of the age, the "women who dealt in roots," unscrupulous herb sellers who, like certain modern plant nurseries, were not above giving alternatives without authorization. But the grand plan was rendered defunct and the tyranny of ignorance assured for a few more years by the English Civil War.

This politico-religious struggle was elevated by both sides into a life and death struggle for liberty. The two friends preferred that which was offered by church and king and Johnson, the younger by eight years, joined the Royalist army—moving from his mild world of hunting plants to the more vigorous pursuit of Roundheads. As a herbalist-apothecary he was an unusual volunteer, but by no means the square peg his superiors might have expected. Undoubtedly his letters to Goodyer would have contained far more information about the plants he found while campaigning than news of the war or his own commissioning by the king and eventual promotion to the rank of lieutenant colonel. Then the letters stopped coming and Goodyer had news which thoroughly disheartened him. His friend had been in command of the defending garrison at the investment of Basing House in Hampshire.

*Basing.* It was a name Royalists could remember with pride. Yet the painful, brave story was pathetic, too, because tactically the post had not mattered. The royal position was neither bettered nor worsened by the result of the siege. But the gesture mattered a great deal because morale was always stronger in the Parliamentary army where the pay was fairly regular. A noble, if frankly useless, gesture might vivify the king's soldiers and so Basing House had been held for as long as possible. It was in the final phase that Thomas Johnson received a ball in the shoulder. The wound corrupted, and it finally killed him.

After his friend's death Goodyer abandoned all idea of the British flora and hardly ever botanized out in the field. His grief was as deep as it was quiet. When the war was over he set himself a monumental, time-consuming task, that of writing out the whole of Dioscorides both in Greek and in an English translation. It meant little more to him than lines written out by a punished schoolboy—filled four and a half thousand pages of small and careful handwriting and took three years to complete.

The Royalist cause found a sympathetic following among several noted plant collectors; Robert Morison, for example, who fought at the Battle of the Bridge of Dee and was in exile during the Commonwealth. He returned with Charles II to become Physician Royal, and professor of botany at Oxford, and was run over and killed by a coach in the Strand. Then there was Sir Thomas Browne who, though his primary interests were natural history, antiquities, and anything quaint or curious, also made collections out in the field. He practiced medicine in Norfolk and London throughout the English Civil War and at heart was a Royalist.

Thomas Willisel was the only considerable plant hunter to fight on the side of Parliament, and it is probably not a coincidence that he served under General Lambert who was a firstclass plantsman though not himself a collector. As the discoverer, among many other rarities, of the Nottingham catchfly and the red catchfly, Willisel was very well thought of by his contemporaries. They also admired his indefatigability, for he was a hardy, lean man who could live on next to nothing, if necessary. Many years after the English Civil War, Morison, the Cavalier botanist, hired Willisel to hunt out plants in Jamaica, but the soft and deceitful climate leached his strength and, within a year, he was dead.

The attachment of these plant hunters to king or Parliament was the exception rather than the rule. It has been remarked already how many collectors in this era were indifferent to, or unaware of, the commotions and conflicts which so thoroughly upset everyone else. On the Continent it was true, also. Unless they were physically caught up in it, collectors lived through the bloody Thirty Years' War secure in their own religious convictions, and far more bent on botany than on battles.

A supreme example in England of the detached plant hunter was John Ray of Essex. He died in 1705, two years before Linnaeus was born and, because of the latter's two-name system of plant nomenclature, Ray's *Catalogue of the Plants of England and the Adjacent Islands* and the much larger *Synopsis of the British Flora* were quickly made obsolete. This is perhaps why he is less familiar than he deserves.

Ray had much in common with William Turner the Tudor plant hunter. Both were of humble origin; Turner being a tanner's son, Ray a blacksmith's. Both pulled themselves up by the bootstraps to attend Cambridge. Both lost their livelihood because of religious scrupulousness. But whereas Turner was extremely sensitive to the political climate of his day, Ray barely noticed such cataclysmic events as the English Civil War and the Glorious Revolution.

While Lieutenant Colonel Johnson was defending Basing House, the Reverend Mr. Ray, a Fellow of Trinity, was pottering about the water meadows by the Cam and making expeditions "north to fenland, west to breckland, and south to the knobbly Gog-Magog Hills," collecting and drying plants and working on the local flora. When finances allowed, he made expeditions all over England, and even penetrated well into Wales and the Scottish borderlands. This he did mostly alone and on horseback, sublimely indifferent to the dispositions of campaigning troops and constant danger from footpads, discharged soldiers and deserters.

The Act of Uniformity after the Restoration drove Ray from Cambridge which, happily for botany, forced him to broaden his horizons. He spent three years abroad and then continued his hunting over little-known parts of Britain.

The result was a mass of new information and a list of plants which made a pygmy of Turner's *New Herbal.*

At this point in his career Ray lost his friend and companion on many botanic expeditions, Francis Willoughby of Windermere, and he chose to retire to the country—to return to his native village, Black Notley. There he married, fathered and raised four daughters, and wrote (in elegant Latin) the results of his plant hunting over many years. At the conclusion of a successful and, ultimately, tranquil life he died of ulceration. He was seventy-eight years old.

More is known of these collectors of wild plants than of their compatriots who hunted out exotics. But the most petted and fêted, the most lavishly and frequently described, and undoubtedly the most famous plant of the seventeenth century was a tender alien introduced to England long before the Civil War. Affection for the orange spread like a fever among the gentlemen dilettanti of Europe. In England it was all-important in the span of years between the Tudors and the Hanoverians, and the culture of over 169 varieties, in pots and tubs on little wheels— which were wintered in substantial and often very beautiful orangeries—was the height of fashion and gardening delight.

The fruit was widely championed by people as diverse as the eccentric Celia Fiennes, who rode over rough roads and marshy tracks through many English counties, and Sir William Temple, the concocter of that useful word "sharawagdi." But it was the scholarly John Evelyn who was the English orange grower's cicerone. He advised his friends "of the Quality" on orangery management, invented his own hothouse stove, an apparatus made of crucible earth pipes and heated with "a plain single furnace" (such as chemists use in their laboratories for common operations) and published his observations in *Kalendarium Hortense* and *The Art of Gardening.* It is not clear from his diary or his other writings whether or not Evelyn himself collected plants out in the field, but there was no doubting his immense indirect influence on those who did. Moreover, by knowing and lov-ing plants so well and writing of them so tantalizingly, he beguiled people into becoming patrons of exotic plant hunters:

*About Michaelmas (sooner or later as the season directs) the weather fair and by no means foggie, retire your choice greens and rarest plants (being dry) as Orange, Lemons, Indian and Spanish Jasmine, Oleanders, Barba-Jovis, Amomum plin, Citysus lunatus, Chamalaca trioccos, Cistus ledon clusii, dates, aloes, sedums, etc.*

Nurserymen were quick to meet the demand made by Evelyn's admirers and, having the equipment, primitive forcing houses and orangeries, they cultivated and bred the many plants he recommended. In 1648, though it was the climacteric year of the king's final defeat and trial, authorities at the Oxford Physic Garden published a list of the plants grown there. Exactly fourteen hundred—that is two-thirds of the whole collection—were exotics; which meant that at some time or another they had been introduced from abroad.

When and why, and who in the first place hunted them out, is largely a matter of conjecture. English collectors forced into exile owing to the political and religious intolerance of the age were not uncommon, but it seems certain that the majority of exotics, and undoubtedly those from beyond Europe, found their way into English "hybernizing houses" by way of diplomatic couriers, merchant seamen and other travelers. Many a sailor's keepsake, brought home as a souvenir of distant lands, had a commercial value. It was in the interests of nurserymen to have paid agents at the docks whenever shipping made the Port of London. But, more often than not, plant hunting was a subsidiary to some other occupation.

Spirited adventurers, refugees, social outcasts and misfits were free to make a new and tolerably safe life on the east coast of North America. As they settled and multiplied, driving the native Indians over the Appalachians, the administration of the Colonies demanded a supply of clergymen. It was inevitable, too, that, in a century engrossed in religion, the Anglicans and Protestants of England and the Roman Catholics of Spain and France should send out missionaries to the ungoverned outposts of European civilization and to the benighted Indians. Not all, but very many were sufficiently interested in natural history to collect plants and send home seeds and vegetative parts.

Henry Compton, Bishop of London, was one of the most famous collectors of exotic plants in the century. Being born at beautiful Compton Wynates must have seeded his love of gardens and plants though he did not have an opportunity to indulge it fully for many years. As a young man he was a mercenary soldier in Flanders, and on a sudden notion, or divine inspiration, made an abrupt *volte-face* of career and returned home at the time of the Restoration to be ordained. Compton's father was Earl of Northampton, high in the favor of the restored sovereign, and his other connections were so influential that not many years passed before he was consecrated and enthroned as Lord Bishop of London—with the gardens of Fulham Palace at his disposal. These had already been well stocked with foreign plants by Bishop Grindal in the reign of Queen Elizabeth, and they delighted Compton. At once he set about the construction of conservatories and the nurturing of plants. Moreover, a chronicler of the day recorded that the new bishop was "very curious in collecting as well as in cultivating." He was, indeed. "The Americas" lay within his jurisdiction and he had the responsibility of supplying resident clergymen and itinerant missionaries. On their appointment they were made to understand that an adjunct of their priestly duty to the Colonists and Indians was to supply their Lord Bishop with exotic plants. This they did to such good effect that the gardens at Fulham soon contained the largest single collection of exotics in the kingdom. Then, because, like most contemporary bishops, he could not keep his finger out of political pies, James II suspended him from all clerical duties—thereby giving him the freedom to enjoy his plants to his heart's content.

One of the best known of Compton's strategically placed clergymen-plant-hunters was John Bannister who proselytized for the Church of England in Brazil to small effect, but found there, to his bishop's joy, the graceful silver-leaved climber named after him *Banisteria argyrophylla*. After extensive travels he settled as a parson in Virginia; writing Compton long botanical letters, sending him plants, and working on a flora of the Colony. He must be accounted one of the first botanical casualties because he fell off a cliff while fingering small plants from crevices, and broke his neck.

Loyal always to his botanical clergymen, Bishop Compton saw the *Virginian Catalogue* through the press and, busy as he was with this and the palace gardens and conservatories, he was not altogether pleased when James II's suspension was withdrawn and he found himself at liberty to resume his episcopal duties. In fact, the same contemporary chronicler noted that the change in the state of affairs appeared to make little difference to the Bishop's way of life:

*There were few days in the year, till towards the latter part of his life, but he was in his garden, ordering and directing the replacement or removal of his trees and plants.*

Happy Bishop Compton!

In concluding these notes on collectors and patrons in the Orangery era, a place has to be found for the most peculiar of all plant hunters. Like the missionaries, collecting was his secondary occupation. His first occupation, though, was far less virtuous than theirs.

William Dampier was orphaned as a small child. Thereafter he made life such hell for everyone that his guardian was delighted to turn a blind eye when the boy ran away to sea. Hydrography began to interest him, and he applied himself to learn as much about it as he could on voyages to Newfoundland, Bantam, Jamaica and the Bay of Campeche. On the rare occasions he stepped ashore he showed an equal interest in botany, collecting specimens for drying, and recording his observations in a journal. In the conflict of interests—or more likely involvement in something disreputable—plants won over water and he skipped his ship in Mexico. In either event, he spent two years among the foresters of Yucatan, a crew with no laws, no code of behavior, and no respect for anything or anyone. A willing learner in this school of villainy, young Dampier graduated to piracy. He joined a band of buccaneers who plundered, raped and murdered their bloody way across the Isthmus of Darien and southwards down the Colombian coast. Dampier, with his collecting kit as well as cutlass and his readiness to examine a plant on his way to firing a village or desecrating a church, was the living prototype of many fictional villains; of the cutthroat, for instance, with an appreciation for porcelain, or the torturer with a high regard for family life.

By this time he was acknowledged as a gifted leader and he began his career as a pirate chief by seizing a Danish ship at Sierra Leone. The escapade paid dividends on the voyage he made from Chile to Mexico, then across the Pacific to China and down to Australia, and it made him the first Englishman to reach the Antipodes. But, off the Nicobar Islands his officers and crew decided that he was not such a gifted leader after all, and they abandoned him ashore. He must have had great courage as well as resource, for he set out into the frightening vastness of the India Ocean and made his way all alone in a frail native canoe well over two hundred miles to Sumatra.

"Poor Captain Dampier!" exclaimed the Dutch authorities when they had heard his piteous story; and they promptly shipped him back to England.

London lionized him for a time. Well-armed, well-dressed, wigged and powdered, and with all the charm and salty humor of a good talker and seasoned traveler, "Captain" Dampier was impressive. Very soon he was being generally admired as the author of an exciting volume called *A New Voyage Round the World,* and acknowledged by leading plantsmen as the authority on tropical exotics. The Admiralty became interested in such a firstclass navigator and, totally ignorant of his buccaneering background, the authorities gave him the command of a voyage of discovery to the South Seas where he was to report on the possibility of colonizing Western Australia. Pepys and Evelyn wined and dined him well and asked him to be so good as to collect plants on their account. He consented.

This second voyage was a remarkable feat of navigation, a necessarily limited but otherwise excellent exploration of the northwest coast of Australia, the coast of New Guinea and New Britain, and the archipelago and strait which bear Dampier's name. He had a poor opinion of the Australian aborigines, calling them "the miserablest people in the world . . . and setting aside their shape, they differ but little from brutes." The flora pleased him far more. Looking for fresh water in the Dampier Archipelago he took the bumboat to an island and, while his men dug for water, he and his water spaniel happily botanized.

*There grow here two or three sorts of shrubs, one just like Rosemary; and therefore I called this Rosemary Island. It grew in great plenty here but had no smell. Some of the other shrubs had blue and yellow flowers and we found two sorts of grain, like beans. The one grew in bushes, the other sort on a sort of creeping vine that runs along the ground, having thick leaves and blossoms like bean blossoms but much larger, of a deep red colour looking very beautiful.*

His "creeping vine" was the parrotbeak glory pea named after him *Clianthus dampieri.* For hunting out this plant alone he deserves fame; though, like him, it is an enigma, being particularly difficult to propagate.*

The expedition almost ended in disaster for the ship sank off Ascension Island, but Dampier and his crew managed to get ashore where they lived on turtle and goat until they were seen and rescued two months later. In the shipwreck, Dampier lost most of his collections and his notes and sketches, but forty percent of his dried plants survived and can be seen today in the Oxford Herbarium.

By this time the strain of being a respectable, seagoing captain was proving too much for Dampier. He began to vent his spleen on the nearest person at hand, his first lieutenant, and was so atrociously cruel to the poor man that when they made port back in England he was denounced by the crew and court-martialed.

To be tried and found guilty of cruelty in the Royal Navy at a time when, in Winston Churchill's memorable phrase, "rum, buggery and the lash" were keeping it together and beginning to make it great, was in itself remarkable. Then, only three years after being convicted, to be reappointed to an even higher command in exactly the same navy, was even more so. But this is what happened.

In his new venture to the South Seas Dampier had overall command of two ships. The captain of one (improbably enough) was a London physician and the inventor of a sweat-producing sedative called "Dover's Powder." The master of the same ship was Alexander Selkirk, a scamp from Fife who fell out with the doctor and, at his own request, was put ashore on Juan Fernandez to become the

* The compilers of some gardening dictionaries are sanguine to say that cuttings root well in sandy soil under glass, or that the plant can easily be propagated from seeds. The experience of weathered gardeners is generally to the contrary. The parrotbeak is obstinate. It requires pampering. It must be constantly nourished and invigorated by a more robust shrub. This means sowing seeds of the bladder senna in thumb pots, and two weeks afterwards, sowing the parrotbeaks. When the latter are still minute (before they have formed their first true leaves), they have to be grafted onto the bladder sennas. If they take well, thereafter they will thrive, but the actual grafting is a tricky job requiring deft and little fingers.

prototype of Robinson Crusoe. On the voyage Dampier's navigation was superb, and his plant hunting highly successful, but his old devil outed again.

This time when Dampier's little fleet reached home port again he was accused of excessive brutality and drunkenness and even the fruit of both, cowardice. He wrote an angry *Vindication* but it made no difference. His reputation was gone, and he was unemployable as a commander. In view of this it is surprising that he should have found his way into *Gulliver's Travels,* and that, later, as "a rough sailor but man of exquisite mind," he should have inspired Coleridge to write *The Ancient Mariner.* But there could be no satisfaction in this for Dampier. For the present he was an ex-officer, thoroughly vexed and depressed, until adventure and travel and the wild plants of the South Seas reasserted their spell over him.

As a result when, precisely four years, four months and four days after his marooning, Alexander Selkirk was taken off his island by a privateer, he found that the navigating officer was none other than his old commander, and that bloodthirsty botanist, William Dampier.

LANT hunting in the seventeenth century, it has been suggested, was first motivated by the need to know more of medicine, and then by the desire to find either interesting native and exotic "greens" or suitable *par terre* flowers for the *broderies* of geometric gardens. In the following century, plants were primarily collected in a spirit of scientific inquiry. The botanist's day-book and herbarium, his microscope and vascula became more important than the apothecary's laboratory and the garden bed; and from this point in time the field widens so far (and continues to widen up to the present day) that no more than a cursory history of hunters *en masse,* or thumbnail sketches of a representative few, is in any way possible. Deciding what material shall be included in a book is often less difficult than deciding what shall be left out. In this study the opposite is true; but, metaphorically throwing all the principal botanical collectors of the age into a sieve, three will not drop through with the rest. They were almost exact contemporaries as well, all dying in the 1770's: Linnaeus of Sweden, Commerson of the Dombes, and John Bartram of Philadelphia. They are selected as representative, no more; which is not to deny the historic importance and the influence of the botanists, plantsmen and hunters from other backgrounds and from other places —for example, Virginia or Vienna, Potsdam or Peking.

The eighteenth century has been called the "Age of Reason," despite the sublime superstitiousness of the time; and the

"Age of Elegance," which appeared to pay small regard to the reek and the encrusted dirt beneath the scents and silks. With complete justification it has also been called the "Golden Age of Botany," for it was the century of classification, of systematic plant hunting, of professionalism, and, within degree, of experiment.

A good deal of this was due to the work of Carl Linnaeus.*

The number of known plants had increased each year. By the date of his birth, in 1705, the local and regional, national and international floras—based on Dioscorides-Aristotle or on personal observation out in the field—had grown top-heavy. There were also competing systems of classifying plants which, with the overlong names and descriptions, and the meretricious, herbalist claptrap that had clung to plants down the centuries, resulted in a jungle of muddle and mistaken identities. Someone with a clear mind and a keen eye was required either to clean up the mess or to abandon it and suggest an acceptable alternative.

Linnaeus was the man.

His father was the pastor of a country village in the south of Sweden. As frequently happens with sons of the parsonage, he was destined for the ordained ministry of the church, but—like many another parson's son—he managed to evade it. In fact, this was not particularly difficult. From the time he was able to run Linnaeus showed such a liking for being out in the fields and such a loathing for any sort of schooling that his father was seriously advised to apprentice him to a tailor or a cobbler. The local doctor checked this by taking him into his own house and encouraging him to study medicine. So, when the boy went up to the University of Lund he went to be taught medicine, not theology.

Linnaeus' year at Lund and the following years at the larger University of Uppsala were not easy. He was a poor country boy without even the money to have his shoes mended. They were patched, inefficiently, with folded

---

* It is convenient to refer to him by his Latinized surname, though Carl Linné was his real name. In his fiftieth year, he was ennobled and given the sought-after "von."

paper. And he was often hungry. But at both universities he was befriended and looked after by men in comfortable circumstances: at Lund by the amateur botanist, Doctor Stoboeus, and at Uppsala by a Doctor Olaf Celsius, priest and botanist, who chanced upon him in the academical garden,* and promptly took him home, gave him board and lodging and the use of his extensive library. As a token of his gratitude Linnaeus tutored the doctor's son in botany, and then, when he discovered he had an aptitude for teaching, instructed his fellow undergraduates. Quite soon he showed such promise that the university authorities appointed him assistant to the professor of botany and, even before he could settle to the immensely hard work and minute income of this post, the Academy of Science elected him to explore and hunt plants in Lapland. He had not yet taken his degree, but there would be time later, and he was young, and the offer was a marvelous one. He accepted the election with delight, and set off on a journey of hundreds of miles through unmapped territory writing up his journal each day, trying to develop his embryonic ideas on classification and making a collection of dried plants.

It was 1732, a time when people dressed according to their class and wore the same kind of clothes whether they were playing football, gardening, or attending an execution. It did not make for great comfort though the young Linnaeus appeared not to notice this:

*My clothes consisted of a light coat of Westgothland linsey-woolsey cloth without folds, lined with red shaloon, having small cuffs and a collar of shag, leather breeches, a round wig, a green leather cap, and a pair of half boots.*

His equipment was as light as he could make it: a shortsword, a fowling piece, a pocketbook and passport and a little leather bag which contained:

---

* It is singular that three of the most famous plantsmen have been chanced upon in botanic gardens and promptly befriended: Linnaeus by Doctor Celsius, David Douglas by Sir William Hooker, and Joseph Paxton by the sixth duke of Devonshire.

*One shirt, two pairs of false cuffs, two half shirts, an inkstand, pencase, microscope and spying-glass, a gauze cap to protect me occasionally from the gnats, a comb, my journal, and a parcel of paper stitched together for drying plants.*

False cuffs seem an unusual requirement for a plant hunter in a largely uninhabited area.

It was an exhilarating trip. Linnaeus returned home with one hundred dried plants, hitherto unknown, to establish his reputation as the author of the *Flora Japponica*, and to fall in love with a sweet, young girl who adored him in return.

The girl's father, though, would not hear of her marrying a penniless botanical collector. Linnaeus must take his degree, practice as a physician, and settle down. The father was reasonable enough to provide the necessary expenses and, as the money was available, Linnaeus sensibly decided to see a little more of the world and go to a foreign university.

While plant-hunting his way through Northern Europe the young man's zeal for scientific accuracy caused him to be heartily disliked in Hamburg. There the city fathers were custodians of an ancient and prized "seven-headed hydra," a "relic" of the Crusades to the Holy Land. Linnaeus, as a humble student, asked for permission to see the marvel which he then examined with care. His thoroughness established that seven weasel heads had been skilfully sewn together, attached to two clawed feet, and covered with snakeskin. The triumph of scientific observation entirely failed to please the city fathers who, up to that time, had enjoyed a small but regular income by putting the creature on show, and Linnaeus wisely hurried on his way.

He took his degree in Holland, and for two years was the curator of the Hatrecamp Botanic Garden. For a long time he had been perfecting his system of plant classification, which had its foundations in Sébastien Vaillant's observations on the precise sexual functioning of plants and, at last, he published his theories.

They were widely acclaimed because his approach was so unusual and commendably simple; his system asking no more from a botanist than that he count the numbers of a flower's stamens. The total, noting certain other characteristics, would place the plant first in a division and then in a subdivision. Identification was as easy as that.

But it had its faults as such an artificial system must have * and, though explicable in Linnaeus' Latin original, it was open to bizarre interpretation in foreign translations. For example, in one late eighteenth-century version, in English, endless complications and ludicrous situations arose through calling the stamens "husbands" and the styles, "wives." This caused one plant to have "twenty husbands or more in the same marriage"; and another plant "four husbands, two taller than the other two." As a result there was a farcical outcry in Wesley's England against the Swede's lewd and salacious botany.

Linnaeus' most enduring contribution to botany was his formalizing of Gaspard Bauhin's idea of giving two names to all created things. He undertook to name and classify everything "from buffaloes to buttercups"; and undoubtedly his work on indexing plants, published later in his life in 1753 as *Species Plantarum,* made something orderly out of the casual, chaotic botany of preceding years, and stabilized nomenclature forever.

The young Swede's reputation was already considerable. Because the owner of the Hatrecamp Botanic Garden was an English East Indian nabob it was natural that Linnaeus, as director, should visit England. When he did he was touched by the warm welcome he received from many of the distinguished botanists of London. Fame pleased him and, recalling that prophets on the whole are not honored in their own country, he might well have decided to stay away from Sweden. But he was still young and that girl was awaiting him in Stockholm. When he did return to marry and practice medicine he was gratified to find himself as

---

* Nevertheless, stamen classification remained the dominant system for a long time.

well-known in Uppsala as he had been in Western Europe.
But neither marriage nor doctoring suited him. The sweet,
young girl turned almost overnight into a dragon. All his
life he was to regard her "with respect and terror." And, as
to being a physician, he expressed himself truthfully (but
clumsily, it is to be hoped) when he said that he was
"fonder of meddling with plants than with patients."

Liking neither wife nor work, he considered improving
the latter by leaving Sweden but, fortuitously and just in
time, he was elected professor of anatomy at the University
of Uppsala. He did not care for the subject but he accepted
the chair and it was a step in the right direction towards his
real vocation as a teacher. Moreover, not very long after he
was able to exchange his professorship for the less lucrative
but far more congenial chair of botany, materia medica and
natural history.

Teaching, sharing his own pleasures, and enjoying the
company of adoring students was to fill the rest of Linnaeus'
life and make him supremely happy. His influence was
huge. At the beginning of his teaching career as professor,
Uppsala had five hundred registered undergraduates. The
number gradually increased to three times that number.
Students came to him from all over Europe. At his death,
the number dropped once more to five hundred.

Included among his followers were some who were to
become leaders in the natural sciences throughout the
world. People of distinction, from bishops to leading botanists, would travel to Uppsala and attach themselves as
extramural students for the weekend, simply to enjoy the
privilege of hearing Linnaeus lecture.

The amount of enthusiasm he generated was astounding
and, when the malignant Swedish weather allowed, his
twice-weekly botanical expeditions would attract as many
as two hundred undergraduates and more; often so many
that they announced fresh discoveries to each other with
bugle calls like huntsmen in the field. At the end of the hunt
they took their trophies to the professor to hear him ap-
praise the best of them. If he judged any to be of particular

interest they would honor the plant and its discoverer with a celebration—singing, as they marched home in a long crocodile, to the beat of drums and fanfares from bugles and trumpets.

The party that evening would be held in a hall or garden with much dancing to fiddle music, and drinking as only Scandinavian students could drink. Their professor would sit smoking his pipe and enjoying their exuberance. And then he, as well, would be pulled to his feet to share in the dancing. At this, too, he excelled. Not only was he an internationally renowned botanical collector and classifier and their inspiring teacher, but he could also outclass them all in the footwork of a Polish jig.

In contrast to the social plant hunts of Linnaeus' later years—when legions of students carried the vascula and presses and all the paraphernalia of collecting, and would, had it been necessary, have carried their professor, too— John Bartram of Philadelphia chose to be as solitary as possible in forty years of plant hunting along the eastern Colonies of North America.

This man became a legend in his own lifetime. It was partly because he was so reckless in penetrating wild Indian country at a period when the Pennsylvanian communities dreaded the Iroquois away to their north, and the Chicasaws and Shawnees to the west of the Alleghany Mountains. But it was also because the *mise en scène* of Bartram's whole life was intriguing, to say the least.

He was the son of a Quaker English farmer who reached the Colonies in 1680, "before there was a single house in Philadelphia." Old Bartram was a singleminded individualist. On the death of his first wife (John's mother) he handed his children over to their grandmother, quarreled with the local Friends, defied the "Meeting" when it enquired into his personal affairs and promptly emigrated to

North Carolina. There he remarried, bred two more children and ended his rambunctious life speared and scalped by Yamasee Indians beside the Cape Fear River.

John Bartram was as unable to escape polemics as his father had been. He, too, was hailed before the "Meeting" and told to account for his peculiar views. Like his father he denied their right to pry into his private affairs. Instead of walking out, though, he remained where he was while the "Meeting" drew up a final "Letter of Irrevocable Disownment," and he politely took his seat each Sunday thereafter in the Meeting House as if nothing at all had happened. The perplexed and embarrassed Friends did not quite know what to do in the face of such eccentric behavior, so they did nothing.

The average Colonist was a farmer and John was no exception. Bred to ordinary husbandry he showed a talent for imaginative farming which was far in advance of his times; regularly feeding his fields with a rich, liquid manure, spreading rotted compost over virgin and impoverished land during the winter months. This gave him lush hay "outside a donkey's dreaming," and he drew an average of thirty-three bushels of wheat from an acre while his neighbors averaged only twenty.

He needed to do well for he had a large family. His first wife had died in 1727, after four years of marriage, leaving him a widower with two small children. A year later he bought a tract of land on the banks of the Schuylkill River which edged on the wilderness. This he farmed. He threw together a timber shack, remarried, built a larger house round the original, and added to it as ten children were born of the marriage. One of them, William, was to be as keen a botanist as his father and, towards the end of his life, accompany him on some of his plant-hunting expeditions.

How, in the first place, John became interested in plants has been the source of two romantic stories. The first was that he found a colony of birdfoot violets, *Viola pedata,* in a water meadow, admired the flower so much that he dreamed of it the following night, and woke at dawn a perfervid devotee of the science of botany. The second, told by his French friend, the scientist, Crèvecoeur, had the same basis of sudden revelation, but the cause, in this case, was a single daisy. Bartram was ploughing, saw the daisy, plucked it, pulled it to bits out of curiosity, and then (according to Crèvecoeur) chided himself in the following Quakerish fashion:

*What a shame that thee should have been employed so many years tilling the earth and destroying so many flowers and plants, without being acquainted with their structure and uses.*

Which remarkable self-rebuke caused him to hire a man to continue with the ploughing while he himself went to Philadelphia to buy a book on botany and a Latin grammar to make it explicable.

Later in his life Bartram made it clear to his London friend and patron, Peter Collinson, that from the age of ten he had been mildly interested in plants; and that, as the years passed, the interest expanded until it grew beyond his control and it became an obsession.

The second Mrs. Bartram did not care for this at all. She had married a farmer with prospects, and there he was, studying and collecting unprofitable weeds, and hiring a hand to do the farmwork with money they could scarcely afford. To begin with, their life was indeed difficult, and Bartram had to temper his enthusiasm in order to meet the needs of his farm and ever-growing family. Not being able to get out and hunt plants in the wilderness as often as he wished, it was at this time that he personally laid the foundations of his famous five-acre botanic garden. Then good luck, nothing else, put him in touch with Peter Collinson.

Collinson was a London merchant who traded with the American Colonies. He was also an amateur botanist and plantsman who had a wide circle of similarly minded friends in England. From the plant introductions made by young John Tradescant and, after that, by traders and missionaries in the Colonies, he estimated that the flora of the Americas must be fascinatingly different from the flora he already knew. He tried his hardest to persuade settlers to send him supplies of plants. Some obliged, but the majority of his friends in the Colonies shared neither his interest nor his knowledge. Even those who were willing and able to collect for him could only be asked once, or twice at the most. To pester friends for consignments of plants would be ungracious. Collinson plagued his business agents to find him a professional plant hunter. It was outside their job and their attempts were only halfhearted. Then good luck, nothing else, put Collinson in touch with John Bartram.

To begin with, both were shy. Neither wished to embarrass the other and jeopardize the future. One was delighted to pay five guineas a box for plants and seeds, and the other equally delighted to have a reasonable excuse to indulge in his passion; but, in the first place, they were modest in their hopes and demands—Collinson not daring to hope Bartram would agree to *send* a second or a third box; Bartram not daring to hope that Collinson would *wish* for a second or third box. In the event, there was no question of second or third boxes. For thirty-three years John Bartram hunted American plants for Peter Collinson, sending hundreds of boxes on the long journey across the Atlantic. During the Seven Years' War some consignments were lost, and even in peacetime only a small percentage of plants could be expected to reach England in good condition, exposed as they were to dangers from weather, salty spray, and the understandable pococurantism of seamen. Vermin added to the dangers. Collinson once found a rat's nest, complete with young, in one of his precious boxes, all of them well and apparently content "amidst a ruin of roots and dead greenery." But the percentage of success was large enough to make the enterprise worthwhile.

Collinson gathered together a syndicate of botanists and plantsmen willing to pay an annual subscription of ten pounds for a share in Bartram's boxes. And he also found private patrons for his protégé in Pennsylvania. The most considerable of them was Lord Petre who would underwrite the cost of a complete expedition, but their number also included the Dukes of Richmond and Norfolk, and the Earl of Bute, at one time, prime minister. Bute became a martyr to collecting when he was out botanizing, fell out of a tree and was killed. He also hired Bartram on behalf of Frederick, Prince of Wales—better known as the "Poor Fred" who died in the arms of his dancing master. With such influential patrons it is not surprising that Bartram's highly successful plant hunting was officially recognized, and Collinson was able to write him:

*My repeated solicitations have not been in vain, for this day I received certain intelligence from Our Gracious King that he had appointed you his Botanist, with a salary of £50 a year.*

As Collinson's protégé, and, in particular, as King's Botanist, Bartram was in the position to do much as he wished. Though until his boys grew up to take his place he stayed on the farm at sowing time and harvest, his interest and most of his energy was reserved for plant hunting in the American virgin forests, and mountains and on the plains.

In scores of places he was the first white man to penetrate into the interior. On occasion he came across "White Indians," that is, men and women who had been captured by Indians, and reconciled to their customs preferring them to the white way of life. Bartram did not like them. He was notoriously not Quakerlike in his illiberal attitude toward the Indians and the Whites who had "gone native," though, as the son of an Indian victim, it was understandable. But there was less language problem with them than with real Indians and sometimes he used them as guides. On Bartram's trip to the Great Lakes, for example, one of his guides was called Shicckalamy and professed to be chief in a village of Delaware Indians, though he was in fact a Frenchman from Montreal. His interpreter on the same expedition was Conrad Weisser, a refugee from the Palatinate, who had tried his hand at being a recluse in the Seventh Day Cloister at Ephrata, Pennsylvania, but far preferred belonging to the Maques Indians. Bartram called them savages and "gone wild whites," but they were useful.

Generally, though, when hunting plants he was alone, and because he was often in totally unexplored country and used his own names to identify geographical features, it is not always possible to discover precisely where he went. His maps were hypothetical and most of his ringing, descriptive names like the "Impenetrable" and "Endless Mountains" and the "Dismal Vale" were never adopted. Nonetheless, it can be safely taken that he traveled widely, even during the Seven Years' War against France, and that he went deeply into Indian country as well.

He carried little with him; a bedding roll, a change of linen, books, tools and firearms, and two panniers attached to his saddle for plants and seeds. He took salt and flour but otherwise lived on what the country offered; eating berries, nuts, fruit, edible stems, the game which he shot and the fish which he caught. If the Indians were friendly he would eat with them; confiding to his journal his high opinion of their cooking. Fresh eels cooked over embers and eaten with boiled corn and watermelons won his special commendation; and so did a bowl of boiled beans mixed with Indian dumplings made of new and soft corn scraped from the ear. Accustomed to frugal and exceedingly plain living at home he grew quite excited about the Indians' capacity to make a feast of wake-robins. And a banquet of wild huckleberries and maize seethed in venison broth drew from him the equivalent of a Michelin gastronomic star:

*"Noble entertainment. Too good to leave any at all."*

Bartram has been credited with introducing more than two hundred American "discoveries" to the gardens of the Old World. They included the Magnolia, *M. grandiflora,* which was exceedingly popular and became "as essential to a fine Georgian house as the walls that supported it," and

*Lilium superbum* which, when it first flowered in Peter Collinson's garden in 1738, threw him into such a state of enchantment that his family and the servants were seriously alarmed.

Patron and protégé became fast friends and corresponded regularly, notwithstanding the fact that the mails were so slow that a large packet of numbered letters would be delivered instead of a single communication. Bartram was a great reader and longed for books from London. Although it was costly, Collinson did his best to oblige him, but when it became evident that Bartram's appetite was insatiable, he sent a mild note warning him that even Solomon did not get all his knowledge from books. Bartram replied wryly:

*I love reading dearly, and I believe if Solomon had loved women less and books more, he would have been a wiser and happier man.*

The king's botanist of Philadelphia is justly regarded with pride in the United States. The five-acre botanic garden by the Schuylkill River which he called his "garden of delight" is mostly extant as a part of the present-day Philadelphia park system; his most enduring memorial, though, is the accolade bestowed upon him by Linnaeus himself. In admiration inspired by his immense, self-taught knowledge and his assiduousness in hunting plants, the great classifier called John Bartram "the greatest living botanist in the world."

Linnaeus, in his *Glory of the Scientist* of 1737, exclaimed:

*Good God! when I consider the melancholy fate of so many of (botany's) votaries I am tempted to ask whether men are in their right minds who so desperately risk life and everything else through their love of collecting plants.*

Unknown to the Swedish savant he had written an apt description of his admiring disciple, Philibert Commerson. Certainly Commerson thought so when he read it, shyly admitting to a friend that he had what he called "botanomania." He had, indeed. Pasfield Oliver in his life of Commerson * underlined the point:

*The mere suspicion of a plant unknown to him was an irresistible attraction. He thought nothing of scaling almost inaccessible mountains, and both risked his life and ruined his health by his exertions . . . On his botanical expeditions he always went by himself, taking with him scarcely any money or provisions. He would return home sick, scarred with wounds, shaken by falls and accidents of all kinds, as well as utterly worn out by his exertions and by the violence of his own enthusiasm.*

There was always a luminous air of unreality about this vital, frenziedly energetic, and prodigious tornado of a plant hunter. Even his beginnings were rooted in fantasy for he was a true Bourguignon, born in the Dombes, then an independent state lying between the rivers Ain and Saône, comparable to those present-day curiosities, Monaco, Andorra and San Remo. In theory, the Comte d'Eu was sovereign prince; in fact, the place was outside any legal authority. There was no security for life or property except "the ancient habits and customs of the Dombes" until France first purchased and afterwards formally annexed the territory in 1762.

Commerson was born in this strange place in 1727, when the country was reputed to be an unhealthy seat of agues, rheumatism and a species of malarial fever. Though a plateau, it lay so low that it was perpetually dank, and, being a desolate, uninviting, unwanted tract of shallow valleys, coppices and stagnant pools, it was a refuge for hundreds of thousands of waterfowl (some of them ex-

---

* *The Life of Philibert Commerson* by Pasfield Oliver, edited by G. F. Scott Elliott (John Murray, 1909).

tremely rare), and the habitat, as well, of many unusual plants. Had he chosen it, Philibert Commerson's bizarre birthplace could hardly have been more appropriate for an incipient naturalist.

His first love was for fishes, which in such a sodden environment was barely to be wondered at, and particularly so as the Dombists practiced an unusual fish husbandry. Over roughly twenty thousand acres they rotated fish and corn as commercial crops. Lakes and ponds were drained, the fish taken, and grain sown on the muddy bottoms. After harvest they were refilled and restocked with fish. These fattened on the gleanings of grain, provided ready food for the Dombists and manured the mud which, in two years' time, would once more be a field of growing corn. This extraordinary rotation of carp, tench and other fishes with oats and barley gave young Philibert a special interest in fishes. He collected them with gusto and conceived a highly original idea for preserving them; that is by drying the little ones between sheets of heavy-gauge paper just as though they were marsh plants. But the boy was fickle in his affections. From fishes, birds and birds' eggs, even from the fascination of reptiles and fossils, and the cohorts of brightly colored insects, the plant world stole his heart away.

Though he had his quiverful of fourteen children Philibert's father was rich enough to set them all up. Seeing his second son's obsession with botany he sent him to Montpellier University, not as large as some, and in a draughty part of France, but the nursery of l'Obel, l'Ecluse and many other botanists of stature. It had, moreover, a botanic garden of some distinction and so, evidently, it was exactly the right place for Philibert.

It would have been if the boy's absorption in plant hunting had not led him to forget there were such things as petty larceny and the law of trespass. It was, and remains a common practice among many plantsmen to take cuttings and filch. bulbs and seeds, even whole plants. If outright purchase is impossible and proprietors will not be persuaded to part with plants, looting seems to be the only solution. Commerson had precedents for his behavior. Joseph Pitton de Tournefort, the adventurous French botanical collector of the previous century who, in a plant-hunting expedition to the Levant collected 1,300 specimens, was given to looting the gardens of his friends, and, sometimes, those of total strangers. On one occasion he was caught in the act by an outraged gardener who bombarded him with a fusilade of rocks and brickbats, and with such devastating accuracy that Tournefort—who was on terms of intimacy with the king and had thought nothing of plant hunting through thirty-two Aegean Islands in stormy and pirate-infested seas—was obliged "to save his life by extreme agility and the fleetness of his feet."

Tournefort was deeply admired by Commerson and faithfully imitated. It was bad enough that very soon the young man was in trouble with a large number of smallholders around Montpellier, but worse when he was actually caught collecting specimens for his herbarium in the University Botanic Garden—and not merely by a gardener or keeper but by François Boissier de Sauvages de la Croix, the professor of botany himself.

It was a sign of the advanced state of Commerson's botanomania that he was outraged and truly considered himself an injured party when he was barred from the garden. The interdict was only temporary but he never forgot it, and years afterwards he was still criticizing the professor who had caught him helping himself to university plants.

In botanical circles Commerson was quickly recognized as a brilliant, but apparently lunatic, plant hunter; and it is clear that between leaving the university and his marriage in 1760, he became almost a compulsive collector—a magpie of living plants, herbarium specimens, botanical treatises, books and catalogs—in fact, any absorbable piece of information. The risks he took for the sake of plants were quite extraordinary, and if he had not been exceedingly sharp-witted, athletic and lucky he must, surely, have succumbed to one or other of them. On one dramatic occasion he heard the roar of an avalanche above him and, not waiting an instant (for it was imperative to beat the avalanche in the gravity race), he hunched his knees to his chin and rolled like a ball down a fiercely steep gradient to safety. On another occasion he was collecting along the steep banks of a swollen mountain stream when he slipped and was caught, like Absalom, by the hair in a bush. To free himself "he was obliged to cut his hair and fell into the stream by which he was carried away and very nearly drowned."

Marriage calmed him. His wife brought him fortune and gave him a greatly loved son, Archambault, but two years later she died.

Grief stirred Philibert up again. He became determined to be a "practical" botanist, and not shy away from the hardships and the hazards which hunting plants involved. The study, the microscope and the herbarium were not sufficient for a botanist like Commerson. "Glory," he wrote, "requires, like Fortune, a race of men alike hardy and tenacious."

Chance gave him the opportunity to gain and deserve just such glory; the king appointed him Botanist Royal and sent him off on a circumnavigation with that prodigy of many arts and sciences, Louis Antoine de Bougainville. Besides being a favorite of the king, and described by a contemporary as "plus orné, plus dix-huitième siècle," Bougainville was also widely admired as an advocate at the Paris Bar, a diplomatist, a mathematical genius and the author of *A Treatise on the Integral Calculus,* a Fellow of the Royal Society of London, an eminent soldier and navigator, explorer and linguist, and so sympathetic in his understanding of the North American Indians that he was joyfully accepted into the tribe of the Tortoise.

Notwithstanding his friendship with the French royal family, Bougainville survived the terror to serve France under Bonaparte; and this he did in no sense as a Gallic "Vicar of Bray," but with his honor and integrity intact. It is ironic, perhaps, that so noble and brilliant a pantologist should be best remembered today merely because of the exotic plant named after him, the *Bourgainvillea*. Both having such an exuberant taste for scientific enquiry, the expedition's commander and the Botanist Royal were bound to get on well.

Before he left, Commerson handed over his son, Archambault, to the care of an uncle and solemnly made his will. It was an enlightened document in which he specified that, if he should die in a place where there was a medical school, only his heart should be buried and the remainder presented to the nearest theatre of anatomy. He also "attached in perpetuity the capital and interest of two laundries near Châtillon" for the founding of "a prize of morality"—whatever that might have been. He made several bequests, provided for his housekeeper, Jeanne Baret, and left the rest to Archambault.

Then he raced to Rochefort, extravagantly changing horses as often as possible, and in an agony of suspense all the time because he was a little late. He need not have troubled. His ship, appropriately named *La Boudeuse,* kept to her moorings for several days after Commerson's breathless arrival. This delay, though vexing, gave him the opportunity to stow and arrange all the scientific equipment with Jean Baret, his young botanical assistant.

When they did sail, Philibert found that he was a poor sailor. The heave and the rock of his new home made journal writing difficult. A brief entry headed "4th-7th February" makes everything plain:

*My dinner and supper are but loans, which I am exact in repaying one hour or half an hour afterwards.*

The French king's commands had been loosely phrased —"to proceed to the East Indies and so circumnavigate the globe." The idea was to achieve for the glory of France what had already been achieved by the English, and—in passing —to claim and name pieces of unexplored territory. The west coast of New Holland, as Australia was then called, had already been partially explored and claimed. So far as anyone knew, the east coast had not. At a later date the French venture was quizzically described by its commander as, "Bougainville's Failure to Discover New Holland." In fact, like Scott of the Antarctic, he was just a little late. Territorial considerations aside, his circumnavigation was a triumph of seamanship and a great success, especially in the fields of anthropology and natural history.

A list of Commerson's plant discoveries alone would demonstrate his outstanding contribution to the expedition. There were at least sixty new genera and three thousand new species. But, as naturalist to the expedition, his work was by no means confined to botany.

His journal and the ship's log show how versatile were his activities and interests.

As an illustration, when they reached the Rio de la Plata he saw at once why the Spanish explorers of 1513 had named it the River of Silver, for billions of white zephyr lilies, *Zephyranthes candida*, were in bloom and the plains gleamed with a silvery sheen. The sight proved to be but an appetizer. The exquisite beauty of Brazil delighted him. "I had a fearful sore on my leg which appeared at sea," he noted; but it did not prevent him from botanizing and, among other major discoveries, he found a pink species of the zephyr lily which was named for him, *Zephyranthes commersonii.*

Afterwards, in Buenos Aires, he relinquished botany long enough to hunt jaguar with two gentlemen adventurers, a German prince and a French chevalier who had paid to join the expedition.

Then, still further south, on the littoral of the Bahia Grande, where the cold was so devastating that the hardiest seamen wore all they possessed and still were chilled to the bone, Commerson and his assistant hunted a less ferocious but no less elusive quarry, adding handsomely to their collection of discoveries. Jean Baret earned his master's warm praise on this expedition for his fortitude, his ingenious attempts to ameliorate their discomforts, and for his willingness to carry so large a share of the firearms, forks, vascula, provisions, drying papers and presses, sketching blocks and other equipment.

The snow-water they took on board at the Straits of Magellan gave everyone sore throats, and it was Commerson the naturalist, and not the ship's surgeon, who provided a remedy: ordering that each barrel of water should be laced with a pint of vinegar and mulled with red-hot bullets.

On the strength of this original cure they made Tierra del Fuego, and there the ship's blue-grey cat, which had attached itself to Commerson, so captivated the natives that they offered him one of their loveliest young girls in exchange. Cat worshipers will be gratified to hear that, under the circumstances, he felt bound to refuse.

Like countless ships before and since, *La Boudeuse* appeared to hesitate in apprehension before facing the Horn. But Bougainville's confidence was caught by everyone on board. His seamanship and navigation were never in doubt. As calmly as if he were promenading in the Bois de Boulogne he carried them safely through that region of icy peaks and piercing, shrieking, never-dying winds. Then they breasted the Peruvian Current and made good way, all sails ballooned by the southeast tradewinds.

Commerson's absorbed interest in natural history was again temporarily suspended by seasickness. But he was certainly in trim and ready for everything when they made landfall at Tahiti where the prototype of Rousseau's "noble savage" eked out his paradisiacal, *al fresco* existence with public lovemaking, fruit and pig eating, and (on occasion, in case there should be vengeful gods) with the excitement of a human sacrifice. Commerson confided to his journal a conviction that, in fact, the Tahitians knew no god but love. The distractions from botany were formidable but he did manage a little plant hunting in the thirteen days of their stay. At sea again, his time was partly filled with examining marine life and pressing and preserving small fishes as he had done in the Dombes as a boy. Always on the alert for scraps of miscellaneous information, he noted in April, 1768:

*16° s. lat. & 170' e. long. Gold-tailed Dolphin affords excellent eating when cooked with butter and capers.*

Commerson's even, contented life suffered an abrupt upheaval on Mallicolo Island in the New Hebrides when his shipmates were made aware of a singular fact.

A local chieftain, admiring Jean Baret and free from Western inhibitions, seized the young botanist and would have made off with him if a shore party of seamen had not prevented it. In the scurry Baret's clothing was somewhat disarranged.

Bougainville noted the facts with dignity and detachment.

*M. de Commerson's servant (Baré by name) . . . confessed to me, her eyes streaming with tears, that she was a woman. She told me that at Rochefort she had deceived her master by presenting herself in men's clothes at the very moment when he was about to embark.*

Pasfield Oliver, writing for Edwardian readers, assumed a cautious tone: *

*It is best, after the lapse of one hundred and sixty years or so, to add no comment whatever to this extraordinary story.*

More recent research and a Puckish irreverence to the subjects of thumbnail biographies have suggested there is a close resemblance between "Jean Baret" (or Baré) and the

---

* At least in refraining from comment and not concealing facts he was more honest than the overfastidious Victorian "editors" of plant-hunters' journals. Joseph Hooker, for example, bowdlerized Banks' robust account of his South Sea voyage in search of plants to such an extent that a modern authority has described his work as "not so much a journal as a piece of carnage."

housekeeper "Jeanne Baret" mentioned in Commerson's will; and has provoked, as well, the legitimate question: was the botanist naive, wily, or frankly stupid?

One delightfully unlikely story has it that, in consequence of the discovery, poor Commerson, being old (he was forty-one!) and much mortified (and he an eighteenth-century Frenchman, by no means averse to the pleasures of the alcove!) was so embarrassed that he decided to exile himself forever; and that Jean changed her name to Hortense and stayed to comfort her master until his death, after which she went home to Paris, married a clockmaker, and gave her name to the commonest garden hydrangea, *H. hortensia.*

In fact, it seems that Jean rather naturally changed her name to Jeanne, that she married a soldier, and that she returned to France where she settled near Commerson's family in the Dombes. At her death she left everything to Commerson's son, Archambault. Commerson, in his turn, honored her by naming a genus *Baretia* though, a prior name having been established, it is now altered to *Quivisia.*

Clearly the naturalist and his assistant meant a good deal to each other, and Commerson never did go home. The reason for this is clouded. He left Bougainville (and presumably Jeanne Baret) at Mauritius, and fetched up in Madagascar. Promptly he set about the flora of the island, and to such effect that he had it pigeonholed in record time. Then he was recalled to France, his appointment canceled and his salary stopped. This, anyway, was how he put it when he wrote a vexed letter to a friend in Paris, exclaiming: "My plants, my beloved plants have consoled me for everything."

But, probably, the communication from Paris was neither as brutal nor as mysterious as it appeared, bearing the reasonable interpretation that Commerson's appointment and stipend inevitably would have finished when he left *La Boudeuse,* and that he was summoned home again in order to reclaim the post of Botanist Royal. The truth remains elusive, but it is probable that the plant riches of Madagascar outweighed for a time the attractions of Paris and the

Dombes, and certainly he had less liking for the necessary court attendance of a Botanist Royal at the Tuileries or at Fontainebleau than for his work as a botanist out in the field.

Whatever the reason, Commerson remained in Madagascar, enjoying the society of the natives whom he described as "idle and intelligent, mild and yet terrible," making gardens, putting his portfolios in order, and plant hunting to the last. He wrote to the same friend in Paris:

*One cannot abstain when in the sight of the rich treasures scattered so freely over this fertile land, from a feeling of pity for those gloomy indoor theorisers who pass their lives in hammering out vain systematics.*

The prodigious collector died in 1773 at the early age of forty-six. Eight days afterwards (when they could not possibly have been aware of his death), a full assembly of the Academy of France elected him a member by unanimous acclaim. It was a unique honor because no member had ever before been elected in his absence, and it showed his country's high regard for Commerson's work in the field of botany.

He ranked and still ranks as the most prolifically successful of all plant hunters making, quite literally, thousands of new discoveries. He claimed to know over 25,000 species of plants. When he died his inventory contained fifty-six huge lists of dried plants collected on his voyage from Rochefort to Madagascar. About 1,500 specimens are now in the possession of the Linnaean Society in London, and twice that number are in the Delessert Herbarium. The rest are scattered, but all have been accounted for—except the collection he made on that island of distractions where accommodating ladies danced the timorodee and where ship's carpenter's nails were prized far more than gold. Philibert de Commerson's Tahitian collection was in the first place small, and then altogether lost.

ATHER less than a year after M. de Commerson, naturalist aboard *La Boudeuse* had left Tahiti, there arrived in Matavai Bay Sir Joseph Banks, naturalist to Captain Cook's expedition, aboard the *Endeavour*. Sir Joseph was the "Grand Cham" of botanical collecting at the end of the golden age of botany. And he was a marvelously lucky man; silver-spooned, as it were, from his birth in 1743 right to the end of his long and momentous life. Somehow he managed to be at both Eton and Harrow and he had a considerable income from estates in Yorkshire. His health was excellent until he was crippled with gout in later years, and even then he was blessed with a sufficiently equable temperament to put up with his misfortune. He was happily married, had a devoted sister who wrote up his notes, and he treasured the friendship of George III as well as that of humble students, illustrious scientists, and the influential statesmen of his day. He was president of the Royal Society for forty-two years, enjoyed immense popularity (except with those who envied his position and constant good fortune) and kept court at his house in Soho Square where the library was cared for by the Swedish botanist, Jonas Dryander. Anyone with a curiosity to sell, knowledge to impart, an idea to air, or an interesting tale to tell was sure of a warm welcome— and, if he needed it, a meal and help on his way. But though Banks was a Maecenas, a patron of patrons, he was primarily an active collector, an astute plant hunter whose work on Captain Cook's circumnavigation earned him international honor. To his contemporaries he gave the appearance of being the cock robin of British Science, but only his enemies refused to acknowledge that he was also the owl. He was that unbeatable combination of a visionary and a practical man, and in a study of plant hunting his chief importance lies less in his own distinguished career as a plant hunter than in his encouragement and training of other collectors to work for Kew.

Kew in the eighteenth century was not as it is now. It was royal, not national, property; * exposed to the caprice of Hanoverians; to the uncertain taste of "Poor Fred's" widow (characterized by Thackeray as a "shrewd, hard, domineering, narrow-minded" princess); to the benevolent but not very intelligent interest of her son, George III; and, of course, because the family set the pace in energetic breeding, to the influence of their bevy of relations. The Hookers, father and son, were to make it the greatest botanic garden in the world, but only Banks' spadework made this possible. His friendship with George III, his private fortune, and his high prestige both as a practical botanist and as president of the Royal Society enabled him to materialize many of his excellent ideas without a great deal of financial or bureaucratic trouble. It was due to an idea of Banks that Linnaeus' library and herbarium were bought outright by an Englishman and established in London—to the surprise and the chagrin of the Swedes. It was also due to his suggestion that Botany Bay became a convict settlement. Yet the most imaginative of all his plans was surely the establishment of a "mart and exchange of plants" at the royal garden in Kew.

What is known of Banks' personality suggests that, had it been humanly possible, he himself would have dearly liked to do all the collecting. But he was a realist, and he had gout. Moreover, he knew that he could come closer to satisfying his scientific appetite if he remained at the center

---

* At the beginning it was solely a private venture which (according to the *Kew Illustrated Guide*, p. 2) "explains how it comes about that the most famous botanical garden in the world is situated on a soil so infertile and sandy."

of things, and just at that particular time he could do no better than stay in London—for London then was England, and England then had a world influence and power it had never had before and would never have again. His decision was to organize from London, to send out his trained collecting commandos, and arrange the disposition of what their hunting brought in. Most of their plants and seeds found a first home at Kew, but some went to one or other of the botanic gardens in Jamaica, St. Vincent and Ceylon, which were also brainchildren of the energetic Banks.

The training scheme at Kew was not elaborate, and the success of Sir Joseph's collectors all over the world was more than anything else a tribute to his assessment of their character and his ability to fire them with enthusiasm. That he himself had met many of the dangers he expected them to face was in itself an encouragement. Armchair theorizing is one thing. Being warned by an experienced practitioner is another.

Banks was frank. He told his young men that plant hunting required single-mindedness, stamina and a cheerful indifference to discomfort and to continuous disappointment; and, too, that their vocation (he thought of it as nothing less) might involve them in extremes of heat or cold, hunger and thirst, tropical fevers and contact with revolting diseases and creatures, shipwreck and sudden death. The warning came well from a plant hunter who had all the necessary character qualifications himself, and who, in his adventurous collecting, had suffered from exposure in Tierra del Fuego, malaria on the Malay Archipelago, near shipwreck off Newfoundland, total shipwreck off Australia, and who, again and again, had had to face the high probability that, at any moment, his ship would founder on coral reefs, capsize, or be pooped by Pacific breakers. Moreover, as he had noted in his 1769 journal during a storm off the North Island of New Zealand—

*The almost certainty of being eat as soon as you come ashore adds not a little to the terrors of shipwreck.*

The youngsters would gaze at the fabulous Sir Joseph, admire his sangfroid and candor, and keep him in mind when they encountered dangers in the service of Kew.

Three of them in particular discovered that he had in no way exaggerated, neither overestimating the glory nor underestimating the difficulty of being a plant hunter, and to this day they are remembered among gardeners and plantsmen.

Francis Masson of Aberdeen, trained in plant and seed preservation, actually earned the distinction of being termed "indefatigable" by the indefatigable Banks. He collected twice in South Africa, and in the Iberian Peninsula, Madeira, the Canaries, the Azores and West Indies, and finally in North America where, it is thought, he froze to death in the icy winter of 1805. He worked for £100 a year with the right to £200 worth of expenses. His triumphs were considerable. Apart from introducing Cape Heaths—which so pleased the gardening public that within fifty years over four hundred kinds were being cultivated—he was also the first to appreciate the value of Cape Pelargoniums, sending home fifty varieties which gave rise to the common garden geranium so much loved by the Victorians; and he also introduced varieties of proteas, aloes, and the unique Green Ixia, *I. viridiflora* which, on account of its sea-green flowers with the dusky middle, caused a minor sensation at Kew.

Against the triumphs must be set Masson's disappointments and hardships. In South Africa there was a wealth of savage animals as well as plants. He was fortunate and mostly escaped their attentions by taking proper precautions, but often, when he trekked into the hinterland to botanize, his life was in jeopardy from hostile Africans. His rule was to penetrate as far as possible into the veldt; that is, until he met armed natives who made it abundantly clear that he could go no further. On his second expedition to South Africa, anti-British Boer settlers were even more menacing than the Africans, and it was not safe to travel more than fifty miles from Cape Town. One especial torment confronted him close to Cape Town when a chain gang of escaped convicts tried to capture him and use him as a hostage. He had an irrational but ineradicable dread of being held prisoner, and he knew quite well that if they had not been chained together they would have caught him. As it was he spent a terrified night, crouched in hiding with a clasp knife in his hand, while the convicts, growing more and more desperate and threatening, searched for him through the brush in long sweeps. Though on this occasion he escaped, his fear twice materialized in later years: once while he was serving, very unwillingly, as a British conscript at the fall of New Granada in the West Indies and was taken prisoner by the French; and afterwards, while sailing to America when he was captured by French privateers. His unenviable death in 1805 brought to an end thirty-three years of sacrifice and strenuous plant hunting in the service of Kew.

David Nelson's career as a Kew Collector was shorter and even more dangerous. Banks sent him off on Captain Cook's third expedition as botanist aboard the *Resolution*. It was an immense voyage which took four years and, in the course of it, Nelson was to hunt plants in arctic, temperate and tropical regions. With him on board the *Resolution* was one of Banks' protégés from Tahiti; a youngster named Omai who had been lionized as a curiosity by London Society, painted by Reynolds, taken to the theatre and the House of Lords and (improbably enough) grouse shooting on the Yorkshire moors. He was now to be returned to Tahiti—complete with a pension from King George, an electrical machine, pots, pans and cutlery, a suit of armor, and a portable organ.

The voyage out was eventful. Having delivered Omai —though not to Tahiti where, as an expatriate, he was no longer welcome, but to a neighboring island—and having attended a human sacrifice,* when the butchering of pigs, the heat of sacrificial fires, the wailing and the drumming, and the piercing shrieks of a little boy which was symbolic

---

* John Webber, the *Resolution's* artist, made a drawing of the ceremony.

of divine gratitude, must have been nerve fraying even to a Kew-trained plant collector, they sailed north to the Sandwich Islands and there, in a scurry on the beach of sunny Kealakekua Bay, their commander, Captain Cook, was stabbed to death. To the men on the expedition it was a calamity beyond belief. Not only had Cook been much respected, drawing hero worship from many of them, but undoubtedly he had been the greatest sailor and navigator of his day. Now that they had to do without his genius and his infectious air of confidence, the quite ordinary dangers of the exploration which were bad enough would seem to be multiplied many times. But, perforce, they were obliged to do without him; and they sailed successfully up beyond the Arctic Circle, then south again towards Japan and China, through the strait between Java and Sumatra, and by the Indian Ocean and the Cape, back home again to England.

So shattering a voyage would have been enough for most young men, but not for David Nelson.

One of Sir Joseph's less successful ideas was to introduce breadfruit to the West Indies where he considered it would make cheap and palatable food for Negro slaves. Two expeditions were necessary to accomplish the introduction, and to prove in the end that he had been oversanguine. Both voyages were commanded by a Captain Bligh, his ship on the first occasion being the *Bounty*. Banks sent his trusted plant collector, Nelson, with a Kew trainee, William Brown, to look after the botanical side of things.

The astonishing, virtuoso performance of the late Charles Laughton in the film of *Mutiny on the Bounty* has made Bligh into an irredeemable villain. It appears from historical account that he did have a sharp manner, but that he was no more and no less a brutal disciplinarian than other sea captains of the day. He has been described as a mariner second only to Cook. Certainly his feat in crossing the Pacific in an open boat and, at the same time, keeping a tight control over his fellow-passengers was a testament to his seamanship and to his power of command.

Indirectly, it was the breadfruit which caused the famous mutiny. Like a banana, the plant is mainly propagated by shoots from old stock, though it can be grown from seed. Banks' instructions had been explicit. In order to make sure the enterprise did not fail, Nelson and Brown were to carry both propagating stock and young seedlings, and this necessitated waiting in Tahiti while seeds were sown and grown into seedlings sufficiently robust to withstand a long sea voyage. Five months in the languorous siren island, where there was very little to do, and each man had his girl, heavily underlined the unattractiveness of life below decks on one of his Britannic Majesty's men-o'-war.

The parting from Tahiti was not easy. Some of the crew were genuinely devoted to their vahines. Lotus eating is delicious, but to self-discipline it is poisonous. The scupper-gash and bilge-boys who formed a large part of the crew hated the breadfruit plants as the cause of their leaving the island; just as much they hated the captain who apparently was indifferent to the pain of their departure. After a few days at sea, chafing in their cramped and sweltering quarters, and resenting the ration of fresh water lost each day to the breadfruit, they were ripe for mischief.

David Nelson now had two, new experiences added to his record of privations: to be abandoned in a small boat in the middle of nowhere; and to see the destruction of his plans and hard work—a line of mutinous seamen passing over a thousand breadfruit plants from hand to hand to be dropped over the side. His assistant, William Brown, found himself willy-nilly on the side of the mutineers and obliged to join the chain of seamen destroying his beloved breadfruits. Later he was useful to Fletcher Christian on Pitcairn because of his knowledge of plants and husbandry, but he ended sadly in his own back garden as the victim of a stray bullet.

Nelson's death was of another kind. At the conclusion of that truly terrible forty-seven-day voyage of 4,500 miles in an open boat he died in agony of a lung fever.

Bligh recorded in his log:

*The loss of this honest man I much lamented; he had with great care and diligence attended to the object for which he was sent.*

And, having seen to his decent burying, he noted:

*I was sorry I could get no tombstone to place over his remains.*

Irascible or not, Bligh was high enough in Banks' regard to be sent out on the second and successful voyage to collect breadfruits from Tahiti. And, after Bligh had distinguished himself at the battle of Copenhagen under Nelson, it was at Banks' suggestion that he was appointed governor of New South Wales to pull together the colony's muddled and slender economy. Bligh's regime there was short, and the quality of his government is still open to dispute, but his continuing part in this study is important because there he met and became very friendly with the third of Kew's outstanding collectors, the Yorkshireman, George Caley.

As a boy, Caley had written to Sir Joseph Banks stating bluntly that he intended to be a botanist. He enclosed with the letter some plants and, as one or two turned out to be fresh discoveries, Banks replied with a warning that botany brought small financial rewards but, if the boy were genuinely keen to learn, a job of weeder at Kew at ten shillings a week was his for the asking. Caley took it, and for two years he learned as much as he could when he begged to be sent abroad. Banks at first demurred, then relented, paid for his passage out to Australia and gave him a letter of introduction to Governor Bligh.

For ten years Caley hunted plants in some of the wildest and least known parts of Australia; sending valuable seeds and stock to Kew, and with them loquacious botanical descriptions; on one occasion describing thirty-one packets of seeds in 318 close-written pages. His was a lonely life. After one expedition deep into the interior he told Governor

Bligh that in the whole journey the only living creatures he had seen were two crows, adding gloomily that, in his opinion, even they had lost their way. No doubt because of the monotony he tended to explode whenever he returned to civilization, quarreling with all his neighbors, threatening once to thrash a missionary, paying overt attentions to a widow and to convict women—one of whom, interestingly enough, was Margaret Catchpole, the smuggler's moll from Suffolk.

Captain Bligh liked Caley; but, then, Bligh was Bligh.

Banks, occasionally severe with errant plant hunters, told Caley to behave himself. But even this Olympian warning made little difference, so Banks cut off his income, giving him a choice of returning to England or remaining in the Antipodes. Caley chose to return, and took with him an aboriginal manservant named Dan.

Banks had neither the will nor the heart to be stern any longer. He forgave Caley and welcomed him, and because his many plant introductions had been valuable and of great interest, he appointed him superintendent of the St. Vincent Botanical Garden in Jamaica. A blunt Yorkshireman —in fact, rugged—to the last, Caley fell out with the Jamaican "Quality" and closed the gardens on Sundays—the favorite day for visiting—because, he said, they were a light-fingered lot who helped themselves to seeds.

On the death of Sir Joseph Banks in 1820 a Whig Government began to retrench at Kew. The garden's allocation was reduced and many of its plant hunters called in.

One of the recalled collectors was Alan Cunningham, although he was the king's botanist; and he was actually refused his claim for compensation for his firearms, tent, provisions and plant-hunting kit which had been stolen by escaped convicts on Norfolk Island. Another, James Bowie, who had served Kew well in South Africa sending home a quantity of valued plants, including the progenitors of the modern Gladiolus and the first *Clivia nobilis* to be seen in England, found himself unwanted and in financial difficulties. He was obliged to become gardener to a German baron until he was befriended by the remittance man, Mr. George Rex—a happy-go-lucky bastard of George III, and, therefore, another of Victoria's "wicked uncles."

Kew's prestige fell and was not to rise until Sir William Hooker became the first official director of the National Botanic Garden in 1841.

In these twenty years the chief patrons of plant hunting were a number of recently founded botanical and horticultural societies. They had to pass through the awkward stage and suffer growing pains, some to wither away, others to mature into the well-known societies of today. They were responsible for a continuance of the scientific emphasis in plant collection, for encouraging any enterprise which would add to botanical knowledge, and their eyes were instinctively turned to the richest plant repository in the world, when the obduracy of imperial mandarins had made hunting impossible.

At this point it is appropriate to look back in time and examine, although only superficially, the first hesitant and often clumsy plant hunting undertaken by Westerners in mysterious Cathay.

In the immense history of Imperial China dynasties have altered, though not often, and imperial pleasure grounds, of course, have undergone some change, but the august passion for plants and gardens appears to have remained constant. The first recorded gardening emperor was the illustrious Chin Ming who reigned absolute over a large part of the Chinese Dominions from 2737 to 2697 B.C. The last Manchu emperor of China, though obliged by political circumstances to call himself "Mr. Henry Pu Yi," died in 1967, aged sixty-one, and—still true to the tradition of the Dragon Throne—he died classified as a weeder in the Peking Botanic Gardens. There can be no record quite like this in the whole history of civilization.

China gave gardening to Japan, where from the earliest times there was an equally high regard for trees and flowers, for water and for rock formations. But neither country could or would communicate its high culture to the rest of the world.* Largely for political reasons their front doors were kept shut for as long as possible, which made trading difficult and a systematic investigation of their wild floras quite out of the question. Their cultivated plants, grown for centuries in Oriental gardens and small holdings, gradually found their way to the West and, being unknown and strikingly beautiful, they aroused a furor of interest and, of course, a longing for more. But next to nothing was known of other flowering plants, except that there must be large possibilities. The reports on economic plants sent home by missionaries whetted the thirst of Western botanical collectors long before it was legally possible to hunt plants in the Far East.

The Portuguese merchant adventurers took and held Macao. Much later the Dutch tried to do the same with Formosa, but they were driven out by pirates and had to make do with a tenuous footing in Japan. Their base on the small island of Deshima off Nagasaki enabled servants of the Dutch East India Company to report on local horticulture and the island's flora, no more. For the privilege of using the base, the fattest of the Dutchmen were obliged to go into Yedo (later called Tokyo) once a year and pay a peppercorn rent of self-degradation. They had to turn somersaults in the street and spit on the Cross. The former

---

* Inevitably, for want of the stimulant of fresh ideas, Oriental gardening became formalized and mannered; it almost atrophied into a fixed tradition. When Westerners were first able to examine the tradition, they were enchanted. Chinoiserie in the eighteenth-century, and Japanesery in the nineteenth, were all the rage.

humiliation would have hurt their pride but it is surprising that they submitted to the latter—simply for a trading concession.

Spain, Portugal and England, and even China, found their trading with Japan strictly supervised. The English East India Company did have a factory on Hirado Island from 1614 to 1623, but it proved highly unprofitable and they withdrew. Their factory at Canton, on the other hand, made a sufficient profit to justify its maintenance but the Chinese were as difficult as the Japanese. The liberty of English sailors and traders was seriously restricted. They were forbidden, for example, to move away from their factory, to employ native servants or to learn the Chinese language; and the supercargos could communicate with the government only through a selected list of Chinese merchants.

The tyranny was endured because in time the trickle of trade became highly lucrative. But it hardly allowed for the collecting and exporting of wild Chinese plants, and it is astonishing that as early as the late seventeenth century a company surgeon named Cunningham was able to collect and dry up to a thousand species, among them seeds of the conifer which bears his name, *Cunninghamia sinensis*. Though officially serving as a surgeon, Cunningham was, rather, a negotiator for the company whose duty it was to establish contact with the mandarins and try to open trade with Cochin China. At this fairly high diplomatic level he failed, and so badly that he was the only survivor of a concerted attack on his negotiating party and spent two long years in a Chinese prison. But, afterwards, as a persuader or briber of Chinese guards and coolies, he was an absolute master.

Across the China Seas a German physician named Engelbert Kämpfer was enjoying the Dutch Company's hospitality and carrying out a superficial study of the local flora. His work was necessarily scanty. He had special privileges and, in fact, saw enough of the country to write a *History of Japan,* but his liberty was by no means unlimited. The likelihood of having his ears pinned to a wooden post and the tender parts of his anatomy slowly mutilated if he went beyond permitted boundaries must have deterred his botanic ardor.

A hundred years later the circumstances had barely altered. In the main, Japan rigorously barred foreigners. The Swede, C. P. Thunberg, who, within limits, was allowed to collect at the end of the eighteenth century, and who introduced to Europe the barberry, *Berberis thunbergii*, was very much the exception. And there was hardly any improvement in China. Officially, by that time, some of the Chinese ports were open to trading but it was not worth the cost of bribing officials with large presents or permanent pensions. The Dutch foothold on Deshima, and the ports of Macao and Canton continued as the only outlets to the West, and then Canton itself became threatened. The English government reacted by sending a plenipotentiary, Lord George Macartney, to the imperial court at Peking.

It was a strange mission: rather overstaffed, certainly ill-equipped, and altogether improbable in that not one of the prime officials could speak any of the Chinese languages and they had to rely entirely on the thirteen-year-old son of the Secretary. But the mission was cheerful, its optimism founded on that marvelous English notion that honor and integrity ought, in the end to prevail, but that if they didn't there was always the threat of grapeshot, the cavalry and the flag. As rough-and-ready diplomacy it proved highly successful in a long history of empire building, but with a wise and inscrutable sovereign like the ancient Emperor Kien Lung, who had his own views on honor and was politely deaf to the claims of commerce, it was a miserable failure.

The restrictions on trading and traders were to continue, and even tighten, and only one thing prevented the failure from being total. Sir George Staunton, the Secretary, was an enthusiastic amateur botanist and the inimitable Banks had, of course, suggested that two gardeners be added to the British suite. As a result, a certain amount of discreet plant hunting took place on the journey, and some interesting species were introduced to Europe for the first time.

There was never a large output of cultivated plants through the Dutch trading posts, but the captains of British Indiamen found it sufficiently profitable to buy plants in the nurseries (called *Fa-tee*) of Canton and Macao, and ship them back to European posts. The "Eastern Four," that is, varieties of camellia, chrysanthemum, peony and azalea, were in constant demand. Other genera were introduced casually, by chance, or by an enterprising seaman. Over ninety "Chinese" plants were listed in Banks' Kew Catalogue of 1810–1813, but, by far, the larger part had been introduced by private travelers or by East India Company servants making a side-shilling from rich gardeners in England. It was unthinkable that Sir Joseph Banks should not poke his finger into this particular pie. No one had a quicker or a clearer eye for a plant and from the ninety in his Kew list he would have made a shrewd estimate of China's possibilities. So, in 1803, he sent William Kerr, a Kew gardener, out to Canton, and if he had not been crippled with gout very probably he would have gone himself.

Banks' vicarious collector did well enough, sending home the first tiger lily which was an immediate favorite, Japanese honeysuckle, the sulphur-yellow pygmy water lily, the vigorous, white climbing rose which he named *R. banksiae* as a compliment to his master, and another climber which he named *Kerria japonica* after himself. He was based out in the Far East, at £100 a year, plus expenses, for no less than nine years; botanizing in Java and the Philippine Islands, but spending most of his time in Canton. There he fell foul of the company's senior surgeon, John Livingstone, a fellow-botanist of uncertain temper. Without particularizing, the doctor complained to the fledgling Horticultural Society, of which he was a corresponding member, that Kerr had behaved badly in Canton. Moreover he blamed Kew as well as Kerr because—

*his salary was too small for his necessary wants and conse-
quently he lost respect* \* . . . *I have not the slightest doubt
but his failure is to be attributed, chiefly, to the necessity he
was under of associating with inferior persons.*

The pompous note excites curiosity; and a longing to know
precisely what Kerr was up to, why, how, and with whom.
To describe his work as a "failure" seems overstrong for at
the time this peevish letter was written he had been given
an appointment at the Colombo Botanic Gardens and evidently had Banks' approval and support. Kerr himself was
silent on the matter. He never even explained how he managed to get hold of his plants when the restrictions against
foreigners were so stringent. A happy conjecture suggests
that he was helped by the "inferior persons."

The continuing illiberal attitude of the Chinese mandarins was a source of irritation to the British government.
The East India Company complained. Again and again it
asked for firm support. Ultimately the government was
stung sufficiently to send out a second mission under the
leadership of Lord Amherst as Ambassador. It promised to
succeed better than the first for the embassy had a Chinese-
speaking Secretary; in fact, the very same Staunton who, as
a boy of thirteen, had been the only person able to communicate with the Chinese on the Macartney Mission. Sir
Joseph Banks chose a Doctor Clarke Abel to travel as the
ambassador's naturalist, and provided him with two collectors. It was, moreover, a propitious time to send out an
embassy because the victory of Waterloo had just made
Britain's power plain. Even the Chinese emperor, it was
thought, would have heard of Napoleon and been
impressed by his defeat.

But he had not. Or, if he had, military campaigns and
victories were as unimportant to him as the claims of commerce.

---

\*This is difficult to follow. £100 a year plus expenses appears to have
been the regular Kew salary for a collector out in the field, and the Horticultural Society's own collector in the Far East, Robert Fortune, was engaged for precisely the same figure.

Again the mission was a failure.

On the day of Lord Amherst's arrival, when protocol demanded that he immediately present his credentials at court, he excused himself on the grounds that he was indisposed. No doubt he was after the journey up from the coast. But ambassadors have made greater sacrifices for England than attending court while suffering from traveler's dysentery. It counted against Amherst, as did his reaction when informed by an imperial functionary that protocol also demanded that he should prostrate himself before the Dragon Throne. He threw a thoroughly British huff and declined to do any such thing.

Making indignant gestures from a position of strength is one thing. From a position of weakness it is another. The emperor simply declined to see such a proud, pert man and dismissed the embassy. Having achieved precisely nothing Amherst was forced to go home.

On the way back to the coast Abel's two collectors hunted plants. He himself was in a delicate state and he had been a nonfunctioning naturalist from the start, but he used his influence to persuade the mortified ambassador that, if they slowed down their pace to suit the collectors, the embassy might have at least something to show for all its trouble. Such candor was not calculated to soothe, but Abel was more concerned with botany than Amherst's wounded pride, and, being frank, he got his way. The pace was slowed down and, as they pottered their way to Canton, the collectors foraged alongside the route. They were under considerable pressure, being obliged to keep an eye on their Chinese escort and after a time they had to abandon the general practice of taking duplicates. Nevertheless, their collecting was thorough and successful; a rich haul of seeds and plants which, without any doubt, would impress the authorities at home.

But fortune continued to frown on the Amherst embassy.

Doctor Abel gave the few duplicates into the care of the embassy's Secretary. The rest was consigned to H.M.S.

*Alceste,* and this vessel, driven by a storm, was holed on a coral reef off Borneo, and the main botanical collection went to the bottom of the Java Sea.

In the story of early plant hunting in Cathay, John Reeves holds a distinguished place, not so much because he was an assiduous collector but because he was methodical. He was especially aware of the difficulties in transporting plants over long distances, game to make endless experiments, and never discouraged even when his consignments were lost at sea and he had to make up collections for a second or third time.

In the official ranks of the East India Company one of the most exalted was the post of Chief Inspector of Tea at Canton. Reeves held it for seventeen years and only twice in that long period did he take leave in England. The rest of the time he was wielding a large influence over gardening and botanical affairs, both in the Far East and in Europe. In fact, he held a comparable position in China to that of Sir Joseph Banks in England. It was he who entertained visiting botanists; giving hospitality, advice and every encouragement to plant hunters sent out from England.* Inevitably he was Banks' friend and correspondent, and he wrote regularly as well to Secretary Sabine of the Horticultural Society and to Secretary Lindley who followed him. In Canton he made a willing ally of Chief Surgeon Livingstone, and together they devised plans to make the export of plants less haphazard than it had been.

Though a man of such importance, even Reeves was not allowed into the interior and he had to keep within a restricted area round Canton, but, being an administrator of great ingenuity, he organized illegal squads of coolies to hunt for him in the hills and he paid painters to make a record of the plants that were brought in just in case any should prove to be obstinate travelers and refuse to live through the long journey to England. These colored drawings were sent to the Horticultural Society in London, actu-

---

* Two gardener-collectors of the Horticultural Society, appositely named Potts and Parks, acknowledged Reeves' kindness in their journals.

ally sold when that society came to grief, and only found their way back to the refounded and renamed Royal Horticultural Society in 1936.

The monopoly enjoyed by the East India Company in China gave plant hunters the opportunity to collect in the immediate vicinity of Canton and Macao, but one large land frontier to the north was entirely outside the company's sphere of influence and it was there that Russian botanists made their explorations.

For some inscrutable reason a Russian imperial ecclesiastical mission was housed permanently in Peking and the Chinese authorities permitted the mission a staff of three scientists. In 1830, Doctor Alexander von Bunge, the athletic botanist celebrated for his plant hunting in the desolate heights of Mongolia, was appointed botanist to the mission in Peking. Unfortunately he had most of the attributes of redhaired men, and no patience at all with the lunatic bureaucracy of the Celestial Empire. Within a year he was causing diplomatic upheavals and his *permis de séjour* was withdrawn. But even in that short space of time Bunge made fabulous discoveries: among them winter jasmine, the chicory-blue leadwort, *Ceratostigma plumbaginoides* (sometimes wrongly called *Plumbago*) and the spindle tree which has his name, *Euonymus bungeanus*. A doctor named Kirilof was attached to the same mission and he was in Peking ten years, but his collections never matched von Bunge's. They included, though, a specimen of *Panax ginseng,* a plant so rare and so highly valued as an aphrodisiac that the emperor mounted an expedition every year to hunt for the plants in Manchuria.

The Russians knew something of China's flora, the settlers in Canton and Macao a little more; but the territory actually explored was only a fractional part of the great landmass of China.

Japan, too, remained a fortress, though a Bavarian doctor named Philipp Franz van Siebold had managed to accomplish something. He was attached to the Dutch Station on Deshima and had the inestimable luck to be an eye specialist as well as a botanist. The Japanese, with their noted eye troubles, found it in their interest to allow him special privileges, and he managed to make collections far larger than his predecessors in Japan, Kämpfer and Thunberg. His life, however, was not without risks. Bartering his ophthalmic skill for a license to move freely on the main islands, he had seduced the myopic Imperial Astronomer into letting him have a copy of a map of Japan, a secret document of great importance, but on his way back to Deshima he was shipwrecked and the map discovered. Japanese heads rolled—but an eye doctor was an eye doctor. Siebold was sentenced to two years' confinement to Deshima, to be followed by banishment. In 1830 he took 458 plants with him to Holland; in itself a considerable achievement. But he had seen the possibilities on his trip to the main islands. He described them. Botanical appetites in Europe were stimulated.

At the beginning of the nineteenth century forbidden interiors of both China and Japan held golden promise and the restrictions must have been agonizing to plant hunters of imagination and spirit.

Away to the west in North America there were no restrictions beyond those imposed by wars, wild Indians, deplorable conditions and dangerous terrain. Because of their preoccupation with settling the land and spreading frontiers, establishing agriculture and commerce, and fighting Indians, Englishmen and the French, few American-born Colonists had had time for plant hunting. John Bartram was an exception, and so were Lewis and Clark and Long all of whom collected on their expeditions to the west. Otherwise, the scientific botanizing in the States had been undertaken by Europeans, by André Michaux who collected for the French government, by an Austrian, Frederick Pursh, by two Englishmen, Nuttall and Goldie, and by two Scots, Archibald Menzies and David Douglas. The last made his collections when Kew was at its lowest ebb and the Horticultural Society of London tumbling into ruin, and, without any doubt, he was the most intrepid and successful hunter ever known.

ROBABLY it has no significance, but it is nonetheless remarkable that, whereas emperors, holy popes, kings, electors, reigning dukes and bishops have generally been enthroned on worthwhile articles of furniture, the kings of Scots have not. Their throne has been stone; simply a rock, greyish-blue in color, cold to the touch, roughly the size and shape of a church hassock. Scone, where the coronations took place, once had a substantial royal palace. After the union it fell into desuetude. What was a royal city, a meeting place of Parliaments, shrank and shrank to finish as a decayed, run-down hamlet with a handful of cottages and a church.

It was there, right at the end of the eighteenth century, that David Douglas was born.

His father called himself a stonemason, which meant that he turned out a tombstone or two and cut lettering, but otherwise was the district's jack-of-all-trades. He was noted for being short-tempered, unsmiling and mulish.

All three handicaps were inherited by his second boy, David. The resulting clash of wills was so alarming that Mrs. Douglas got the boy out of the way by sending him to the village school at the tender age of three. This, at any rate, is what she hoped; but David defied the schoolmistress' authority, played truant, and behaved so badly that he had to be taken away. Either that or he was expelled—and all before the age of seven.

At his new school the master believed in using the tawse—a double-ended strap of hardened leather—very hard and very regularly, but it made small difference to young Douglas. He was no more respectful or punctual than before, neither was he any more thorough with his school-work. Probably the only thing which prevented this bumptious delinquent from developing into a thug was his consuming passion for natural history. It humanized him, and good luck helped as well for when, to everyone's relief, he left school at the age of ten, just the sort of job he wanted was waiting for him on his own doorstep.

No large garden was within reach of Scone until about the time David was ousted from the village school when the old palace was rebuilt by the Earl of Mansfield. Considering Scone too close to the palace, he had the hamlet moved, literally, two miles further away. The parish church was taken down, its stones numbered, and rebuilt on the new site. Over £70,000 were spent on the mansion which had 125 rooms, ninety of them bedrooms, and this magnificence was matched in the grounds. The gardens, already becoming well-known for their excellence when David Douglas left school, were superintended by a friend of his father, the head gardener, William Beattie.

Scone gardens and Mr. Beattie worked like an Aladdin's lamp on the boy. His pigheadedness and his idleness in school changed overnight to a willingness and eagerness to learn. In his seven-year apprenticeship he became a master in the practical details of working ornamental, forcing and kitchen gardens. He became proficient, also, as a botanist, collecting wild specimens in the hills for drying and pressing, or transplanting to his father's garden. He became thirsty for knowledge; reading travel books, works on natural history, the Bible, anything he could lay his hands on; and when, at eighteen, he was recommended by Beattie to a post in the famous gardens at Valleyfield near Dunfermline, he seemed well set on the path to distinction as a master-gardener himself. But the large collection of exotic plants at Valleyfield suggested a fresh and very original idea to Douglas. Instead of a gardener, he would be a botanist, and not an ordinary, stay-at-home, microscope and notebook botanist, but a collector out in the field, a real hunter.

It has already been remarked that the rise to fame and fortune of botanists from humble circumstances reads very often like a fairytale. David Douglas' good fortune was no less exceptional.

To begin with, his employer at Valleyfield gave him the privilege of using his own, private, botanical library and he took such advantage of the opportunity that in two years he was able to apply for, and get, a place on the staff of the Botanical Garden at Glasgow. There he caught the eye of William Hooker, one of the foremost botanists of the day, and professor at the university. The country boy from Scone and the professor of botany became fast friends, and botanized together on the Scottish Highlands and islands. So high was Hooker's regard for his young companion that he recommended him to Secretary Sabine of the new Horticultural Society of London, and, at the tender age of twenty-four, Douglas was given his heart's desire by being appointed to collect information and plants for the society in the east of the United States.

A map of the United States in 1823 looks quaint.

Parts of the country were unexplored, huge areas unsettled, even unmapped. The horn of Florida had recently been bought from Spain. The present states of California, Nevada, Utah, Arizona, New Mexico, Texas and three-quarters of Colorado were colonies of the Mexican emperor. The states of Washington, Oregon and Idaho were still English, and Alaska was Russian. Though New York boasted a population of 125,000, there was a neglected twenty-acre garden where Rockefeller Center now stands, and the city scavenging department was composed of a herd of gutter-rooting and very healthy pigs.

Douglas' job was to find new plants if he could, but principally he was to study American fruit growing in the east, and beg or buy specimens of trees.

The voyage out from Liverpool took fifty-nine whole days. On the second week fresh water was rationed, and tobacco became so scarce that the crew used it twice over— chewing it first, then drying it in the sun to make it smokable. Getting ashore at New York must have been like escaping from prison.

Douglas' first expeditions at once illustrated his determination and singlemindedness. He met some colorful characters, among them William Coxe, an orchidist, who gave him, for presentation to the Horticultural Society, two bottles of seven-year-old cider, and an ex-governor of New York, DeWitt Clinton, who consigned to his care six wild pigeons, boxes of minerals, apples, pears, moccasins, books and written speeches. He traveled by various conveyances —stage-coach, horse-drawn canal barges and paddle steamers. In one of the latter they hit a storm and a paddle was swept away. He saw some fine sights, too; the house of exile of Joseph Bonaparte, Napoleon's brother and ex-king of Spain, Niagara Falls, and the gala opening of the Erie Canal at Albany. But he thought of little except natural history. The botanical gardens at Philadelphia and Bartram's "Garden of Delight" at Kingsessing mattered a thousand times more to him than the pleasure grounds of Bony's brother. The best part of his trip to Niagara was the opportunity to botanize on the river banks and on Goat Island. And while Albany had a riproaring time at the canal opening with the firing of guns, bands, processions, fireworks, liquor, barbecues and general uproar, Douglas was locked in a hotel room arranging his collections.

His is one of the most extreme examples of a boy's hobby turning into a man's fulltime job, of an interest becoming an all-absorbing passion—what, quite rightly, is called "a craze." Very probably the citizens of Albany regarded their Scottish guest as crazy.

Douglas' trip, anyway, was successful. He carried back to England many plants of interest, notes on their distribution, habitat, seeds, dried specimens and living plants; and, in addition to the gifts from Coxe and Clinton and other well wishers, he took with him some living wood ducks and quail.

The voyage home was shorter and more comfortable; barely thirty days. Curiously enough, only the ducks were seasick.

Douglas' other trips for the Horticultural Society of London could be called his "Great Adventures." In them he often trod where no white man, and perhaps in some cases where no one at all, had ever been before. They were in the wilds of Canada under the protection, so called, of the Hudson Bay Company or on the undeveloped, mostly unexplored western coastline of North America.

The easy way to the west coast was around Cape Horn and on his first long voyage out aboard the *William and Ann,* in 1824, Douglas was delighted to have the company of a youngster he had known at Glasgow University; John Scouler, aged nineteen but already a doctor and ship's surgeon.

Scouler was as much a magpie collector as Douglas. At Rio, for example, we hear of him returning on board one evening looking extremely odd. The japanned collecting tin on his back was jammed tight with plants, so much that they spilled out of the top. His pockets were full of pieces of granite. His hat, inside and out, was pinned all over with insects. Both arms were full of plants, and somehow he also managed to be carrying one of the most venemous of Brazilian snakes.

He and Douglas packed two boxes of rare orchids and other plants and sent them back to London from Rio, and on the voyage south to the Horn they continued their observation of natural history; measuring seaweed sixty feet long, and catching several albatrosses, one with a twelve-foot wing span. What the superstitious sailors thought of this is not recorded.

It was a happy voyage for both of them. The captain being tolerant (he was rewarded for his patience by a silver medal from the Horticultural Society), they turned his ship into a floating laboratory. When they made landfall at Fort George (now called Astoria), and while the *William and Ann* was being refitted and revictualed, Surgeon Scouler was given permission to botanize with Douglas. Apart from the company of a few enthusiastic amateurs among the "gentlemen" of the Hudson Bay Company and the "employees" who were mostly French Canadian, Indians, halfbreeds with a few Sandwich Islanders, or friendly Indians whom he trained to collect for him, Douglas thereafter was a lone plant hunter.

On New Year's Day, 1826, after six months in the Columbia River region, and having already suffered a great deal for the sake of botany, Douglas wrote in his journal:

*I am now here, and God only knows where I may be next. In all probability, if a change does not take place, I will shortly be consigned to the tomb.*

Of Douglas' three main expeditions, the first to the east coast, the second in the northwest and across British North America and a third in California and the west coast, the second made the greatest demands upon him.

He proved his devotion, or craze, by once undertaking an extended journey into unknown territory provided with hardly any clothing at all, simply so that he could carry thirty quires of paper, weighing 102 pounds, for drying and packing the plants he hoped to collect. On another occasion, when snowshoeing through the Rockies with a party of hungry, half-frozen company men (an appalling journey on which they had to ford a racing mountain river fourteen times in a day by plunging up to the waist in the bitterly cold water), one of them was lucky enough to see and shoot a gamebird renowned as excellent eating. But no one had a taste of it. Douglas was there first, and not having seen such a fowl before he refused to give it up, stuffed it on the spot, and added it to the heavy load he was already carrying. He named it "Franklin's Grouse" and the very specimen which he roughly preserved about 150 years ago, high in the Rockies, may still be seen in the Royal Scottish Museum in Edinburgh.

Apart from the sheer fatigue of traveling huge distances over uneven ground on foot, he faced some very real dangers. He made friends with a few of the Indians, especially among the Chinooks, who called him "The Grass Man" for obvious reasons, and who considered he must be one of King George's great white chiefs. These were friendly, and from others he bought friendship with beads, buttons, rings, gimcrack trinkets and plugs of tobacco, but quite frequently he found himself threatened by hostile Indians. There was always the risk of meeting a war party or of employing a treacherous guide.

He had to put up with worse trials; long bouts of hunger so extreme that he was almost starved and reduced to eating all the berries and seeds he had been at such pains to collect, the roots of wild arrowhead and liquorice, the skins of the animals he had dried to send to England, and "twice being obliged to eat up his horse." Then there were natural dangers such as slime pits, snow drifts, chasms, avalanches, half-hidden rocks and other river snags that tore the bottom out of a canoe as well as rapids, waterfalls and floods. He lost his entire collections twice in the same hazardous place. There were fevers, too, which only the toughest of the Europeans could withstand and which decimated the Indians. Attacks of fever weakened Douglas, as did a festering knee caused by a rusty nail, and he began to suffer from a severe irritation in his eyes which made seeing more and more difficult. Vermin were an additional menace. Pack rats ate up all the seeds he had recently collected while he lay asleep, gnawed through a bundle of dried plants, carried off his razor and shaving bowl, and did not wake him until they began to drag away his portable inkstand. This disturbed him. He stretched out for his gun and shot them dead. He also had a bad experience with "an indescribable

herd of fleas" in an Indian hall. He escaped from them to
sleep outside, where immediately he was attacked by "two
species of ants, one very large, black, three-quarters of an
inch long, and a small red one."

Poor weather was so commonplace that for days and
nights on end Douglas was never dry, and the storms could
be wild and frightening:

*The rain, driven by the violence of the wind, rendered it
impossible for me to keep any fire, and to add misery to my
affliction my tent was blown down at midnight . . . Every
ten or fifteen minutes immense trees falling produced a
crash as if the earth was cleaving asunder, which with the
thunder peal on peal before the echo of the former died
away, and the lightening in zigzag and forked flashes, had
on my mind a sensation more than I can ever give vent to.*

His fortitude was nothing short of heroic and it is
barely surprising that his already short temper grew shorter.
Candidly he admitted it:

*. . . travelled thirty-three miles, drenched and bleached
with rain and sleet, chilled with a piercing north wind; and
then to finish the day experienced the cooling, comfortless
consolation of lying down wet without supper or fire. On
such occasions I am very liable to become fretful.*

Most of us would weep, turn up our toes, and die.

It was on this, his second American expedition, that Douglas found and introduced to Europe the pine which bears his
name; a massive but graceful tree, and so tall that, in its
native forests, the branchless trunks soar upwards like ca-
thedral pillars of green-gray marble. And the Douglas fir
was only one of his many finds among the conifers. In a

letter to Hooker in Glasgow he wrote: "You will begin to think that I manufacture Pines at my pleasure."

Perhaps the sugar pine was the most beautiful of them all. Certainly it led him the greatest dance.

Right at the beginning of his exploration he had found Kalapooia Indians chewing large, sweet-flavored pine seeds, and learned that they came from an outsize tree which grew far away. A little time after, having established that the trees grew in the mostly unknown country of the Umpqua Indians, and learning that company fur hunters were about to explore that region, he attached himself to the party.

The fur hunters rode but the plant hunter preferred to walk and use his horse as a baggage carrier. They had to rely for food on what they shot and, game being in short supply, quite soon they were hungry. This was not the least of their trials. One of the party was treed and partly savaged by a grizzly. By the time they had reached the site of the present city of Elkton, the fur hunters were exhausted through hunger and from hacking a trail through thick undergrowth, and their horses were worn and winded.

The indomitable Douglas pulled in his belt another notch, went on botanizing on his own, toppled into a deep gulley, and lay unconscious for five hours until some Kalapooias found him. His chest was very painful, so he gave himself a drastic kill-or-cure treatment, bled himself from the left foot, and took a bath in the ice-cold river.

Against all the rules, he recovered.

At this point he decided to leave the main party and set out after the sugar pines guided by Centernose, the son of a chief.

It was a terrible journey.

They had enough food for one meal a day, were drenched and frozen in a storm, and the botanist caught some sort of chill. His head was racked with pain, his belly tightened with cramps and he had such dizzy spells that he could barely see. He cured the chill by sweating it out and then tramping thirteen miles.

Eventually, when walking by himself, he met an Indian

who strung his bow at the ragged collector and would have shot him. Douglas quickly laid down his own gun, gave the boy some beads, shared a pipe with him, and by sign language discovered that he was about twenty miles from the sugar pine country.

He reached his objective some hours later and, forgetting his tiredness and hunger, was transported with delight.

The trees were too vast to be measured as they stood, but one, which had been blown down by the wind, had a total length of 215 feet, and at its fattest was fifty-seven feet, nine inches. Douglas carefully noted these details and others, and then set about shooting down a few of the foot-long cones from the tops of the trees.

There he was, blasting away, chipping them from the branches with ball, when he found himself surrounded by a party of eight Indians in full war paint who were armed to the teeth and looked anything but friendly.

A battle of nerves followed: the Indians with strung bows aiming at Douglas, and he six paces away with a cocked gun in one hand and a pistol in the other. It went on for eight, nine, ten, tense, silent minutes, until the Indian leader abruptly asked for tobacco.

The tension was broken. Douglas promised them tobacco if they fetched him more of the cones. They agreed and disappeared.

He picked up three bright green cones he had shot from the tree and ran as fast as he could back to his camp. There, unable to converse with his guide, not daring to light a fire, and supperless, he spent an uneasy night in constant expectation of an attack.

No attack came. Instead, three grizzly bears turned up at dawn. Douglas shot two of them.

He then made his way downriver. Meeting the main party, they built fires against the possibility of Indian attacks, pulled in their belts—for they were all famished—and, the strain getting the better of them, quarreled fiercely among themselves.

Douglas' worst experience came near the end of the

journey, when, in swimming a river, he lost by far the
greater part of all he had collected in the past weeks of
continual hardship. Happily though, he still had his precious sugar pine cones.

After such a harrowing adventure anyone less than
David Douglas would have taken a rest, particularly as he
suffered afterwards from severely swollen ankles caused by
walking so far in the wet and cold. But, once his feet were in
trim again he could not sit still. He was off to the coast
by himself to collect seaweeds and shells—and there a tempest dashed his canoe to pieces on the shore. He crawled to
safety and took refuge from the storm with an Indian friend
who fed him dried salmon and salal berries. This unsuitable
food gave him such severe and weakening bilious attacks
that his long trek back to the company's base was a torment
of exhaustion and hunger. He arrived there on a Christmas
Day, rather more dead than alive.

Douglas had his rewards. His successes were enormous.

After this expedition he made the difficult journey
overland to take ship on Hudson Bay. When he reached
York Factory on the southwest shore he had traveled by
canoe, or shallop, or on horseback, snowshoe or on foot over
ten thousand miles in a little over two years. Without a
companion or crampons, alpenstock, snow goggles, or even a
walking stick (and simply as a diversion in the middle of a
long trek) he had climbed the two highest peaks in the
Rocky Mountains and named them in honor of Brown, the
botanist, and his great friend, William Hooker. He had set a
record in finding and ultimately introducing to England
more plants than ever before had been introduced by any
individual from any country.

Fate played a last, little trick on him a few days before
he was due to sail on the *Prince of Wales*. Because of
shallow water the ship lay out at some distance from the

shore and Douglas, with a party of three and eight oarsmen, rowed out to visit her riding at anchor. On their way back they were caught in a hurricane, swept out into the bay. The waves were many feet high. There was tremendous thunder and rain. The cold was intense. Rowing was impossible; all they could do was try to keep the boat afloat by bailing continuously with their hats. This they did all night, all the next day, and well into the second night before they could use the oars. By this time they were seventy miles out without a compass and in the pitch dark. It was a miracle, nothing less, that eventually they got back to York Factory; all the same they had suffered severely from the cold and the exposure. Douglas, especially, was in poor shape, and he had hardly recovered the use of his limbs before the *Prince of Wales* made landfall at Portsmouth on October 11, 1827.

David Douglas had been out of the country for a little over three years. He was twenty-eight years old and already famous.

The magnificent achievement of their salaried collector was genuinely appreciated by the Council and Fellows of the Horticultural Society of London, and, too, by a far wider circle of admirers. Douglas was elected a Fellow—and without the obligation to pay fees or subscriptions—of three learned bodies, the Linnaean Society, the Zoological Society, and the Geological Society. Arrangements were made for his journal to be published.

He was gratified by the honors and, to begin with, he enjoyed being made much of in London drawing rooms and committee rooms, even ballrooms. Then, either it went to his head or (and this is more probable) he became bored. Certainly, at what could have been one of the happiest times of his life, he was discontented, surly, anxious to find fault.

He had some cause. To have made such sacrifices for the Horticultural Society—and then discover he was being paid less than the porter who opened and shut their front door would have inflamed a less excitable man than David Douglas. And his bad temper was nourished when he discovered that some of the natural history specimens that he had so carefully sent home in 1825 had been thoughtlessly stuffed in a corner. They were motheaten, crushed, and useless.

He quarreled with Secretary Sabine. He quarreled with the committee members. He quarreled with the Fellows. He would have quarreled by post with Hooker if Hooker had allowed him to. Hooker, more than anyone, knew what was wrong, that restlessness was at the root of the trouble, and being lionized and made much of did not suit David Douglas of Scone.

The Scots, like Slavs and most European Russians, are noted for their taciturnity. If it is relieved by a sense of humor, however wry, all is well. Douglas was simply taciturn, as unsmiling as his father.

The Scots, like Texans, Arabs and the hill tribesmen of India, are fiercely independent people—which is honorable and praiseworthy if it is not spoiled by pigheadedness. Douglas' early history showed how large a share he had of stubbornness.

He was a misfit in London society; dour, humorless, suspicious and cantankerous and, in the end, ill-mannered. Had he someone to love he might have been different, but nothing in the nature of a love letter has ever come to light in all his private correspondence. He respected and admired a few friends. He was devoted to a small Scots terrier called Billy, which from this time was hardly ever away from his side. But he gave his heart to plants only.

None of this says that by nature he was an unhappy man. Dickens might have made a mistake in supposing that old Ebenezer Scrooge was miserable simply because he was unlike everyone else in *A Christmas Carol*. In his own grouchy, Scrooge-like way, no doubt he was quite content without human companionship, goose and plum pudding. And Douglas may have been the same. In London society he behaved badly because he was as much out of his proper element as a fish in a tree or a bird in a goldfish bowl.

Hooker knew this. Writing many years later, he described Douglas' low spirits and irritability and the cause of both:

*His temper became more sensitive than ever, and himself restless and dissatisfied; so that his best friends could not but wish, as he himself did, that he were again occupied in the honourable task of exploring northwest America.*

There was widespread relief when the Horticultural Society sent him off on another expedition to the western coast of North America. He was to travel by way of the Horn and the Sandwich Islands and concentrate most of his attention on the flora of California. The Zoological Society sponsored him in a small way, as did the British Colonial Office which wanted accurate maps of the Columbia territory. He was shown how to fix geographical positions with their longitude and latitude, given a sextant, chronometer, barometer, thermometer, hygrometer, compass, the most expensive apparatus for making magnetic observations, and taught how to use them.

Douglas was being sent back into his proper element under the patronage of the British Government, the Royal Navy, the Hudson Bay Company, the Horticultural and the Zoological Societies. As he noted himself, it was "not the journey of a commonplace tourist."

He sailed away on October 31, 1829, and never saw England again.

His previous hardships had told on Douglas. When he reached the Columbia region after an eight-month voyage, his old acquaintances noted the alteration in him. During his absence the Greenwich Naval School had sent out several youngsters to be trained by the company. One of these boys, who had never seen the thirty-year-old botanist before, described him as "a fair florid partially bald-headed Scotsman of medium stature gentlemanly address about forty-eight years of age."

He was still tough, though, under his battered surface. He hired a man-o'-war's deckhand to carry his equipment when he went collecting, and, for the time being, his journeys were neither as long nor as adventurous as before. But he had the resistance to survive a bout of fever so terrible that whole Indian villages, of 450 inhabitants and more, were totally wiped out, twenty-four of the company's men died, and trading, for a while, was at a standstill. Douglas apparently kept himself on the go with what he called "healthful perambulations"—in other words, arduous botanizing trips.

By the time he judged he ought to be moving south to California, he had collected a consignment of dead and living quadrupeds, birds, reptiles and insects for the Zoological Society, and for the Horticultural Society, three chests of seeds, and over a hundred new species of plants—including six unknown pines.

As the Indians in the sugar pine country between Columbia and California were restless and dangerous, and Douglas felt less inclined to take risks than he had before, he decided to travel by ship.

Archibald Menzies, naturalist aboard the *Discoverer* on Vancouver's exploration of the western coast of America, had landed in California even before Douglas' birth. He had collected a few plants and written careful and tantalizing descriptions of others. At the time of Douglas' visit it was a Mexican colony where the vine, the olive and the fig, and even bananas and sugar cane were cultivated; but the larger part was unpopulated and generally unknown.

Douglas showed the uncertainty in his mind of what might lie ahead of him by the list of provisions he bought before leaving Columbia. Apart from the obvious necessities like shoes, shot, cod line and candles, he included ten pounds of tea, nine gallons of brandy, two large black silk handkerchiefs, a large mooseskin, and a jew's harp. He paid off his deckhand servant, and with Billy, the terrier, took a brig sailing south.

"Don David," as Douglas was called because he was an *"hombre de educación,"* was enchanted by California: its rich flora, the kindness of the inhabitants, the hospitality and help given him by the Franciscan friars who "loved the sciences too well to think it curious to see one go so far in quest of grass."

The only drawbacks to this otherwise perfect place were the presence of two other botanists * and the intense summer heat. He made friends with the former and they swopped finds like schoolboys, but he could do nothing about the latter and it was "hot enough to suffocate all fleas."

The spring was unbelievably beautiful and it was then that he had to work speedily before the heat parched up the vegetation. In his first year, Douglas arranged and cataloged a number of unknown genera and over eight hundred species, many of them new.

In California he found, and later introduced to London, the Garrya which in its male form is one of the most striking and elegant evergreens under the sky. Its egg-shaped leaves are the color of emeralds above, and underneath are furry and gray. The catkins—a foot long in the States, but barely half that in England—are like closely linked necklaces of jade. This, with the introduction of the Monterey pine and a number of brilliant, annual flowers like wild

---

* Dr. Thomas Coulter who was collecting there for a Swiss patron, and Ferdinand Deppe, a German naturalist who traveled the world as a supercargo.

heliotrope, blazing star and Californian bluebell, gave him fame far beyond Great Britain. For example, a duplicate set of one of his collections was sent to the botanic garden at St. Petersburg.

The especial value of Don David's Californian expedition was that he stayed nineteen months there and was systematic in his collecting. In the end he had about sixty new plants, but his collections consisted of hundreds of species, together with seaweeds, mosses and liverworts.

In the soil attached to their roots were flakes and spots of a yellowish mineral. Douglas knew what it was, but he did not guess how much of this yellow mineral there was. If he had, perhaps the great Californian Gold Rush of 1848 would have taken place seventeen years beforehand.

Douglas returned to Columbia, via the Sandwich Islands, for another collecting trip, and heard there that the Horticultural Society which employed him was in a turmoil. His patron, Sabine, was such an enthusiastic gardener that he had handed the everyday affair of the secretaryship to a clerk—who then had embezzled the society funds. At the same time it was discovered that certain Fellows, including the king, a duke, a marquess, thirteen other peers, and twelve clergymen, owed outstanding subscriptions. Sabine resigned. Douglas, out of loyalty, resigned with him. Thereafter, all his collections went to Hooker.

But this was not to be for long.

A project approved and backed by the czar and the Russian governor of Alaska, that Douglas should botanize across Alaska, Siberia, Russia and Europe, ended only 1,150 miles after the start of the journey.

Even covering that distance was a heroic feat because Douglas' eyesight had worsened. He was completely blind in the right eye and had to wear smoked spectacles to protect the other. As a result his temper had shortened and sharpened. He had quarreled with a company trader on the journey and had been challenged to a duel—which he had declined. He learned that the Indians ahead were unfriendly. He was low in spirits and could not face the prospect of months of travel through unknown country. For the first time, he turned back. A week later came disaster.

His party was canoeing down to headquarters on the Frazer River when, in the rapids at Fort George Canyon, the canoe was ripped and smashed to pieces. Douglas himself was carried down to a whirlpool and swirled round and round in dizzy turbulence for an hour and forty minutes before being washed out like a cork onto a rocky shore. Providentially, all the travelers escaped with their lives, but Douglas had lost a collection of four hundred species of plants and—this was the real disaster—his volume of field notes in which he had listed, against numbers, the precise location of all his important Californian plants. It was a serious loss to him, and has been to botanists ever since.

He reached the Columbia River, exhausted. Three months afterwards, and with enormous reluctance, he decided that he would have to return home. To do so by the Sandwich Islands, where he could collect from the tropical vegetation and examine the volcanoes, made the thought of London fractionally more bearable.

He and Billy sailed in the company's brig in October, 1833—touching for a time at San Francisco—"a few dilapidated buildings"—where Douglas camped and botanized on an eminence which is now roughly the center of modern San Francisco. Then he sailed to Honolulu.

Douglas enjoyed his months in the Sandwich Islands. He was intrigued by the natives' notion that fatness is attractive, and noted how they stuffed themselves with *poi* —a starchy dish made from taro. He hired porters, a cook, a birdcatcher and a guide who carried his spy glass and umbrella; shot black pigs and wild cattle (the descendants of those brought to the islands by Captain Vancouver); botanized, finding some interesting ferns as well as many mosses and lichens; and traveled the islands in turn, making magnetic and geographical records and observing extinct and half-active volcanoes.

By the end of June he was familiar with all the islands and felt obliged to face the depressing prospect that, when a ship bound for England made landfall at Honolulu, he would have to leave for home. While waiting, he undertook to show a visiting missionary the wonders of Hawaii. They agreed to meet at a village on Hawaii called Hilo.

The meeting never took place.

Douglas walked the long route over the mountain. He was unable to hire a porter and carried his own small bundle and equipment. Billy trotted with him. He stayed the night at the house of a man named Davis, and, early the next day called on an English ex-convict, Ned Gurney. He was warned that about two miles further on there were three cattle traps, that is, crudely made pits disguised with branches, leaves and earth.

Some time after, two of Gurney's natives heard the unmistakable sounds of a trapped beast in one of the pits. They looked in. Snorting with fear, and stamping in the debris of soil and leaves which had caved in under its weight, was a terrified wild bull. Beneath it, half-covered with fallen earth, the clothes rent, lay the gored body of a man.

In the pathway, a little black dog was guarding a bundle which the natives recognized. The dog howled and howled and would not stop.

No one could be sure whether Douglas had met his death by accident or not. Old jailbirds are never free of suspicion. It was said that the botanist had had a bag of money on him when he set out, and that this was never found. An American cattle hunter examined his body and expressed the view that the wounds and gashes could not have been caused by a bull; there was sufficient doubt for the local missionary to embalm his body so that it could be sent to Honolulu for expert examination. There the experts said the wounds had been caused by a bull.

To this day there are unconvinced people who believe he was murdered, but it seems probable that Douglas heard the bull's bellows and, like the natives after him, peered into the pit—and slipped. His end, with no chance at all of escaping that maddened beast, must have been a terrible one.

He was mourned by men of science all over the world. But he left only £50 and a bundle of dried plants collected in the Sandwich Islands.

Billy was sent back to England.

# ❧ Part Two
# The Techniques of Collecting

## one / Fieldwork

*Equipment: taking Herbarium material: Notes and Maps: Transporting Exotics: a Short History of the Carriage of Plants: Particular Difficulties on Sea Voyages: Experiments, Recommendations and Complaints: Transporting Seeds.*

## two / Nathaniel Ward of Wellclose Square

*A Portrait from Deduction: the Caterpillar Jar: Ward's observation and reasoning: the Prototype Design: Terraria—their decoration and contents: the Fern Age: 1834, the* Annus Mirabilis *because Ward's thorough experiment succeeded: Sages and the eminent acknowledge their debt to Ward: the Use of Wardian Cases in introducing economic plants: a dramatic change in the prospects of Plant Hunters and their Patrons.*

OTANIZING can be an excessively costly business. The rich man who has flunkies to carry his kit and, maybe, uses a portable transmitter to summon his chauffeur to a rendezvous is the Croesus among collectors. Yet botany can also be the least extravagant of hobbies. Equipment for fieldwork may be diverse and complicated: vascula of varying size, sheath knife, penknife, scissors, magnifying glass, portable press with drying papers, grapnels for pond weeds, a trowel for digging roots and tubers, a bottle for duckweeds, stout gloves for brambles, jeweler's labels for instantaneous numbering, tweezers, razor, pencil, notebooks, floras, maps, antiinsect ointment, sandwich box and hip flask. Alternatively, the kit can be primitive and simple; fingers and jacket pockets being sufficient, though the enterprising will also carry an old cocoa tin, a knife and a plastic bag or two.

These facts have been demonstrated again and again in the habits of illustrious plant hunters. Linnaeus, for example, while collecting in Lapland, was content with very little equipment and his own company; yet the younger Hooker, while collecting in India, preferred to have the assistance of an attentive valet, coolies, seed gatherers, runners, cooks, tree climbers, plant dryers and pressers, an instrument mender and taxidermist, and, naturally, sepoys to guard the lot. Moreover, whereas Linnaeus loved to lie on his back and watch the rosy light over the Lapland taiga and tundra, Joseph Hooker found himself equally happy being grandly received by a rajah swathed in yellow silk, and crowned with a pink hat "from all sides of which hung floss-silk," seated on a six-foot, brocade and wicker throne.

Nevertheless, however austere or luxurious the plant-hunting expedition, several principles of collecting remain constant.

The first of these is the necessity to take means of identification from field to laboratory or garden. A written description, however worthy of a literary or scientific prize, is never enough. Nor, today, is a photograph, in color or in black and white, because of the tricks a camera lens can play, and the obvious difficulties of dimensions. For the latter reason, too, drawings will not do, unless they are botanical sketches drawn with the aid of a microscope. A specimen of the plant has to be gathered, dried and expertly pressed, to be kept as evidence of the find in a particular locality or for identifying later by specialists.* The finicky demand that all parts of a plant should be preserved—that is, bud, flower, fruit, roots, stem and leaves; but as, in most cases, this would require three takings or gatherings, it is not generally a practical possibility on a plant-hunting expedition. The dried plant can easily be transported and, if the presser has not bungled his work and deformed the natural shape of a flower's parts, it remains identifiable for a long time. The Tradescants' herbarium, which is three hundred years old, contains easily recognizable specimens, and though no one now knows their secret processes, or how they preserved tints and made up gums, the essential colors are still there.

The taking of herbarium material always has been an important part of botanizing and, from the earliest days, hunters had no more trouble in looking after their dried

* Once the binomial system was established and classification became a matter for careful analysis in a botanical laboratory even the collectors, who were firstclass botanists in their own right, would send in their dried plants for authoritative identification and final arrangement. David Douglas, for example, had his best collections worked over by Sir William Hooker, and William Barton of the University of Pennsylvania spent years sorting and classifying the dried plants collected on the Lewis and Clark and the Long expeditions.

collections than we have today; except, of course, that to keep nibbling pests at bay they had to use less complex chemicals than paradichlorobenzene.

A second, constant principle attached to plant hunting is the necessity to keep notes and up-to-date maps. Apart from its importance to the developing science of geobotany, it is vital to know a plant's location if, later, seeds have to be taken from it—or, should the first stocks have failed to take in an alien habitat, if it is necessary to return for fresh supplies. A plant so outstanding, so beautiful, or so scientifically intriguing that its original whereabouts is instantly burned into the collector's memory is uncommon. Photographic memories among collectors are as rare. Therefore, maps made up each day are of the greatest importance to the plant collector. His descriptive notes of plant habitats are equally so to the gardener who later has the care of them. This principle was long overlooked or impossible to fulfill in the earliest days of plant introductions; whereas it must have come close to driving a collector mad to have the fruit of his fieldwork literally destroyed by an incompetent gardener at home, it must have been equally maddening to the gardener if—as often happened—the collector's description of the plant and its habitat was grossly inadequate. All in all, it is astounding that so many exotic introductions to the West were nurtured and bred by enterprising plantsmen who often had to guess what sort of surroundings and soil, temperature, food and water, humidity and light, a tender and alien plant might like.

The third and obvious principle is that, if possible, living stocks or viable seeds should be transported home. Moving plants from one habitat to another never has been as easy as it is today.

Queen Hatshepsut's hunters had the right idea in 1482 B.C. when they transported trees and plants in reed baskets and jars of soil, but they merely had to carry them through favorable climatic conditions from the Land of Punt to Egypt, and moreover, they had at their disposal pharaonic slaves to carry fresh water, work fans, adjust sunblinds and do anything else necessary to the health of their green treasure.

Not a great deal of progress was made in the next 3,316 years. True, David Douglas had rolls of oilcloth in which to pack his dried plants, waxed containers for his sleeping bulbs, corms and rhizomes, and little seed packages treated (ineffectually) against vermin and bugs, but he was alone and without the help of helots, and the ship which carried his collections on the long journey from Vancouver Island to London hardly made more speed than Egyptian vessels barging up and down the Nile. Douglas sent living stocks as well, but, like Gobi crossers, only a tough or lucky few got through. In fact, the chance of keeping plants alive on long journeys when communications were, to say the least, sluggish, was about equal to the chances of messages in bottles and those attached to gas balloons arriving safely at their proper destination.

Even hunters on elaborate expeditions who had the advantage of coolies to carry boxes of plants found that over large distances it was difficult to guard against killing the weakest plants outright, and making valetudinarians of the strongest by subjecting them to extreme variations in temperature, humidity and altitude. South America has always bred extremes in almost everything—not least in the difficulties a plant hunter encountered in transporting his finds to the coast. The journey would be dangerous, long and tedious, often lasting many weeks. It would involve waiting for fresh mules or porters, for canoes and native rafts and steamers, for transport of all kinds at different points along the route; sometimes for tracks to be cleared of fallen rock, bridges rebuilt, for floods to subside and dried-up rivers to refill. At regular intervals the boxes would need to be opened and their contents inspected, the diseased and damaged plants jettisoned, the rest repacked. The plants would feel the change from climate to climate, of varying temperatures, humidity and light intensity, as they were carried through swamps, grass plains, difficult jungle country, primeval forests, over high mountain passes and on the breast of wide rivers either foul in tropical heats or made turgid by the rains. Orchid hunters in particular discovered that in South America it was not sufficient to have a nose for a plant and the courage and stamina to follow its lead. They had to be expert, also, in transport problems and plant management, capable of dealing with muleteers, overseers, rivermen and supercargos.

At the port the hunter's responsibilities ended. His anxieties did not. For all he knew the captain would redistribute the cargo out at sea; have the plants moved forward where the danger from sea spray was a hundred times greater, or stowed below where the conditions were exactly right to ferment the plants into putrid scraps of vegetable matter. It would be done "in the interests of good seamanship," but, in reality, for the captain's own personal comfort. Not many enjoyed having their poops and their living quarters cluttered up with plants.

Even supposing the captain was a plantsman himself, or that he had a particular, personal, commercial interest in the consignment arriving safe and sound, the rate of plant mortality was increased by disinterested and idle sailors. Shifting the boxes to scrub the decks beneath was extra trouble and unlikely to be done unless the bo's'n happened to be by. It did not need much salt to ruin the plants. Sea water sloshed carelessly against the boxes day by day was more than enough. In the torrid zone it was vital to air the plants by lifting the lid of each box for a specified length of time, but in the torrid zone it was natural for seamen to do as little as possible. The least exertion increased their discomfort. *Ergo,* the lids were often untouched.

Rats belong to ships as eggs belong to bacon. Notoriously, they will eat anything, and certainly they would not jib at the fresh wood of plant chests nor the salading which grew inside them. On the occasions, too, when insects were shanghaied from their native land on the leaves or stems of plants, their meals during the voyage were at hand.

With all these avoidable hazards was the shock to plant systems caused by the continuing variations in climate. A specimen collected in the high forests of Eastern Asia, and intended for Europe would have an immensely long passage and meet great heat, both humid and dry, and, worst of all, surprisingly rapid changes of temperature and humidity. Such changes, which vexed the human spirit, were frequently the kiss of death to plants. Finally, in the storms which lashed shipping round the Cape and the Horn and on the last run through Biscay, the first thing to be jettisoned was always the consignment of plants.

All in all, the safe transit and safe arrival of exotic plants destined for Europe was in doubt from the moment they were uprooted. John Claudius Loudon's calculation—and he was thorough with his figures—which gave the number of successful introductions, is both interesting and impressive. He noted that, at the beginning of the nineteenth century, 13,140 plants were being cultivated in the British Isles, of which only 1,400 were natives. The remainder, at some time or other and in various ways, had successfully made the journey from overseas.

The experiments carried out in order to lessen the mortality rate of plants in transit were novel and diverse. John Evelyn's advice was that plants stood a greater chance of surviving long voyages and the bucketing of foul weather at sea if they were stowed in barrels. Packing individual plants in paper wrappings and suspending them in nets from the main cabin roof was another proposal and it had a moderate success on brief voyages. On longer ones the plants were threatened by lack of light and moisture and the airless fug so much relished by seamen when they go below. Peter Collinson could only guess at Bartram's difficulties in keeping plants alive on his long expeditions into the interior; but he made some practical experiments in London and wrote to suggest that the American put his plants in bladders, sprinkle a handful of moist loam over the roots, and tie the bladder's neck round the plant stem. The advice has a modern ring. How much easier Bartram's work would have been with a supply of plastic bags of varying size. Another of Bartram's patrons, the rich Doctor Fothergill of Upton, made proposals for the effective shipment of propagating stocks; that they should be planted in open chests and protected from salt spray by canvas over a cane framework. In good weather the canvas could be folded back to let in light and fresh air. Alternatively, the stocks could be planted in chests with removable lids, and if the lids were glazed with talc or thick glass so much the better. Within the limitations of the day this was sound scientific advice, and Fothergill proved his wisdom by adding that the most important thing was to bribe captain, ship's officers and crew.

John Livingstone, the chief surgeon in Canton who was Reeves' friend and Kerr's detractor, wrote about plant transport in a letter to the Horticultural Society in 1819. Characteristically—for his temper was sharp and scolding second nature to him—he complained of this and that, but the letter was sufficiently informative and useful to be printed in the *Transactions* for distribution to fellows. His observations on the actual cost of shipping plants from China are astonishing:

*From my own knowledge and observation . . . I am of the opinion that one thousand plants have been lost for one which survived the voyage to England. Plants purchased at Canton, including their chests and other necessary charges, cost six shillings and eight pence sterling each, on a fair average; consequently every plant now in England, must have been introduced at the enormous expense of upwards of £300.*

At such a price it is something of a wonder that contemporary Al Capones and Giulianos failed to have a hand in so profitable and manageable a market.

It was natural that Livingstone should find the whole thing deplorable. He made recommendations based on observations he and Reeves had made in Canton. Because plant-pot gardening was customary in the Orient the nurseries carried large stocks. But many of the plants were forced, which gave them sufficient vigor to last their time in a garden before being replaced, but quite insufficient to stand a long journey to Europe. Other, more spunky stocks ought to be obtained or specially grown.

The growing medium was important, too. Nursery stocks in Canton were generally planted in local clay, which was excellent for their needs in the violent rains and long droughts common to that part of China, but inappropriate for a sea voyage. A more fibrous, loamy medium would have to be used, and plants settled in their pots a good two months before being put on board. A third important recommendation which broke with long tradition was that plants in transit should not be taken ashore at the island of St. Helena. This custom may have been originated by a sentimental and unscientific sea captain who, aware of the benefit a run ashore was to his crew, considered it would be equally beneficial to the plants he had on board. In fact, the mild, moist climate woke up the partially dormant plants and started them into growth, a dangerous procedure which leached the reserves of strength they needed later in northern latitudes.*

There is no doubt they were excellent recommendations. But, insisted Livingstone (blowing clear, single notes on his own trumpet), this "more certain method of gratifying the English horticulturalist and botanist" would also fail, and all his own research, ingenuity and competence in the understandig of plants be entirely wasted, unless something was done about the appalling inefficiency at the Port of London. Jacks-in-office who held on to cargo manifests and slapdash stevedores could, between them, ruin a valuable consignment—and they often did.

It followed that trouble should be taken by the Horticultural Society to speed up the unloading and clearing of plant consignments at the docks. It fell to the society as well to provide a full-time gardener in the East to undertake the

---

* On one of his two journeys to England, Reeves demonstrated the worth of all three recommendations by successfully transporting ninety out of one hundred plants from Canton to the Thames.

selection of good plant stocks and their hardening and acclimatizing in preparation for the voyage west. Scrupulous in detail, Livingstone counseled:

*He should reside at Macao, having a suitable establishment, a house, garden, and native assistants.*

And, as a spur to keep the man on his toes, he should be paid by piecework:

*—a certain handsome sum for every new plant with which he enriched the horticultural and botanical stores of England.*

These last were, perhaps, counsels of perfection. Certainly in that category lies his recommendation that collections on shipboard should be put in the sole charge of a gardener. Yet, only by careful application of the principles he advocated could the rate of plant mortality in transit be reduced.

Fourteen years after Livingstone's letter had been received in London, Nathaniel Wallich, another botanist who was a foreign member of the Horticultural Society, sent in a paper on the same subject. His chief experience had been in transporting plants from India and, while generally underlining the recommendations from Canton, he particularized in practical matters. Plants, he advised, should always be mature—"already advanced in age"—and grafts should have been firmly established for at least three years before considering them for shipment. They then should be well established in square, wooden boxes and placed in a glazed chest; eight boxes fitting snugly to each chest. This allowed for easy removal and replacement in case of deaths in transit. The little boxes should have three drainage holes bored in their bottoms and stand on a layer of broken glass and pebbles. The containing chest, on the other hand, should stand on small feet. This would sweeten deckhands who could swab underneath them, and because the chests were painted, ironbound and really the product of cabinet-makers rather than joiners, their elegant appearance would please captains who "are very unwilling to allow their deck to be occupied by unsightly objects." Air and water would be provided for by opening the cases at dusk and shutting them at dawn and by allowing one pint of water to each plant a day, half a pint in the forenoon and half at night. Although glazed with Chinese oyster shell, stout glass, or plating of thick talc, the rows of chests were to be protected from flying spray with painted canvas. These elaborations had proved successful as Dr. Wallich observed:

*Such has been the vigour with which plants thus treated grew, that it was frequently necessary to have recourse to the knife in order to check their luxuriance.*

As a description of plant transport in 1831 it sounds over-sanguine; wishful thinking rather than statistical fact. Only two years afterwards, *The Gardener's Magazine* was congratulating the purser of an East India merchant-man for successfully carrying eight out of twenty-nine Chinese azaleas from Canton to London. Being congratulated for a less than fifty percent success seems a more accurate picture.

Because, at the present time of quicksilver communications, more seeds are transported than living plants, and because a seed's obvious advantage over a living plant is the small amount of stowage space it needs, it seems surprising that more plants were shipped than seeds until a hundred years ago. Some collectors of the quality of Bartram and Douglas collected more seeds than plant stocks, but the very first record of a large-size seed collection being made was on the mortifying Amherst embassy to the emperor of Cathay. Doctor Abel's assistants then boxed up three hundred lots of seeds, though shipwreck prevented most of them being germinated under the expert supervision of Sir Joseph Banks at Kew. This was in 1815. In 1822, John Lindley, then assistant secretary to the Horticultural Society, read a paper on the transport of exotics in which he drew attention to the value of seed as a means of introducing new species. To the layman it seems an obvious thing to do. But, apparently, it was not. As late as 1849 Joseph Dalton Hooker collected in the Sikkim Himalaya, and after three months despatched to his father at Kew no less than eighty cartloads of plants.

The general reluctance to collect seed may have been because of the difficulties encountered in learning the techniques of growing perennial exotics from seed. Today there are botanical laboratories where important data can be worked out; a seed's thermal constant, for example, and its proneness to rot, the exact nature of its ferments, and the collection's "percentage purity." In 1849, and for a long time after, the importance of such work was not recognized. In any case, there seemed to be little opportunity to undertake it for a number of botanic gardens were so understaffed or inefficient that huge backlogs of other work arose. The Musée d'Histoire Naturelle and the Jardin Botanique in Paris were inundated with collections of dried plants: for example just four of the many French missionaries sent in more than 233,500 between them. Yet more modest collections were also neglected. Seventy years ago, Emil Bretschneider, the painstaking and wonderfully accurate author of *European Botanical Discoveries in China*, had grounds for complaint. He collected "ripe seeds of interesting plants unknown in Europe" in the mountain regions of the Peking prefecture. These he "transmitted for cultivation to several of the great botanical and horticultural institutions in Europe and America." The results were not altogether satisfactory. The Jardin des Plantes and the Arnold Arboretum won his approval for the care they took, but he was scathing in his view that there was small point in sending seeds to the Royal Botanic Garden at Edinburgh owing to the poor treatment they received. It was fighting talk at the time, and yet nobody of consequence appears to have contradicted him. Exotics were undeniably difficult to raise from seed. Without data from botanical experts professional gardeners must have often met with disappointment, and they would have far preferred to buy a consignment of plant stocks.

It is evident, also, that the carriage of seeds was never easy or certain of success, and though the collecting and packing of stocks was physically demanding it was more psychologically satisfying than collecting handsful of seed. Moreover, the peculiarities of many seeds made absolute reliance on them something of a gamble. There were seeds as fine as dust and seeds like cannon balls; subfusc seeds and seeds as bright as jasper stones; seeds of a regular form and seeds from fantasy, shaped as parasols, as fans, and as little girls in party frocks. Some plants were reluctant seeders, others as prolific as spawning eels; and the cryptogams produced no seeds at all. Then there was the mystery of viability. The short life of rubber plant seeds was demonstrated by the need to charter a steamer to race them from Pará to Kew; yet it has been said (probably apocryphally) that corn sealed in the Egyptian pyramids reacted to moisture, warmth and light, and germinated. Some seeds which have been cared for with all the fancy aids of modern science have died quickly inside their cases; yet a leathery Tonkin bean used for years and years to keep snuff fresh has gaily produced plumule and radicle when moved from the snuff box.

Idiosyncrasies of such a kind doubled a collector's anxieties. They were tripled by the fact that he was seldom in a position to gather seeds at precisely the right moment; and quadrupled because he was too mobile to make elementary germination tests on absorbent paper, felt or flannel, let alone the desirable but complicated tests involving the use of diaphanoscopes, separators, incubators and chemical balances with minute weights. Finally, the collector's anxieties were quintupled because he could not be certain, even if the seeds did make the journey and germinate into seedlings, that they would be true to the parent flower. Rogues are produced less by wild species than by cultivars, but they, nevertheless, exist.

In such a dense fog of anxiety, doubt and difficulty, it is no wonder that plant hunters were prejudiced against relying on seed as a means of introducing exotics.

There were also problems attached to the successful carriage of seeds. They were quite as large as those of transporting plants. Vermin relished nutty seeds far more than leaves and stems and roots. Changes of climatic conditions were also harmful to seeds. In great heat they overripened which lessened their chance of germinating and, in any case, slowed up the whole process. A humid atmosphere softened a seed's cuticle and started a change in its reserve material; precocity which led generally to decay. The recommendation that bags of seeds should be suspended from cabin roofs was all very well, but the cool, drying air favorable to their health was rare. Conditions below decks aboard the old timberships varied between icy draughts and airless fugs.

Doctor Fothergill, who advised Collinson and Bartram on the subject, suggested that large seeds should be crated in beeswax, set in a chipbox like potted shrimps in butter, and the outside of the box smeared thickly with a solution of sublimate of mercury. Smaller seeds, he said, could be wrapped in waxed cotton and treated in the same way. Alternatively, small seeds might be wrapped in screws of waxed paper and packed into glass bottles. But, warned the doctor, it was not sufficient merely to cork the bottles. They ought to be insulated against extremes of heat or cold by being cased in bladders or skins of sewn leather, and packed in a keg with a measured mixture of sal ammoniac, saltpeter and salt. No less elaborate was his third recommendation; to place packets of seeds in jars or cannisters between insulating layers of rice, millet, bran or maize and top the lot with an antiinsect preparation of camphor, sulphur and tobacco.

Doctor Fothergill's advice was hardly bettered for a

century. Then the ingenious Doctor Livingstone experimented in Canton with drying seeds artificially, using one of Professor Leslie's ice machines which worked on the action of sulphuric acid. He was also an advocate of temporarily mummifying short-lived seeds in sugar—especially those like the barberry where the removal of the fleshy fruit to reveal the "stone" appears to shorten the latter's viability. His sugared seeds were put aboard the Indiamen at Canton to be awakened like a regiment of sleeping beauties on their arrival in Europe. And it was Livingstone who suggested that seeds which were so shortlived that they would die on the briefest voyage should be sown in pans at Canton and nursed through their germination by a capable gardener so that they arrived in Europe as robust seedlings. Whether the experiment was made is not known. The Horticultural Society certainly accepted his recommendation and passed it on. But delicate seeds and germinated seedlings would have to survive all the dangers which even Doctor Wallich's three-year-old healthy stock found it an effort to withstand, and it was unlikely that, until 1834, it would have been a practical possibility.

The year 1834 was calamitous in that it marked the premature death of David Douglas, the greatest of all collectors in the history of plant hunting. But it was also an *annus mirabilis* for botany, because in that year an experiment was carried out which proved conclusively the enormous value of a discovery made by a London physician, Nathaniel Bagshaw Ward. His discovery was accidental, but it so revolutionized the transport of exotics that plant hunting up to 1834 might appropriately be called pre-Wardian, and the intensive collecting done afterwards, post-Wardian.

XCEPT for the fact that he was an amateur
naturalist who practiced medicine by necessity rather than choice in the East End of
London, not a great deal is known of Doctor
Ward. By deduction from the book which
he published about his discovery we may
guess he was gentle, probably shy, and acute, but inclined
sometimes to be pompous. Being the kind of man who puts
caterpillars into bottles he was, maybe, either a bachelor or
a widower or beshrewed. Certainly he was a romantic with
characteristic longings for *rus in urbe*, and he recommended
the invention he made because of its power to "induct us
into the quietest regions of vegetable life." It seems improbable that professionally he was a ball of fire; more
likely he was a modest, retiring physician in general practice. Within reason we may see him as a scientific cenobite,
or a recluse.

All this is conjecture, and is probably quite wrong.

What is known is that Wellclose Square, that part of
dockland where he lived, was a Sherlock Holmes sort of
place; not exactly producing lepers, abominable lascars and
wicked Chinamen, but giving that impression all the same.
And had Holmes and Watson been acquainted with their
contemporary, Doctor Nathaniel Ward, undoubtedly they
would have admired his scientific method of observing and
deducing.

What Ward saw in 1827 was by chance: just as, by
chance, the Curies saw pitchblende through their micro-

scope, and Fleming saw, by chance, the fungus which led him to penicillin.

As was his habit, Doctor Ward had placed a caterpillar to pupate in mold at the bottom of a glass jar. He stoppered the jar and then apparently forgot it. When it came to his mind again he found that a tiny fern and an equally tiny blade of grass were growing out of the mold. This would have been an exciting event in itself in a part of London where greenery was as rare as hair on an egg, but the circumstances of the plant growth were of especial interest to the doctor.

*I observed the moisture which during the heat of the day rose from the mould condensed on the surface of the glass and returned whence it came, thus keeping the earth always in the same degree of humidity.*

The cycle had, of course, been noticed before by glasshouse gardeners. Some had discovered it accidentally through forgetting to ventilate their houses on a hot summer's day. Others had deliberately applied the principle to make the warm, moist habit relished by cucurbits and most tropical exotics. But it required Ward's deductive powers to reason why the grass seed and the fern spore should shoot and grow into healthy plants. He concluded it was because they were in "a moist atmosphere free from soot or other extraneous particles" and had light, heat and moisture. He added that it was also because they had "periods of rest and fresh air."

It is not easy to understand exactly what he meant by "periods of rest." Any kind of forcing, either stunting or hastening into precocious growth, would obviously be undesirable. And, left alone, plants rest of their own accord; they do not need "shutting up" like parrots under a green cloth. Nor is it clear why changes of air should be so desirable. Ward's scraps of fern and grass thrived and gave an appearance of being immortal simply because he left the stoppered jar alone. He failed to state the fate of the pupa, which presumably perished, but he noted that the plants lived on in the same atmosphere for four long years—until the lid rusted and raindrops seeped in carrying with it the chemical impurities of Wellclose Square. Fresh air, therefore, would need to be given very sparingly indeed; firstly because it would upset the regular cycle of respiration, temporarily halting it and putting it out of gear; and, secondly, because the freshest of air might contain invisible and insalubrious impurities. It was in fact a feature of his closed cases that they were almost entirely glazed and were kept shut, or opened only on the rarest occasions. The closed cases used on sea voyages in pre-Wardian days were inadequately glazed, and either they were permanently closed (in which case the plants suffered from loss of light), or they were opened as regularly as weather conditions allowed and salt and other damaging particles were admitted with the change of air.

Developing his idea that a clean, even and undisturbed climate was vital to the health of plants, Ward designed a large-scale adaption of his caterpillar jar; instructing the carpenter who made it up that the joinery must be as perfect as possible, and the wood hard and thoroughly seasoned to withstand the effects of condensation from within and "extraneous particles" from without. This case, in which he grew plants experimentally, was the prototype of the hundreds and thousands which were to be made in succeeding years; for an important side-fruit of his discovery was that, in an age of gas lighting and heating by coal fires, indoor gardens became a possibility.

The cases were called *terraria* and soon they were as indispensable a part of the early Victorian parlor and drawing room as the velvet-hung mantleshelf, waxed fruit under domes of glass, "Makart bouquets" made of dried grasses and peacock feathers, and occasional tables laden with bijouterie. Generally they were rectangular, though collector's pieces were made in round and oval form, wedge shaped like cheesedishes, and in the shape of urns and vases. In bizarre specimens the glass was yellowish or faintly blue, and sometimes engraved with arabesques and the profiles of contemporary heroes. Cabinetmakers produced ornate, bowfronted cases with reflectors and prisms on turntables to catch sunbeams, and their frames and stands were massive and made of carved mahogany and teak. Other cases were less ornamental but still solid and built to last. The simplest had cast-iron frames mass-produced by foundries from a limited selection of molds. These were fitted with containers like old-fashioned electric accumulators and stood on turntables covered with red plush or on stands with legs which varied in style from florid Hindoo to elegant Regency.

The contents of the cases varied less. Egregious decorations such as chunks of tufa, seashells, stalactites and blobs of colored glass were fairly rare. The plantings hardly differed in any of the thousands of indoor gardens then kept by the English-speaking peoples, for it so happened that the production of Ward's *terrarium* coincided with a public passion for growing ferns in both England and the United States. It was a fern age. Ferneries, outdoor and indoor, for stove and temperate species, exotics or natives, for abnormal or regular varieties were exceedingly commonplace. Plant tinkers, called "Botany Bens" in England, scoured the countryside and carried baskets of ferns from door to door. Breeders and selectors spent a prodigious amount of time and money in raising crested, tasseled, foliose and plumose forms of common ferns until over a thousand varieties had been recorded and described. There were, for example, no less than sixty-five varieties, hybrids and cultivars of the common Lady Fern. Inevitably the ubiquitous fern had pride of place in Victorian *terraria,* and being indifferent to neglect, resistant to most diseases, and as fond of the gloom as troglodytes, it was the easiest of all plants to grow.

The widespread indoor culture of cosseted spleenworts, rusty-backs and maidenhairs was, though, only an incidental result of Doctor Ward's clever piece of deduction. The phenomenon he had seen told him this might be a means of meeting the difficulties of plant transport so frequently bewailed in the transactions of learned societies. He had this in mind when he designed his prototype. Successful experiments led him to make other closed cases and try more ambitious proofs. In the year 1834 he proved conclusively that plants stood the highest chance of surviving if they were transported in sealed, glazed cases modeled on his caterpillar jar.

Two of Ward's cases were planted with English ferns and grasses, sealed, and fixed in a suitable position on board a clipper outward bound for New South Wales. After a six-month voyage the case was taken ashore at the Antipodes and unsealed. The contents were in firstclass condition. Half the experiment had passed satisfactorily. By the doctor's instructions the two cases were then stocked with native Australian plants, and not ordinary ones, but plants which had already proved to be bad travelers. They included a species of the small creeping tender fern Gleichenia which had never survived any attempt to ship it to England. Ward was determined that his cases should be tested with exceptional thoroughness. Stocked with plants notorious for their tenderness and their reluctance to leave their natural habitat, they were sent on the long, storm-wracked voyage round the Horn. Between Botany Bay and the Pool of London the plants were subjected to variations of temperature from 20° to 120°. They were rolled sideways and tossed backwards and forwards on the swell and the roll of two oceans. But, at the end of it all, when Doctor Ward went down to the quayside and opened his cases he found the plants secure, fresh and green, and full of promise. His confidence in the cases was entirely vindicated.

Thereafter the plant hunter's transport troubles were largely over, though mistakes, of course, occurred. It was possible, they discovered, to "drown" a plant in its own respiration. Given a blazing sun and an excess of moisture in the case it was even possible to boil a plant to death. Inexpert joinery would admit salt. Unless an unbreakable, transparent substance was used for glazing there were obvious hazards on a busy deck. Modifications were necessary and they were made, but the use of Wardian cases—as they came to be called—on overland journeys and long sea voyages meant that, at last, tender plants stood a good ninety percent chance of survival.

It is rather natural to think of these cases as of a standard size under patent. In fact they varied between portable cases, roughly the size and shape of a shoebox, to the huge cases used by Joseph Hooker when he sent a consignment of trees from Tierra del Fuego to his father at Kew. These weighed upwards of three hundredweight, each.

It is doubtful if Nathaniel Ward benefited financially from his invention, though a side perquisite was the sale of his book, *On the Growth of Plants in Closely Glazed Cases*, a blueprint to the design and management of *terraria* and Wardian cases. But he was a man of science who had enough to meet his needs and he valued more than anything the congratulations of sages and the eminent. The gruff Duke of Northumberland, who had an Aladdin's cave of exotics at Syon House, sent word to Wellclose Square that stove gardeners owed the doctor a great deal. His peer and horticultural rival, Charles, Sixth Duke of Devonshire, informed Ward that his case had been indispensable in carrying a specimen of *Amherstia nobilis* all the way from India to the special glasshouse made for it at Chatsworth. Sir William Hooker made a point of telling the doctor what a vast difference his cases had made in the transport of plants to Kew. Distinguished nurserymen like Conrad and George Loddiges of Hackney Wick found that using Wardian cases so greatly reduced their overheads that they were moved to thank the inventor. Other nurserymen, such as the firm of Veitch in Exeter, now considered Ward's cases had made it worthwhile to train and send out plant hunters on their own account. Ward was especially delighted to hear that, by means of his invention, the Cinchona tree had been successfully carried for the first time from its native South America to Java, India and Ceylon, for, as the only source of quinine, the Cinchona was vitally important to the health of Asia.

The East India Company, also, was in the doctor's debt very soon. Experts had advised that conditions in the Himalaya were wonderfully favorable to the growing of fine tea, but the shortlived viability of tea seeds had made it impossible to introduce the Chinese plant. Now, after Doctor Livingstone's suggestion, and under the expert management of Robert Fortune, seeds were sown directly into Wardian cases which germinated during the voyage, and over one hundred thousand vigorous seedlings were planted out in High India. The worldwide game of general post in many economic plants was made possible only by using Wardian Cases. Seeds sent to Kew by consular officials were raised as plants and hardened before being consigned abroad again: cork oaks, for example, to South Australia, better tobacco to Natal, and plants of coffee, cinnamon, ginger and indigo to Queensland. The movement of plants from one region to another in the rapidly expanding United States was also helped by Doctor Ward's discovery. Undoubtedly it made dramatic changes in the prospects of plant hunters and their patrons.

After 1834, in the post-Wardian era, limitations seemed to disappear. Everything was now possible, or appeared to be. At last the whole world had become the plant collector's oyster.

# ❧ Part Three
# A Scramble for Green Treasure

*one  /  From Mexico to Patagonia*

A Catalog of Dangers and Privations: the Mounting of Expeditions: Joseph Hooker's "Antarctic Herborizations": Veitch's Men—William Lobb and Pearce: Unlucky Collectors in the Cordilleras and Selvas: Orchid Stories—the Holy Grail of Orchid Hunters: Benedict Roezl from Old Bohemia.

*two  /  In India and Africa*

Opulent Attractions: the kindly Dr. Wallich: John Gibson's Career: Sir Joseph Hooker takes the Mantle of Sir Joseph Banks: His Adventure in the Himalaya and Assam: the Seductions of Dark Africa: the Welwitschia Affair: "the Savage Life again."

*three  /  The Eastern Tropics*

More Veins of Orchid Gold: Thomas Lobb and Charles Curtis: Extensive Glass-gardening in the West: Beauties, Curiosities and Flesh-Creepers: the sensational Pitcher Plants.

*four  /  The Land of the Rising Sun*

Shoguns and Mikados: Western Gunboat Policies: the Return of Philipp van Siebold: Less Privileged Collectors: the end of the Radical Revolution: Charles Maries, Sargent, Faurie and Japanese Plant Hunters.

*five  /  Post-Wardian China*

The Opium War: Fresh Concessions to the West: Bentham's Flora Hongkongensis: Fortune's Four trips; his Introductions; his Prowess as a Tea Smuggler; his indifference to the Taiping Rebellion: Two Influential Botanists—Hance and Maximowicz: the 1860 Treaty opens a way to the Promised Land.

ASTERS of modern prose have averred that, if they are used sparingly, platitudes, like split infinitives, can have a special force. It would, then, be reasonable to say that plant hunting almost anywhere in Central and South America has never, ever been a picnic. Since 1492 the Panama Isthmus, the West Indies and the Caribbean Islands have suffered constant excitements, varying from the bloody raids of buccaneers and the suppression of slave revolts to more recent and melodramatic upheavals in domestic politics, and even the stoning of the umpire at a game of cricket. The region has seldom been in a sufficiently settled state for the comfortable pursuit of botanizing. As for South America, its history, its peoples, and certainly its botany, have never been without mystery, if not shocks.

The practical difficulty of getting plants down-country to the coast has been touched on. An additional anxiety was that on a continent where revolutions were endemic and, in some parts, *coups d'etat* unbelievably common, no plant hunter when he returned from the interior could ever be sure of the political *status quo*. It made for deep uneasiness. And the actual physical and psychological dangers which confronted collectors out in the field almost defied description. Some, though, in their letters or journals made the attempt.

It will be remembered that Philibert de Commerson enjoyed his jaguar hunt in Buenos Aires. Not so the nineteenth-century collector who complained that in some parts of the country there was "a jaguar every yard." Another inferred that jaguars, however lithe and large and fierce, were far preferable to the vexatious pests which plagued without mercy—clouds of cabouri flies which "settle on any exposed flesh like houseflies upon jam," bêtes rouges, ticks and diggas which bored and burrowed under the skin, stinging marabuntas, ants, the vampire bats which settled on the unwary and sucked and sucked until they fell, heavy and befuddled with blood, to slither into the undergrowth; worst of all, the leeches—black parasitic worms which could penetrate cloth and knew their way into the laceholes of breeches, the eyeholes of leggings, and the laceholes of boots as instinctively as inebriates into their favorite bar. These unpleasant manifestations were also common in the Far East and other tropical jungles, but collectors reported that in South and Central America they seemed larger, more abundant and far more malignant. A French orchid hunter wrote in a jeremiad of his misfortunes that none of the tree climbers he had engaged would climb up into the dense clouds of stinging insects, nor even collect in the scrub where "it was impossible to put down a shilling-piece between the red spiders and other insects." He did not blame them, he said, for some of the ants were two inches in length; but it meant the end of his orchid collecting in that part of Brazil.

The vegetation was formidable, and particularly in the tropical primeval forests. Knives, axes and billhooks had to be used to carve trails through the undergrowth. The dense crochet-work of foliage and hanging creepers reduced light and increased humidity. The tree canopy distorted noises, too: increasing their intensity at night when the jungle sounds were as regular and as deafening as the noises of a busy city, the chatterings and screeches, the warblings and cleaks broken occasionally by the terrible screams of a creature in agony; and muffling them by day when the long periods of deep silence were equally unnerving.

The general effect of trekking in the rain forests was loathsome: hacking a way through slippery, often tacky leaves and tendrils; treading warily on the slimy, uneven ground; watching as carefully as the gloom permitted for insects, ferocious animals, and a hideous variety of snakes.

All these privations had to be endured in loneliness, for it was characteristic of the vast jungles that unless the expedition was equipped and manned on a princely scale, plant hunters were dwarfed by their environment into feeling desolately lonely; and the atmosphere was so enervating that an extensive orchid hunt deep in the forests was not unlike living perpetually in a menacing and murky Turkish bath.

Fevers were feared more than anything else, for the plant hunter was immediately at the mercy of his porters. The unsuperstitious minority of the Indians might remain loyal and nurse him back to health; the larger majority would be more inclined to rob and desert him, or barter him piecemeal to headhunters and cannibals for plugs of tobacco.

This catalog of dangers and privations was thoroughly understood by every potential plant hunter in South and Central America yet, such was the quality of the exotic flora that still they continued to arrive.

Not many went south from the northern continent. The United States of America was growing larger. Year after year, like a shaken kaleidoscope, it wore a different appearance as territories were occupied, conquered, ceded, bought, assigned by treaty or added by revolt. Inescapably, the *zeitgeist* was inward-looking. Botanists and plantsmen had their hands full in dealing with all the wild species indigenous to the new states. The adventurers had taken to exploring, fighting Indians, and the widening of frontiers by the force of arms. The bored and the scamps sailed from New Bedford and Nantucket or Mystic in Connecticut, to join in the bloody extermination of seals and whales in the South Seas. At that time only a few devil-may-cares were prepared to consider plant hunting abroad.

From old Europe, on the other hand, a plethora of private enthusiasts and well-equipped professionals took passage over the South Atlantic bound for Buenos Aires, Rio, Pernambuco, Pará, Kingston and Belize. They were attracted in such numbers by the reports of explorers on the amazing flora to be found in the grasslands and selvas, the cordilleras and the Gran Chaco.

Victor von Hagen in his lengthy book on botanists in South America * gave a skeleton list of the main scientific expeditions undertaken by many nationalities between the Académie des Sciences expedition of 1735 and Richard Spruce's work for Kew in the drenched selvas, up to 1866. It included many honored names: Charles Darwin, Löfling who was a pupil of Linnaeus, Mutis, Humboldt, Wied-Neuwied, Eschwege, Orbigny and Tschudi. By no means were they simply plant hunters. So large was every subject, so wide every horizon that scientific explorers in South America would naturally collect and note everything they could. Nevertheless the quality of their plant collections and their estimate of how much remained to be discovered promised so much to botanists and professional plantsmen in the post-Wardian era that expeditions were quickly mounted and sent out.

Some were very lavish, the general tone being that of Mahomet going to the mountain, and the more opulent private enthusiasts were great sticklers for what was and was not done, and would dine in modified evening attire, even in the torrid zone. But grandeur suited the age and was of great psychological importance. It was strange but true that many Victorian plant hunters in the middle of a desert or the depths of a jungle were better equipped with durable comforts than the tenants of most public housing schemes at the present day. The brandy tantalus, the solid oak traveling desk and medicine chest, the brassbound ditty boxes, the heavy, handmade scientific instruments, and the linen, plate and cutlery compensated for the terrible adventures which lay behind and the terrible possibilities which, maybe, lay ahead. There was no doubt that all this paraphernalia, though heavy, and his strict adherence to the

* *South America Called Them:* Victor von Hagen (Robt. Hale, 1949).

code of the society to which he belonged, kept up the collector's morale and gave him, apparently, fresh supplies of stamina.

There were, of course, a few nonconformists like Emmanuel Thomas who, far from adhering to any code of behavior did precisely what he wanted, and never washed or shaved if he could avoid it. All the same, his skill and his vigor excited Sir William Hooker's surprised admiration: *

*He is never fatigued tho' he carries a great tin Box upon his back as large, and very nearly the shape of a London milk-pail, and in his hand an instrument for collecting plants which resembles a North-american tomahawk.*

The collectors sent out by nursery firms were well provided for. Their equipment, if not as luxurious as that of the private plant hunter, was equally sound. It had to be. Central and South America quickly taught botanical explorers that skinflinting did not pay, that small-scale affairs stood far less chance in proportion of succeeding than the massive expeditions favored by rich amateurs. Nurserymen felt bound to follow suit and be generous in the salary, kit and expenses allowed to the collectors they commissioned. But their policy was less altruistic than businesslike. It was a promising period for plantsmen. The new nabobs were expressing themselves and trying to impress each other with the splendor of their gardens and their glasshouses. The demand for exotic plants was heavy and constant and Doctor Ward had provided a means for shipping plants. It was a sound investment to train and send out collectors, though, having writs to spend very considerable sums if it meant the difference between success and failure, they had to be men of integrity and judgment as well as brave, knowledgeable, practical, resourceful, stubborn and singleminded. Today

* Sir William himself was strictly correct and observed the proprieties wherever he was. When botanizing he wore almost the same clothing as he wore at the University or at Kew; and, top-hatted, high-collared, and equipped with the fobs and seals and watchchain of his class, as well as a vasculum for plants, he covered gigantic distances on foot each day.

such prodigies are government-trained astronauts, and seem to be exceedingly rare. In the last century they appear to have been fairly common.

The first and most notable botanist to collect in South America in the post-Wardian era was Sir William Hooker's son, Joseph. At the age of only twenty-two he was appointed Assistant Surgeon and Botanist aboard H.M.S. *Erebus* on Ross's antarctic exploration which found the South Magnetic Pole. Though still a sprig, through his father he was already well acquainted with many of the leading botanists of his day in America and England, and he became a lifelong friend of Charles Darwin whose *Journal of the Voyage of the Beagle,* published in 1839, had excited him so much that he always kept a copy under his pillow.

Ross's expedition with two ships, *Erebus* and *Terror,* was thoroughly equipped with naval dockyard efficiency, though Hooker recorded that the official botanist appeared to have been overlooked. His own supplies were meager:

*Except for some drying paper for plants, I had not a single instrument or book supplied to me as a naturalist . . . not a single glass bottle was supplied for collecting purposes, empty pickle jars were all we had, and rum as a preservative from the ship's stores.*

The commander was sympathetic and at his own expense provided Hooker with a cabinet. Furthermore, he never failed to encourage him all through the four-year trip. But Hooker's greatest advantage was his own enthusiasm and self-confidence—enough and more for twenty botanists —and he collected with great gusto, and no thought of personal discomfort, whenever he had the opportunity. It was on this apprentice-run that he laid the foundations of his pioneer work as a geobotanist for he collected in so many

different places that he quickly learned to realize the importance of recording the precise location and habitat of every
plant he gathered.

After Ross had found the South Magnetic Pole in what
was to be later called "George the Fifth land," the *Erebus*
and *Terror* made sail to winter north of the Antarctic Circle,
and so Hooker was given an opportunity he had longed for,
that of collecting in that region bounded by Graham Land
and the Falklands, and the southernmost buttonhook of
Argentina. Getting there, though, was a dazing experience.

They met gales of such force that eight-inch and ten-
inch hawsers snapped like strings of raffia, and squalls which
ribboned their storm sails and laid both ships over on their
beams. They righted again and again to be swept on
through ice floes, running the gauntlet of icebergs which
bashed together and snapped apart, or ground together
backwards and forwards, upwards and downwards like
chewing teeth. The barometer stood at 28.40 inches.
Twenty-three degrees of frost solidified wave crests and
spray as they sheeted over the decks. In a night of tempest
the two ships lost contact with each other. On another night
the *Terror* was ablaze for two hours from a fire below. On
yet another night a freak blast of wind caused them to
collide on the weatherside of a cliff-high iceberg. Their shat-
tered topmasts and icy rigging knitted together, and when
the *Terror* was chopped free the *Erebus* was found to be
temporarily disabled, her gig and quarterboats washed
away, and her decks a pig's breakfast or broken spars and
rigging. It was only by Ross's superb seamanship that the
*Erebus* was cleared from the iceberg so that they could
make storm repairs in the belly of that frozen hell.

Limp, battered, bedraggled and in need of extensive
carpenter's and sailmaker's work, the ships made Berkeley
Sound in the Falklands on April 6.

Young Hooker, having been exposed to a longer and
larger succession of perils than almost any plant hunter in
history, continued to be bouncy. He was avid to get ashore
and begin plant hunting. Ross's instructions forbade it. The

purser's party was to go ashore first and collect mailbags. Hooker begged the purser to bring him a handful of plants, and he waited impatiently, dreaming of hardy exotics on the bleak, snowcapped shores. The purser returned hours later, without any mail but with one plant for the eager botanist. It was a tattered shepherd's purse.

Undiscouraged by this beginning Hooker scoured the Falklands on an extensive plant hunt and, though the flora was small, there were some interesting grasses to collect. One of these, the tussac, which resembled the spray thrown up by a bomb dropped at sea, was to be grown at Kew and eventually to take well and prove very useful in the Shetlands. To his father's pleasure (for Sir William was a great muscologist), Hooker found a splendid and rich variety of mosses on an island by Tierra del Fuego where Banks had been with Cook. On Fuego itself he was as fascinated by the flora as Commerson had been, though on this occasion there were no offers of a pretty Fuegian girl for either of the ship's cats. His enthusiasm for geobotany already aflame, he decided that Fuego was "the great botanical centre of the Antarctic Ocean," and his discovery that Britain and Fuego had many lichens and flowering plants in common interested him at once in the possibilities of plant migration.

The botanical drawings he made in this chilly part of the South American continent and the written notes of his plant collecting there were later published in *The Botany of the Antarctic Voyage*. He returned to England even fitter than when he left it, but the expedition had been demanding. Collecting frozen lichens, for example, had sometimes involved prising tufts out with hammer and chisel or, if he had forgotten to take the tools with him, sitting on a lichen until it was thawed by the warmth of his fundament. "Antarctic herborizations," as he called them, made for discomfort, but when a friend suggested that he compensate himself by plant hunting in the opposite sort of climate he confessed that for the time being he would rather stay at home with his father at Kew having "no notion of jumping from cold to hot and cracking like a glass tumbler." Moreover, being by no means ignorant of discomfort caused by heat, he asked: "Have not you botanists killed collectors a-plenty in the tropics?"

The plant hunters up by the equator at that time would have echoed the same view. South America claimed few, if any martyrs to botany through cold. Its heats killed many.

William Lobb was one of the most distinguished professionals to collect in South America. He and his younger brother both hunted for the firm of Exeter nurserymen named Veitch. Thomas hunted in Java, and has a place in a later chapter, while William, a gardener rather than a botanist, was sent out to South America. He had all the attributes of an empire builder, and, in the pursuit of plants, risked his personal safety to the point of lunacy.

Arriving at Rio de Janeiro in 1840, he set about collecting in the hinterland. It was difficult country and largely unexplored. He roamed through parklands and the primeval rain forests along the edge of the Brazilian highlands. Very soon he had sufficient healthy plants to justify Veitch's faith in selecting him, and in the next four years he added to his discoveries in the Argentine pampas, the Andes, and the temperate forests of Chile. It was in the last country that he found a plant which was to establish his reputation as an out-of-the-ordinary collector. In a province inhabited by the Araucanian Indians he recognized a tree which had been first introduced to England by Menzies, the Scots surgeon on Captain Vancouver's voyage of survey and exploration. Menzies had called it the Chile pine, but his introduction had been limited to five saplings, and the specimens were considered more of a scientific curiosity than anything else. Lobb, as a gardener, judged that the tree could become immensely popular in Europe and that it was worth sending quantities of pine kernels back to England. He also changed its name, or rather named the genus *Araucaria* after the Indians whose hospitality he had enjoyed and who used the kernels as a fruit or ground into meal. His instinct had been right. With botanists, his Araucaria from Chile enjoyed fame as being the only known conifer from south of the equator to grow to timber size in a West European climate. With a wide gardening public it enjoyed fame and great popularity as the Monkey puzzle tree.

After his exacting expedition Lobb deserved a long rest as well as his patron's gratitude, but Veitch was too delighted by the success of the enterprise to be patient. Lobb was allowed a short holiday at his home in Cornwall and then dragooned into leading another expedition to South America. He was to search for "the new and the novel" in Chile, especially in the Chonos Archipelago and in northern Patagonia.

It was on this long and arduous trip that he found the lapageria, an evergreen climber with clusters of rose-colored trumpet flowers which became popular enough to cement his fame. It took its name from the French Empress Josephine who, in her mercurial career, had once been Josephine Tascher de la Pagerie, and it was an instant success in Victorian conservatories. In the next few years William found a plethora of worthwhile introductions: the scarlet holly, *Desfontainea spinosa,* a shrubby, flowering holly not often seen today; the apricot-colored barberry, *Berberis darwinii,* with its great and valuable resistance to salty-spray; and the fire bush, *Embothrium coccineum,* which won high praise from W. J. Bean of Kew who wrote: "Perhaps no tree cultivated in the open air in the British Isles gives so striking and brilliant a display as this does." Yet another marvelous discovery was the flame nasturtium, a perennial with a preference for moist, peaty conditions and so hardy that it stood being introduced to the more parky parts of Scotland and the Blue Ridge section of North Carolina.

It was to the United States that William Lobb went after his tougher collecting work had been done, to hunt plants in the Sierra Nevada and to enjoy the benign climate of California before dying of paralysis in San Francisco.

Veitch, whose principal aim now was to find stove plants and suitable subjects for bedding out, continued to invest in collectors. One of them, Richard Pearce, the discoverer of the bright green plum fir, *Prumnopitys elegans,** also introduced the first of the tuberose begonias, *Begonia boliviensis*. With other South American varieties, found at great heights above sea level, it was to be the progenitor of all Veitch's famous cultivars.

After a lifetime of excitement Pearce was lucky to die in his bed. Other stove-plant hunters in the Andes and selvas were less fortunate. One, David Bowman, was robbed of all his possessions, including his plant collections, just before he was due to leave for England. Dysentery or mortification carried him off in Bogota. Another collector, Zahn, the fern expert, got himself drowned in Panama. J. Henry Chesterton, the valet turned Veitch collector, overdid things while hunting orchids and succumbed in Colombia.

His was a not uncommon fate. There was a huge variety of orchids in the rain forests of Brazil and Central America and they had such a commercial pull that hunters frequently risked and lost their lives in searching for new species. Stories abounded about their difficulties. They abounded as well about the orchids. Being voluptuous in character, expensive to buy and to keep, and coming from such mysterious habitats it was inevitable. Disappearing orchids had a prominent place in these romantic stories; that is, a popular species which died out in captivity and somehow had to be replaced.

A well-loved variety of Cattleya orchid called *C. labiata vera* flourished for a time in European stoves; then the plants weakened, refused to respond to treatment, appeared to have no interest in surviving, and, like Victorian ladies in a decline, died out one after the other until only a single specimen was left. In that age of industrial expansion there was money to spare for mounting an expedition to gather fresh supplies of the orchid in South America. But by then no one could recall where the originals had been found.

---

* Poeppig called it *Podocarpus andinus* under which name it is still sometimes listed in the catalogs of nurserymen. Its other common names are plum-fruited yew and Chilean yew.

There were no records; simply the one, living specimen in the conservatory of an English manor house. Gardeners, botanists, nurserymen and expert orchidists consulted one another, but even while they were wringing their hands and wondering how to keep the survivor alive, an act of God in the shape of a holocaust resolved their problem, and manor house, conservatory and orchid went up in flames.

Years passed. Suddenly, colossal excitement was engendered when an old record was found which stated that the original *C. labiata vera* had, in fact, reached England entirely by accident—as a shanghaied plant in a consignment of mosses and lichens sent from the Organ Mountains of Brazil. Expeditions large and small, sponsored and independent, scoured as much of the Organ Mountains as was possible. *Cattleya labiata vera* had become the "Holy Grail" of hunters. And they could not find it. Then, seventy years after its disappearance it reemerged in Europe; rather improbably as the corsage of a lady at an embassy ball in Paris. An orchid enthusiast attached to the British legation saw the corsage. He looked once, twice, in fact as often as a man may, with propriety, at an embassy ball; and, guessing what the orchid was, he doubted his senses. Somehow he got hold of the flower. An expert confirmed his guess. The "Holy Grail" had at last turned up. The trail was followed back to the precise place where it had originated in Brazil and orchid fanciers were able to obtain fresh stocks.

Some orchid hunters had heroic adventures and endured privations which deserved to feature in popular ballads. Walter Davis, for example, crossed and recrossed the Cordilleras of the Andes a score of times, reaching the great height of seventeen thousand feet; and he traveled the length of the Amazon from its principal source to the North Atlantic delta. Gustave Wallis made the same mammoth journey in the search for orchids, but in the opposite direction, from mouth to source, but, unlike Davis who survived to return home, he was killed by a fever in Ecuador, shuddering his terrible way through to madness and death.

In contrast there were collectors who had a remarkable

share of luck and more than their share of comfort. Albert Millican wrote up his experiences in a floridly-decorated volume called *The Travels and Adventures of an Orchid Hunter*. The initial letter on the first page is "illuminated" by the then infant-process of photography, and contains a portrait of the author. He appears to have been naturally cushioned against privations, far less like the lean and leathery plant hunter of one's imagination than, for all the world, like Edward VII caught in a benevolent mood after eating lobster or winning the Derby. Millican's enterprises, though to some extent rewarding, made fewer demands on him than was usual in his profession.

Prince of orchid hunters in Central and South America was a Czech named Benedict Roezl. The majority of his fellow-collectors accepted him as such, and admitted his superior knowledge of the likely whereabouts of orchids in the selvas. His "bags" were richer than anyone's. He introduced different forms of *Selenipediums,* South American cousins of the lady's slipper; varieties of *Cattleyas* and *Stanhopeas,* and curiosities such as the *Masdevallias* he found which had long sepals trailing like kitetails, and the *Miltonia* which was called after him, *M. Roezlii*—a tree-perching orchid with the capacity of Paestum's famous roses for flowering twice in a year. No one outclassed him as an orchid hunter in the steaming rain forests which run between the Bay of Campeche and the Gulf of Guayaquil and stretch from Bolivia to the Atlantic coastline of Brazil, but Roezl won equally high admiration as a general collector, and in this capacity he made plant discoveries in places as far removed as California and Patagonia. They included some well-favored lilies from the wilderness as well as from the cultivated gardens of Spanish settlers; agaves and other succulents from the Mexican plateau and the desert lands of Atacama and Patagonia; stove plants, such as the pygmy *Aphelandra aurantiaca* with its twisted leaves and surprising color of a blushing Chinaman, and, from the West Indies, flamingo flowers, with spathe and radix not unlike those of a wild parson-in-the-pulpit. There was *Anthurium Roe-*

*zlii,* for example, with its white pulpit and port-colored parson; and others with parsons of ivory, vermilion and raw pink.

Such successes ought to have made Roezl a rich man. Joseph Hooker, when complaining of his own meager government grant as a collector in Assam, wrote that "an active collector . . . might easily clear from £2,000 to £3,000 in one season by the sale of Khasi Orchids." He inferred that not many orchids were necessary to raise such a figure. Roezl, although one of his consignments of orchids from Central America actually weighed eight tons, never made a great deal of money. Probably this was because he seldom collected as the employee of a nursery. Working on his own account or on special commissions from private enthusiasts suited his temperament far better. He had been born near Prague, then the capital of Bohemia in the ancient Austro-Hungarian Empire and, rather curiously, he had managed to inherit not one but both strands of the national character. To the stupefaction of his porters he would change, chameleon-like, but for no apparent reason: at one place and time being thin-lipped, silent and wearing a purposeful, doomed, proud look; at another, showing himself irrepressibly optimistic and sunny. He was a stimulating traveling companion, and a genius at tracking down plants, but too impulsive by far and too fiercely individualistic to collect under the direction of financial investors. Later, when he returned to Bohemia and set up as a nurseryman himself, he found trading in plants a fiddling affair unsuited to a man of spirit and his business failed. He was at his best in the roasted Mexican deserts, the swamps of Costa Rica, and the trackless forests of Colombia; modestly accepting the high regard of his fellow-collectors, delighting in finding new quarries, and—depending on the mood of the moment— being either indifferent to hardship and danger or doing his best to laugh them away. He had quite sufficient of both.

Acclimatizing is an enervating and uncomfortable process. Roezl, shifting from climate to climate and altitude to altitude, had to have the stamina of a plant being carried to and fro between tropical stove, temperate house, conservatory and cold frame. If he did not penetrate that part of South America where the plant hunter had complained of "a jaguar every yard," he had his share of close contact with them.

On one occasion he was working in his tent, writing up notes on the day's collecting and pressing specimens, when he was made abruptly aware of a pungent cat stench. He turned to find a jaguar two yards away, and it was neither a kitten nor a benign old grandfather but middle-aged and very evidently disgruntled. It snarled, rubbed its head against the table, and clearly was considering what to do. But before it could make up its mind Roezl came to life, hurled an oil lamp at the beast and threw himself to the floor. The suddenness of the act, Roezl's speed, and perhaps his effrontery, made the jaguar turn tail and disappear with a whimper of fear.

If wild animals were a constant danger, no less so, in that half-civilized place, were the attentions of bandits. Roezl appeared to be bandit-prone. He was held up and robbed no less than seventeen times; though, because he was one of the few collectors of the day to travel when he could both austerely and lightly, he never lost a great deal. One band of Mexican bandits appeared to be so exasperated to find he had barely anything except his horse, his clothes, and bundles and bundles of weeds that some of them were inclined to cut his throat. The knives were out when the chief held up his hand and bade them reconsider. Could this weed collector be sane? They eyed each other. It was bad luck to cut the throats of lunatics. If a man was so crazed as to wander the countryside gathering flowers and grasses and bits of trees, he must surely be under the eye of God. This, anyway, was their happy conclusion, and being in need of good luck at that time, they cheerfully let Roezl go, piously crossed themselves, and rode off to rob someone else.

It is clear that Roezl had a Benjamin's share of good fortune. The skills he learned and acquired as a hunter, and his own special talent for nosing out rarities, mattered less than luck. A propitious sign of his luck was a heaven-sent gift of plants in 1871. He and a native boy were canoeing down to the Pacific coast after an unrewarding plant hunting expedition up in the mountains. The river was swollen with recent rains and flowing swiftly. Alert to every danger as they rocketed downstream, Roezl found they were overtaking a floating tree which must have been uprooted and torn from the bank far away upriver. Its branches and bark were festooned, as though for a floral carnival, with epiphytic orchids, ferns and mosses of every shade of green, and (most astounding of all) a crimson monochaetum with furry leaves. Roezl and the boy quickly moored themselves to the tree and collected plants from its branches as they traveled downriver. The rich haul completely made up for the disappointments of their expedition.

Luck must have been with Roezl in at least ninety percent of his enterprises, not to have succumbed to the human, animal, insect, vegetable, geographical and climatic perils he encountered so often (and with such aplomb) in South and Central America. He died, moreover, of natural causes back at home near Prague. He merited the statue raised to his honor as the most eminent plant-hunting son of old Bohemia.

FTER 1498, when Vasco de Gama cast anchor in the harbor of Calicut, India was like a candleflame to moths in the minds of imaginative Europeans. It promised opulence. Faustus, tempted by the "evill Angell" longed for spirits to "flye to India for gold." Moreover it promised mystery, novelty and enormous opportunity to adventurers, explorers, traders, soldiers, empire carvers, administrators, religious proselytizers, civil engineers and, ultimately, to plant hunters. The land of Warren Hastings, Clive and Lord William Bentinck was also the chosen plant-hunting territory of several botanists and plantsmen.

The long-established rule of the East India Company and, after the transference of power to the Crown in 1858, the order imposed by British India, gave Anglo-Indians (the term was not then abusive) a secure feeling of "belonging." There was no feeling of temporarily camping out, and the more solid attributes of Western culture were soon in evidence. Among them were botanic gardens.

Nathaniel Wallich, who had made sage recommendations on the carriage of plants before Ward invented his case, was a director of the Calcutta Botanic Gardens. He was himself a collector of renown and his herbarium material eventually fetched up in Kew, but, like Reeves in Canton, his chief service to plant hunting was really the help he gave to fellow botanists and to gardeners sent out by the great. In particular he had the wit to guess the stresses under which the latter worked. To begin with, they depended absolutely on succeeding. It was at the back of their minds that, if they did not track down and transport what they had been ordered to find, their livelihood and their whole future might be affected. It was unlikely, but it could happen. Also, they would be homesick, and, in the class-conscious societies of the nineteenth century, they would be either too shy to ask for help from the upper-class English and French residents, or—made bold by necessity—they could so easily appear arrogant and overbearing in their demands. Plant hunting in India was difficult enough without adding an extra load of tensions such as these, and it was Wallich's special talent to help. It was he who met the gardeners personally at the dockside. It was he who smoothed out the difficulties, soothed the real or imaginary hurts, and made sure they were well looked after and respected all the time they were in British India.

Wallich's care of John Gibson, who arrived in 1835 (that is, in the first year of the post-Wardian era), was illustrative of his general concern to be as useful as possible. The young man was sent to India by the Duke of Devonshire, or rather by his head gardener, Joseph Paxton; and his instructions were precise. He was to find *Amherstia nobilis* and as many orchids as he could.

Gibson had been chosen because he was considered the Chatsworth "intelligent gardener," but he was naturally predisposed to be overanxious, and as his ship approached the Sundarbans he was dismally convinced he would be an utter failure. No one had troubled to tell him very much about India, but he was familiar with what their local Derbyshire poet Erasmus Darwin had written about a lotus floating on the Ganges.*

*Charm'd on the brink relenting tygers gaze,*
*And pausing buffaloes forget to graze;*
*Admiring elephants forsake their woods,*
*Stretch their wide ears and wade into the floods . . .*

---

* Derbyshire people were very proud of Darwin as author of the best-selling *Botanic Garden.* He was the owner of an eight-acre botanic garden, the writer of "fantastical, extravagant often incomprehensible verses," and grandfather to the great selector.

It was barely surprising that so extravagant a picture failed to correspond with reality, because Erasmus Darwin had never been to India; but the almost total lack of exotic beasts and, instead, the unromantic, dull network of turgid, brown rivers at the delta of the holy Ganges, was something of a letdown to the country boy from Chatsworth. As he later confessed, when he stepped ashore he was disappointed and trembling with uneasiness. Depression had drained him of all confidence. He could not bear the responsibility which faced him. His lavish equipment (no less than thirteen of the new Wardian cases), and all the vast Cavendish wealth which in theory lay behind him and which would have bolstered up most men, merely increased his gloom. The thought of Paxton's elaborate plans to construct a special stovehouse for the Amherstia unnerved him more and more. And he could not bear the heat. No one at Chatsworth had thought to inquire if he enjoyed hot weather. He did not. In fact, he found it unendurable. A temperature of between 80 and 99 made him, in Wallich's words, "dreadfully miserable."

Wallich came to the rescue. He paid small attention to the gaucherie and the long silences of the young gardener. He charmed away his uneasiness; gave him the confidence he needed; promised him that though Bengal could be as airless and blazing as a smelting furnace, and Assam as sodden as a sponge, the plants he saw would give him such pleasure and interest that they would outweigh all inconveniences and discomforts. He was right about both. Carried by boat and wagon and then in a *palkee* by relays of men called his *dawk*, Gibson moved from stage to stage, upcountry through East Bengal and the valley of the Brahmaputra. Lying in the curtained *palkee*, he found the climate unbearable and preferred to walk. However sizzling the tracks, however drenched the forests, his mind was distracted and he found himself spellbound by the vegetation. Where it was sparse it yet outrivaled in brilliance anything he had seen in the soft water-color country around Chatsworth. Where it was lush, its density was extraordinary: thick, choking masses of ferns and mosses, funguses and lichens, bamboos soaring up to the height of a church tower, one hundred feet and more, trees rigged like shipping with shrouds and stays of rampant plants, epiphytes gleaming here and there on trunks and branches; nature so tumid that, in the rare moments of silence from the crying and chattering and calling, the shrieking and screaming, the yelping and roaring, the rate of plant growth, the building up and burgeoning of cells seemed almost audible.

Gibson's self-doubts vanished. He found his Amherstia, and so strenuous and effective was his other collecting that when he sailed away from Calcutta all thirteen of his brand-new Wardian cases were replete with exotic plants. Good Nathaniel Wallich, the inspirer and encourager of his success, saw him safely aboard, helped to arrange the epiphytic orchids which, still attached to their hosts, were suspended from Gibson's cabin roof, and then took the trouble to write to the Duke of Devonshire that his gardener's treasure of Indian plants was "a truly princely one." It was.

The efficient Paxton, forewarned by Calcutta, had a ducal flyboat waiting at the canal basin close to the docks where Gibson's collections were put ashore. From there they were raced by teams of horses to the nearest canal basin to Chatsworth, and then, by sprung wagons. In record time the Duke of Devonshire's new Amherstia House had its first occupant. And besides this triumph which "afforded the Duke great satisfaction," Chatsworth was the richer by more than a hundred species of orchid and, as Gibson himself reported to Paxton, "other fine plants which were not in England when I took my departure from India."

The success of Gibson's first botanical exploration gave him the confidence to make many others, and he became renowned as one of the most experienced of all travelers in the eastern tropics. Because of this he was ultimately appointed superintendent of Battersea Park which he laid out himself. By using foliage plants such as fan and sago palms, tree ferns and bananas and aralias, which Sir William Hooker grew for him at Kew, he attempted, for the enjoyment of all Londoners, a reconstruction of the rich vegeta-

tion he had seen on his many tavels. Very soon the Battersea Subtropical Garden was as famous in London as the
exotic park laid out by Barillet-Deschamps in Paris and
Olmstead's Central Park in New York. But to Gibson himself it was a pale imitation; merely the ghost of the dripping
and matted jade forests enameled with colors which he had
first seen in Bengal and Assam under the aegis of the director of Calcutta's Botanic Garden.

Wallich was celebrated among his friends for what he
called his "little notes." Any excuse to write one was immediately seized on. He would, for instance, present plants to
local botanists and gardeners in Calcutta and then subject
them to a bombardment of botanical *billets doux,* inquiring
into the plants' progress, rate of maturity, health and appetite as though they were children, not vegetables. And he
adored sending good news, writing "little notes" of congrat-
ulation with a boyish glee. A good example was one sent to
Sir William Hooker when his son was elected a Fellow of the
Royal Society. By then Wallich had given up his work in
Calcutta and was able to be present at the election. Barely
had it finished before he was writing to Sir William:

*I rejoice to tell you that your son was elected by a vast
majority . . . much greater than any among eight candi-
dates that were successful. Your Joseph beat them all! Hur-
rah for your Name and for the cause of Botany!*

Wallich's enthusiastic support was not only because he
was a friend of the family but also because Joseph Hooker
was about to go out to his beloved India to collect for Kew
and the Geological Museum, and the young man already
showed promise of being, in many respects, "Elisha" to the
"Elijah" of Sir Joseph Banks. The promise was to be fulfilled. He was to be heaped with honors and elected president of the Royal Society as Banks had been. His influence
was to be as extensive, his knowledge as large, his experience
as a field collector as wide and as rich. In the whole history
of plant hunting there never has been a pair quite like the
two Sir Josephs.

But when he became a Fellow of the Royal Society Joseph was only thirty and not yet knighted. Since his return from the "Antarctic herborizations" he had been overfilling each day with a great number of projects: compiling his *Flora Antarctica,* drawing sets of plants for *The Botany of the Antarctic Voyage,* lecturing at Edinburgh University with a view to keeping the chair of botany warm for himself (though when it fell vacant he was not, in fact, appointed), refusing the chair of botany at Glasgow which was offered as a sop, and turning down, as well, the suggestion that he might like to be director of the Sydney Botanic Garden, considering, and then accepting, a post as fossil botanist on the British Geological Survey, writing essays on coal plants, working on a collection of dried plants from the Galapagos Islands sent to him by Charles Darwin; all this, and falling in love with the daughter of the Cambridge professor of botany.

At this point in his life Joseph might have turned in one of many directions and settled to a distinguished career in this or that. But he could no more sit still at home than Banks before him, and he was no more a laboratory botanist than Banks had been. He had the itching feet of a field botanist, so, when on the Isle of Man he happened to meet the First Lord of the Admiralty who rather improbably offered him work abroad, Joseph hardly paused to consider. The first proposal was that he should go out to Borneo and prepare a report on the British possessions there; and then, on his way home, collect in India. This Borneo project never came to anything. Collecting in India, though, became a firm offer—fossil plants for the Geological Museum and living plants for Kew. Though his writing would have to be neglected, and he would be separated from the professor's daughter, Joseph had no hesitation at all in accepting the offer. It was what he really wanted. The results for horticulture and botany in the West were far reaching.

Far better equipped than on his last plant hunting expedition, armed with last-minute advice from Nathaniel Wallich, and accompanied by Hugh Falconer, the new director who was going out to take over the Calcutta Botanic Garden, Joseph traveled by ship to Alexandria, barge to Cairo, dromedary to Suez and then by the *Moozuffer*, an intensely uncomfortable steam frigate. In no time at all he was working on the first part of his commission and collecting fossils. That done, he made for the Himalaya.

Gibson's prevision of India had been tinted by Erasmus Darwin's extravagant verses. Hooker's had been tinted by an account of Samuel Turner's embassy to Tibet in 1783, and though he was an excellent and meticulous botanist and geologist he was also a dreamer. He was one of those rare and very contented human beings with a capacity for pleasure which included both the scientific and the romantic, and he could enjoy the tiny detail shown through a microscope as well as the scenery which was sublime. The second part of his commission excited him. Sikkim was his objective and, if he could get there, the independent states of Nepal and Bhutan. From all he had been led to believe about the climate he stood a fine chance of discovering many unknown botanical species. This was scientifically satisfying. He was equally delighted by the romantic notion that he would be the first European in sixty-five years to travel in that unmapped region of the Himalaya; and, could he have known that half a century would pass before anyone else followed in his tracks, he would have been enraptured.

In the account which he wrote of his travels in *Himalayan Journals* he showed the bizarre chauvinism and arrogance of a contemporary Englishman abroad which once characterized the spread of red on maps of the world, and the memory of which continues to embarrass the oversensitive, enrage the radicals, cause the breasts of those who have gunboat nostalgia to swell like frogs, and the Puckish to chuckle. Hooker's generalizations were exquisite, little miniatures of Victorian hauteur. The Lepchas he encountered were worthy of some praise though he added the modification: "I believe the Lepcha to be a veritable coward." The Bhotias were "queer and insolent." As for the Khasi people, they were "sulky intractable fellows." Still, he did his duty by them and politely accepted the honors paid him by villagers when they brought him gifts of fruit and vegetables, made sunshelters where he could rest, and bored him with ceremonious beer drinking.

He traveled in some luxury, with a suite of anything between sixteen and sixty servants. This, though, did not necessarily mean that he was comfortable. The contrary was true when bearer replacements failed to turn up at an appointed stage and only after hours of extensive negotiations in teeming rain could he persuade six men to carry his litter while he himself walked the fourteen miles to the next stage. By no means, either, was this an isolated example of administrative inefficiency. On another occasion he had to spend a night in a hut without bed or food because some baggage coolies failed to turn up. Far worse, on his way to Bhomsong in Sikkim where no European had ever been before he was obliged to subsist for eighteen days on eight days' provisions, and was reduced, at length, to an exclusive diet of rice and chili vinegar. And, worst of all, to a zealot like Hooker, because the coolies who carried stocks of drying papers sometimes lagged behind or, mysteriously, were missing when they were most needed, he could not always preserve the plants he found and had to throw away collected specimens. His chagrin when this happened can only be imagined.

He was made testy, too, by local politics which seriously threatened his work and even his liberty. In theory, the rajah of Sikkim was an autocrat. In fact, he was under two thumbs; that of his dewan, a Tibetan, who had a keen appetite for intrigue, and that of the governor-general, Lord Dalhousie, who had an equally keen appetite for annexation. The latter's political agent in Darjeeling met Hooker at Bhomsong and with some difficulty managed to present him to the rajah. Thereafter, though he had not the slightest interest in the matter, Hooker was committed willy-nilly to be antidewan, and affairs reached such a stage that, for no apparent reason, he and the political agent were arrested and imprisoned. The agent, a mild-mannered doctor named Campbell, was put to the torture, and their fate hung in the balance for over a month. Then, by great good fortune, the dewan overreached himself in hatching plots and was disgraced, and Dalhousie was at once pleased to annex Sikkim for its own protection.

Hooker's own report on this piece of history was modest and restrained. Having been released from gaol, he continued botanizing as though nothing had happened. He had his full share of that maddening English sangfroid which enabled him to face angry Sikkim sepoys, far less frightened by their hostility than outraged at their effrontery, and armed only with a foot-long barometer. And the four-year Antarctic expedition had taught him fortitude. Without complaint he endured such excesses of Asian climate as storms of continuous lashing rain for sixty hours at a time, extremes of heat, cold, dryness and humidity, as well as the depredations of fleas, bugs, ticks, midges, and leeches which permanently scarred his legs. With the same modesty and restraint he mentioned, as though in passing, that, in climbing to 19,300 feet, he went higher than any record to that date. He was far more pleased to record his good fortune in seeing the "Specter of the Brocken"—his own shadow cast onto mist with a rainbow nimbus about the head. He happened to be the first Englishman to feel the deep chill on the eternal snows of Kangchenjunga, to know the ceaseless and piercing winds which howled about its precipices, and hear the thunder of its glacial avalanches, but he made no more song and dance about it than in describing the large, yellow-flowered begonia used by the Sikkim Indians as an ingredient in sauce.

Hooker's *Himalayan Journals* show very clearly that his tastes were catholic and his scientific curiosity unusually keen. They do not emphasize, though, that in India he was confirming by personal experience his important theories of distribution. The Himalaya were so immense that on their mountain slopes it was easy to see the variations in plant life at different heights above sea level. His observations were confided, as ammunition for the *Origin of Species,* to his friend Darwin who, in his reply, correctly prophesied:

*I know that I shall live to see you the first authority in Europe on that grand subject, that almost keystone of the laws of Creation, Geographical Distribution.*

It was not only this which marked Hooker's Indian journeys with such interest. His collections were also important. In Sikkim and in "leaning over the border of Tibet" between April, 1848, and November, 1849, they included twenty-eight entirely new Rhododendrons besides a vast quantity of genera and species. "Vast" is the only appropriate adjective. His consignment of plants collected in the three autumn months of 1848 amounted to eighty loads. In Assam, where he collected on his way home from Sikkim, he collected more than two thousand flowering plants including orchids, balsams, ferns and mosses, as well as over three hundred specimens of different timbers for his father's Museum of Economic Botany at Kew. Western gardens were considerably altered as a result of his introductions, especially in the moist peatlands which correspond most closely to the Khasi Hills of Assam. In Hooker's seven-month stay there he measured no less than three hundred inches of rain, an inundation which seems even more impressive if it is written as sixty-five feet. Such Noah's ark downpours are unknown in places like North Carolina and the Scottish Highlands where Hooker's rhododendrons grow, but they are wet and peaty enough.

Three in particular of his many rhododendrons have claims on the discriminating plantsman. *R. thomsonii* produces interest and color from all parts like a good orchestra producing music. Its flowers are colossal and an unforgettable red, but it also gives pleasure with its foliage. The young leaves are frog-colored when they replace the old, and afterwards they turn to a turquoise shade. And from the time the shrub is middle-aged its bark peels to reveal a medley of mellow colors from violet to bullrush brown. *R. nivale* is less spectacular, an arctic shrub appositely named 'Rhododendron of the Snows.' Hooker found it growing like heather at 18,000 feet, and was the first of many to be enchanted by its little blossoms, the color of common thyme flowers, and exquisitely fragrant. The third has a special place in the affections of color connoisseurs. The foliage is large and a bright lettuce green, the flower bud a darker shade, about viridian, and the flower chalices are the palest yellow shot with a third distinctive shade of green. Under the complex filing systems of rhododendron experts the shrub now belongs to the series Maddenii and the subseries megacalyx, but it is better remembered by the name Hooker gave it to honor the seizer of Sikkim, *R. dalhousiae.*

Hooker was one of the few front-ranking botanists to collect in Africa during the immediate post-Wardian era. Plant hunting there before had been in the capable hands of men like Commerson, Masson, Bowie and Burke. During the greater part of the nineteenth century, however, Africa was as dark a continent botanically, as she was in most things, and no extensive collections were made there in any way comparable to those made in Central and South America, Asia and the Far East. Africa attracted Hooker largely because she was romantically "dark." She contained great, untrodden lands as well as neat gardens—some more ancient than many in Europe, and in the most improbable locations. The Nefta oasis, for example, either sizzled with heat or shivered with cold. At noon, 135 degrees in the shade was not uncommon and Norman Douglas, writing in Hooker's lifetime, noted that the Nefta gardens could only be maintained through being "assiduously tended and groomed by relays day and night." And Africa's romantic attractiveness undoubtedly was sauced for Hooker when a Dr. Welwitsch, botanizing in South Africa, came across the genus which bears his name, *Welwitschia.*

Depending on the point of view of the beholder this plant was either scientifically fascinating or a vegetable monster. Hooker naturally held the former view. It was ugly and unique and lived for a hundred years. Therefore its only known variety deserved the name they gave it, *W. mirabilis,* and it was not surprising that for a time it stole Hooker's heart away. Flowering cones and sketches of the plant were sent to him at Kew by the housepainter turned botanical artist, Thomas Baines. Not very long afterwards the real thing arrived from Dr. Welwitsch. Its trunk was the shape of an inverted cone and from it sprang a pair of long, flat, leathery leaves and cymes of scarlet cones. By the time Hooker received this unlovely gift from Africa he was married, a father, appointed his father's assistant at Kew, and busy, as ever, with a dozen different projects. But the misshapen plant devoured all his interest and spare moments for months. Its peculiarities absorbed him. He examined the plant's parts with scrupulous care, an eye glued to the microscope in long vigils of five hours at a stretch, and for a total of three whole days and three whole nights. He lectured on it, talked about it, wrote about it and, no doubt, dreamed about it. Africa, its native land, would appeal to him enormously—especially as he was not by inclination a microscope botanist. He was as restless as any true traveler and confessed to the American botanist, Asa Gray, that he longed "to taste the delights of savagery again . . . to get into the jungle and live in tents."

Morocco, where he chose to go, possessed no jungle, but it was still one of the least explored parts of the globe. Hooker set off with two companions and a Kew gardener called Crump, and though the party was bedeviled with the need to bribe officials and there were annoying setbacks and delays, they combed the Atlas ranges and took home a fine collection of plants.

Hooker returned to a truly Banksian existence as the complete controller of Kew's fortunes, government adviser on botanical appointments, and president of the Royal Society. Later he enjoyed another stimulating expedition, this time in the Rockies with Asa Gray. And he was heaped with honors from universities, learned societies, governments and reigning sovereigns.

Enduring hardships aboard the *Erebus* and in Sikkim, the cold of the Sierra Blanca and the blistering heat of Morocco evidently suited him. He lived on and on. In his great old age he was the benevolent despot of all botanists, and retirement from the responsibilities of administering Kew made little difference to his liking and his capacity for work. His last undertaking was self-imposed and one of the most arduous in all his career. With a microscope and herbarium sheets sent to him from Christiana, St. Petersburg, Berlin, Paris and Kew, he set about the laborious task of classifying the *Impatiens* genus in the balsam family. He managed it, naming 303 new species in the process, returned the herbarium sheets, put away his microscope, and laid down his pen. Four days later he died; it might be said of nothing in particular. He was ninety-four years old.

*three  /  The Eastern Tropics*

ssurance of home comforts—to a surprising degree—for the Western plant hunter on his way out East was provided by the quantity of shipping controlled by Britain in the nineteenth century. The British merchantmen painted in reds and black—some powered by sail, others by steam, and a few by both—were substantial in every respect. There was no nonsense about serving up "foreign foods," and the sofas were as snuff-colored and as heavily buttoned, and the saloons as decorated with potted palms as they were at home. Moreover, because almost all the coaling and cabling stations were British in character as well as in fact, in the oddest places there were British insurance brokers, ship's chandlers, surveyors, marine engineers and victualers. The royal navy dominated and protected the sea routes, so in the great shipping lanes and ports there were generally British warships; the paintwork a glittering white in tropical waters, elsewhere black with orange funnels and white upperworks; the decks alive with barefooted seamen; the bridge staffed by officers as impeccably turned out as the pipeclayed rigging, the polished handrails, the cheesed-down cables, and the gleaming brasswork.

Arriving at Penang or Singapore, Manila or Hong Kong, the plant hunter would have to change ship to a tramp or coaster; that is, from sparkle, spit and polish to coaldust, grease and scruffiness; the sofas and potted palms giving place to cane planter's chairs and canvas punkahs which stirred the fetid air. The food, though, would still be stodgy and more suited to the German Ocean than the South China Sea because a large percentage of small merchant shipping sailed under the Red Ensign and kept to English ways. But then, put ashore at Soerabaja or Geelvink Bay, at Fakfak, Potianak or Yap, he instantly lost touch with the West and found himself on the edge of a wild and alarming experience.

That many collectors persevered and penetrated to the interior of Malaya, Indonesia, the Philippines and New Guinea and their outlying archipelagoes was a tribute either to their vitality and endurance or to the strength of their conviction that the plants of the tropical East Indies were well worth the ghastly risks they ran through the climate and terrain, and at the hands of headshrinkers, poison-dart blowers, ferocious beasts and venemous reptiles. The two great orchid grounds, for example, in Java and the Philippines were full of obstacles; the jungles so densely matted that tracks had to be hacked out, and teeming with huge slugs and leeches, insects and fruit-eating bats. But they were prodigal in beautiful orchids: species of Aërides, Arachnanthe, Cœlogyne, Cypripedium, Dendrobium, Phalaenopsis, Platyclinis, Sarchoehilus, Spathoglottis and Vanda, and the largest tree-perching orchid of them all, Grammatophyllum.

So rich were the veins of orchid gold that professionals were sent out for the sole purpose of finding new species. They were required to note the location of other plants, if possible, but their real business was to collect commercially profitable orchids. Some English nurserymen became internationally famous for specializing in Far Eastern plants: Loddiges of Hackney Wick with a reputation for winning over missionaries, Hugh Low of Clapham who had the advantage of being father to Rajah Sir Hugh Low of Sarawak, Standish and Noble of Bagshot, and, of course, Veitch. They competed with each other in the salaries and bonuses they offered and, because these were often very large, orchid hunting attracted adventurers as well as respectable professionals. Indeed, it seems that some of the former were as

ruthless in their pursuit of spoil as the pearlers and black-
birders who enriched themselves at the expense of everyone
else and who made the Coral Sea between Thursday Island
and the Solomons a living hell for countless divers.

William Lobb's brother, Thomas, was the leading
Veitch collector in the East Indies and undoubtedly their
greatest orchid hunter. He sent back other exotics, including
a collection of tender rhododendrons, but by inclination he
was an orchid fancier. Unlike William, who, so far as conditions in South and Central America and the Sierra Nevada
allowed, was inclined to be a socialite, Thomas was uncom-
municative and when a word could be dragged from his
oyster-like lips it was almost always about orchids. He paid
for his devotion with a leg—lost on an orchid hunt in the
Philippines—but he lived to retire to his native Cornwall.
There he enjoyed a few years of retirement at Devoran,
saying next to nothing and thinking about nothing at all
but orchids. In the church there is a memorial to the brothers:

*Two collectors of plants from foreign countries, who ren-
dered distinguished service to British horticulture.*

And their memory is literally kept green in the graveyard
where four specimens of their introductions flower each
summer in the balmy Gulf Stream climate; a rose-colored
escallonia, a crimson tricuspidaria, a yellow St. John's
wort, and an orange barberry.

Charles Curtis was another of Veitch's orchid hunters
who gave his name to the lady's slipper, *Cypripedium curtisii.* Here was an orchid with a history almost as mysterious
as the lost cattleya which turned up as the corsage of a lady
at a Paris ball. Not that its finding was in any way romantic, as Curtis simply saw it growing in the Penang Botanic
Gardens and sent it back to England. It was much admired
for its violet, clog-shaped lip and leopard-spotted petals, but
either being fêted did not suit it or it pined for the climate
of Penang. Whatever the reason, in time it died, and orchid-

ists gradually came to the alarming conclusion that it had been unique. Nothing was known of its jungle home. Curtis, by this time, was hunting the flora of celestial fields, and the authorities at Penang Botanic Gardens confessed they were ignorant of the orchid's origin. On the theory that most probably it had been found in the Malayan uplands, other plant hunters in that area kept a constant eye open for it and several went out to the East with the primary purpose of finding it. But no one was ever successful. The orchid remained as elusive as the Scarlet Pimpernel himself, but Curtis, apparently, had never forgotten its pretty elegance. At the beginning of this century, a Swedish plant hunter named Ericson was collecting in the Sumatra highlands (once one of Curtis' favorite hunting grounds), and, being forced by a storm to take shelter in a convenient hut, he found a picture of *C. curtisii* painted on the wall. Under it was a scrawl:

*C.C.'s contribution to the adornment of the house.*

It was nothing more than an elaborate doodle, a time passer, neatly painted by Curtis years and years before, perhaps to while away the boredom of being trapped, as Ericson was, by a monsoon. But it showed how clear his recollection was of the orchid which had his name and which had gone perpetually out of circulation.

The repeal of Britain's glass tax in 1845 coincided with the flourishing of industries which produced good materials at a low cost. Moreover, the price of coal for heating glasshouses and labor to maintain them was very small indeed. Everything combined to give the designers of glasshouses their head, and children at their first pantomime could hardly have been more excited. They raised what the poet laureate of the day eulogized as "Tropic Squares," which varied in size and grandeur from backyard leantos for the culture of calceolarias to Decimus Burton's Palm House at Kew, a graceful swan of the glasshouse world with 45,000 square feet of glass tinged to a Stourbridge green. The United States of the time, still too busy internally to be particularly inventive, was content to select and copy the best Europe offered in the way of glasshouse designs. Massive stoves and temperate houses, cold houses and conservatories mushroomed in proportion to American industrial expansion, and with a good many other things the greenhouse followed the railway west.

Filling all these glasshouses created an unprecedented demand for exotics, and the thin stream of plants sent from the eastern tropics in the pre-Wardian era swelled to a sizable river. Hunters scoured the Malay Peninsula, Java, Borneo, the Moluccas and Celebes, Guinea and the Philippines. The ubiquitous orchid was the most profitable quarry but the swamps and forests held many other treasures. Members of the dracaena family were very popular, named after such British military worthies as Sir Garnet Wolseley and Lord Roberts. Then there was the cissus genus, which gave the Californian patio its evergreen grape, *C. capensis,* and the Victorian conservatory a climber, *C. discolor,* with its light green leaves and flowers the indeterminate color of opals. And there were grevilleas, anoectochilus, scarlet glory trees—some deciduous and others evergreen, *Ixoras*—called "prince of stove plants," and crotons with foliage as gorgeously and diversely colored as triggerfish.

These beauties, and many more, reigned in the crystal palaces of Europe and the Americas until the cost of fabric maintenance and fuel and labor eventually made extensive glass-gardening solely the private province of the very rich and the public province of national institutions.

Reigning with the beauties were plants which intrigued because the Victorians dearly loved curiosities. The East Indies was a center of the sort of weird vegetables they liked to see and hear about: swamp palms, for instance, and mangroves, massive bamboos and lilies. Then there were lianas, which grew to a huge size and stifled the forest trees through which they writhed, or—and this was a delicious absurdity—sometimes they would strangle themselves; offshoots and tendrils tightening like fingers around their own throats until they had committed suicide. Still more grotesque was the Sumatran giant arum, *Amorphophallus titanum*, a gross, tropical parson-in-the-pulpit. Whenever the monster flowered in captivity it caused a sensation equal to that of the dramatic sex life of pandas. Not without reason. The parson part is as tall as a real parson. The pulpit is bell-shaped, frilly-edged and has a mauve interior. The whole thing stinks. The flower which bloomed in the New York Botanic Garden in 1937 was said to "reek of the effluvia of drains and all corruption." Another flowered in the Leyden Botanic Garden in 1954 and drew crowds of Hollanders eager to savor its "stench of rotten fish and burnt sugar." But even more fascinating, and given pride of place in Victorian collections of curiosities, were the carnivorous pitcher plants native to the eastern tropics.

Linnaeus, with his sense of the appropriate, had named the plants nepenthes after the cocktail made of an Egyptian drug and wine which Homer described as banishing grief and rage and inducing forgetfulness. To a botanist, explained Linnaeus, the effect of discovering a pitcher plant would be precisely the same. He was entirely correct.

The most bizarre feature of that bizarre plant is that the "pitcher" is not a flower but an extension of leaf midribs. Attached at first by a short thread to the leaf tip it begins as a pale green disc the size of a shirt button, swells, grows in length, and becomes a jug-shaped vessel with a hinged lid and a lip. It is obviously designed to dazzle with luminous, iridescent colors. And because small, honey glands freckle the inside of the jug it promises sweetness. In reality it is a foolhardy trap worthy of Doctor Fu Manchu's most devilish ingenuity. What appears to be an elaborate banqueting hall for insects is their prison and their grave.

The pitcher's lid is involuted, lobster-pot fashion, designed to keep the victims in, and the inside is slippery. An insect attracted by the colour and lulled by the sweetness abruptly finds itself sliding helplessly down into a pool of liquid at the bottom of the jug. If it has the spunk to try to crawl away, it meets downward-pointing hairs, fouls its legs and wings, exhausts itself and topples down a second time to drown in the malodorous mess of digestive juices and water made salty by decomposing corpses. In time, like a body in lime or acid, it disintegrates and leaves few remains.

This carefully contrived apparatus is not a divine whimsy. It has a serious function which falls well within the ordered pattern of creation because, being neither an epiphyte nor with roots in peaty swamps, the pitcher plant needs nitrates. Corrupting crickets, flies and beetles, spiders, ants and butterflies make up for its lack of nitrogen. Moreover the pitcher plant is not the master of all insects. Two parasites use the plant. One is a fly which, as a larva, wriggles into the charnel house to gorge on disintegrating bits of insect; the other is a moth which calmly lays eggs inside the pitchers and these, when hatched as larvae, spin silken aerial ropeways and bridges across the jar so that they will not slip into the death pool below, and then eat away the vegetable walls surrounding them until their host is entirely destroyed.

Rajah Sir Hugh Low had first discovered the pitcher plant in 1851 but, to the mortification of his father, the nurseryman, he failed to introduce it to the West. The silent, orchid-struck Thomas Lobb did manage it. Nepenthes grew for the first time in Europe, but either the stock was feeble or mistakes were made in looking after it for it faded and died. Veitch wasted no time in wringing his hands. As hothouse evergreens, pitcher plants had a future. They shared with orchids what was to him the advantage of being rare and costly to maintain. He judged that, in Victorian society, they would become a much desired caste mark, and that Victorian society, having too much time on its hands and being bored, would welcome a novelty. Furthermore, there was something about pitcher plants which seemed to slot in with the contemporary cult of decadence and esotery. The stuffiness of the time was barely more than a thick coat of paint which hid some surprising realities:

that the Queen smoked, for instance, and discreetly took whisky in lieu of tea when out with the ghillie Brown, and that she, with many high-ranking and intelligent people in the Old World and the New, took an abnormal interest in spiritualism, mumbo jumbo and the occult.

Veitch judged well. The pitcher plant was to become the most delicious hothouse flesh creeper of them all, and was to be honored as a horror by Joris Karl Huysmans, an apostle of decadence in French literature:

*. . . from the tip of each dark, long leaf there hung a green string—an umbilical cord—supporting a greenish urn whose interior was covered with hair.*

The description, sensational rather than accurate, mirrored the plant's appeal which Veitch was determined to take advantage of.

F. W. Burbidge, a plant hunter with exceptional powers of endurance, and with resource and persistence to match, was sent out to the Far East with the sole purpose of collecting pitcher plants. Nothing else. It was 1877. In Delhi, Queen Victoria was publicly proclaimed empress of India. Czar Alexander II undertook to "chastise the treacherous Turk" and marched on Constantinople. Veitch's ironside collector landed in Borneo.

The first pitcher plant had been discovered in Sarawak on the northwest coast. Burbidge estimated, correctly as it happened, that Borneo was the heart of the nepenthes country, and that somewhere in the shady, sodden forests between Bandjermasin and Balakbar he would find what he was after. He did. Shining through the gloomy jungle like cottage lights on a winter's evening he found nepenthes with colossal, brightly-colored pitchers; one species, a deep violet with gaping orange mouth; another, in toadstool array—green-spotted with blobs of crimson; another, green spotted brown; a particularly large species—later named *N. sanguinea*—the color of raw beef; and the *albomarginata* species, a ghostly combination of green and white.

Burbidge's cargo was sensational, and all Veitch's resources and skills were used to ensure that, like haughty brides, they were maintained in the state to which they were accustomed. Within seven years forty-six Far Eastern species had been established in European and American stoves. It became evident that Linnaeus' name was particularly appropriate. Not only did those who hunted the pitchers experience the sort of happy forgetfulness induced by Homer's nepenthes, but their cultivators, too, were daily comforted as they syringed and stoked to maintain East Indian conditions in the stove. And, in the end-of-winter excitement of rebasketing their precious pitchers, they were as entirely oblivious of the painful past as any hero of the *Odyssey*.

APAN's impenetrability continued long after Doctor Ward's triumphant experiment in 1834, and botanists, made greedy for its flora by the reports of Kämpfer, Thunberg and Siebold, pined fruitlessly for the opportunity to go there. Japan was an enigma, and it remained so until 1859. It was known in the West that, though theoretically it was under the rule of a mikado, Japan had been ruled by hereditary shoguns or overlords since 1603, and it was the shoguns' irritating policy to ban contact with other countries and cultures. But it was not known how beneficial this had been to the country: that although there had been occasional religious upheavals, agrarian riots and squabbles between bored warlords, old Nippon, previously so bellicose, enjoyed 256 years of peace and great progress. Inevitably, the West's knowledge of the country was limited and often distorted, and, as often happens, fable stepped in to fatten history. In the process of time the four main islands and their archipelagoes were invested with romance and glamour, heightened by the fact that from the sea forbidden Japan looked strikingly different from any other landfall.

This was not an illusion.

Westerners were to discover later that though, as a nation, Japan was ancient and preserved of a long and interrupted history, geologically it was an infant. The turbulent upheavals which formed her structure had not been honed down by time and rounded off. She was unweathered, and craggy with steep mountain sides and sharp drops where the land had faulted. Most remarkable of all, the earth itself was mutable. Nowhere in the world was land so fevered and shaken with regular quakes and tremors, so threatened with tidal waves. Nowhere was it so thin a crust over the interior subterranean fires. Vocanoes errupted. Hot springs gushed from the mountain slopes. Hundreds of pools of boiling mud gurgled and then vomited up into the sky. These pools were deep, apparently stretching further down to hell than the spires of Western cathedrals stretched up to heaven. Fires were so common that the few Dutch traders on Deshima who attempted the formidable task of mastering Japanese discovered there was a complete language of fires to describe the range of possibilities from a small and easily doused domestic flare-up to a city-consuming holocaust. Their reports of such phenomenon, seen with their own eyes, were hardly believed. But the Western world was fascinated.

Various aspects of historical interpretation account for the overthrow of the shogunate and the opening of Japan.

Down in Yedo (later to be called Tokyo) the shogun ruled as overlord. Up in the old capital, Kyoto, imperial courtiers wore their ceremonial silken clothes, raced crickets in jars, read the sentimental novels of Kioden and Bakin, wrote poems restricted to thirty-one syllables in praise of love or wine or the beauties of nature, gathered together to view the flowering of a cherry or a maple in autumn leaf, organized "moon-gazing parties," composed music for the koto, the samisen, the kokin and the sho, and drank quantities of tea. For far too long they were about as representative of the vitality and will of the Japanese people as the extremely Brittanic Mikado and Pooh-Bah, Ko-Ko and Nanki-Poo of Gilbert's "Titipu." But because their complicated love affairs were so spiced with intrigue they finally learned the fascination of plotting for plotting's sake. And the government down in Yedo was beginning to wear badly. It had many of the faults of old age—shortsightedness, irritability, indiscretion, overconfidence, and a mistrust of change. And, no doubt, even after so long a period of virtual peace and much prosperity, there were real causes of discontent.

Yet an equally powerful cause for the opening up of Japan was the peculiar Western determination to "improve" people. The impertinence of the Old and New Worlds in presuming to interfere in the affairs of so civilized a nation as the Japanese was almost breathtaking; but in 1853 it appeared to be quite natural for a president of the United States to send a letter to the shogun suggesting a commercial treaty—and send it by four, black warships under the command of Commodore Perry. The shogun was a boy. His regent temporized, hoping that old Nippon's privacy could be maintained. Then Russia sent a warship to Yedo Bay on a similar errand, and Commander Perry turned up with a second and far more insistent presidential suggestion, and twice the number of intimidating warships.

With great reluctance certain treaty ports were opened to the West and an extra-territorial concession was granted to resident foreigners which gave them the right to be tried under the law of their own nation and by their own countrymen. As a face saver, the shogun's regent publicly expressed his opinion of the "red barbarians" and "foreign devils" who had forced their gunboat policies on Japan. But the national humiliation was his downfall. The shogunate was discredited, the regent murdered. To their dismay, the plotting courtiers of the mikado had to leave their sybaritic life in Kyoto and take over the government in Yedo. But nothing now could stop the West. Piece by piece the country was opened up to foreigners.

One of the first to take advantage of the new concessions was Philipp van Siebold, the collector whose ophthalmic skill had given him such high credit with the Japanese until he bribed the imperial ambassador to part with a map of Nippon.

Since 1830, when he had returned to Holland with a total of 458 Japanese plants, Siebold had engaged more in polemics than either medicine or botany. If commissioned portraits ever indicate the truth, the painting of Siebold, "a fierce beetling-browed, bearded face surmounting a challenging figure in uniform," might account for this. He had had cause to be vexed. At Antwerp he offered his plants to the authorities and for some unknown reason they had hesitated to accept them. He instantly removed the collection to Ghent where it was cared for in the Botanic Gardens. At this point the revolution of Walloons against the Dutch broke out. It was a stiff contest between Catholics and Protestants, liberalism and autocracy; but the issue was decided at a distance by France and England which, between them, set up the independent sovereign state of Belgium with Queen Victoria's uncle, Leopold, as king. As a Bavarian, Siebold took small interest in the affair, but on Deshima he had been an employee of the Dutch and he was forced to leave Ghent. His plants there were confiscated and, without any sort of authority, distributed among the city's nurserymen.

For nineteen years he quarreled merrily with government bureaucrats, Dutch East India Company officers, and fellow-physicians. In tranquil moments he enjoyed botany and horticulture and the memory of his unusual experiences in Japan, and he consumed his energy by writing a large, illustrated *Flora Japanica,* a *Fauna Japanica,* and a thick *Catalogus Librorum Japanicorum.* Once the Wardian case had been proved as a means of transporting exotics he established a nursery at Leyden to receive and care for imported trees and shrubs from the Orient. Then in 1859, when traders of the Dutch East India Company considered that the troubles between shogun and mikado could be exploited to their own advantage, they invited him to go out to Deshima. They recalled his influence with the Japanese, which would be useful to the company.

Philipp van Siebold went, overjoyed to be returning to the land of bubbling fumaroles and volcanic eruptions, where earth tremors were poetically described as a great subterranean fish waking from sleep and wriggling in ecstasy; a land of tea drinking, bathing ceremonials, cormorant fishing and bribable imperial astronomers. He had the great advantage of being remembered by the Japanese who, because they honored him as an eye physician, were very content to forget his banishment and set him up in a house on the mainland. This made him comfortably independent of the Dutch Company and, because of the extra-territorial concession guaranteed by the government to resident foreigners, he was comfortably independent of the Japanese as well. His obligations to both were merely formal, and were perfunctorily carried out. His house grew into a palace. His influence enlarged at the same rate. In considerable state he made long and highly enjoyable botanical expeditions into the primeval forests where he found a rich variety of trees. There were cryptomerias and Japanese species of hornbeam, hazel, chestnut, pine, cypress, maple, alder, oak, catalpa, birch, beech—one now called Siebold's beech—and fir. There was even a Japanese flowering ash, a lush variety of *Fraxinus ornus* with autumn leaves a metallic violet color. The shrubs growing beneath the trees or in clearings were equally diverse. They included a host of bamboos, almost fifty of them, with euphonious local names like Nahiria-dake, Taimin-chiku, Kan-chiku, Kan-zan-chiku, and Médaké—the species van Siebold introduced to Europe and which, for a long time, was the only bamboo commonly grown there. Another of his introductions, the shrub helwingia, was a botanical curiosity, for its tiny pea-green flowers appeared to sprout from the middle of the tapering leaves. And then there were daphnes, weigelias, fatsias (one species enjoying the notable name of *Fatsia horrida*), a Japanese buddleia, andromeda and box, Siebold's barberry, sweet-scented osmanthus, acanthopanax, and a member of the rue family, a zanthoxylum, called Japan Pepper. To van Siebold's surprise he found another member of the rue family, the orixa, being used as hedging material. The Japanese liked it because its leaves were aromatic and it gave off puffs of scent when brushed by their loose clothes. They appeared not to mind its habit of distributing seeds like a balsam over an area of several feet and which, because the seeds traveled at the rate of peas from a peashooter, made the hedge quite unapproachable at seeding time.

To go on finding, month after month, fresh species of trees and shrubs and flowering plants proved to van Siebold the unsuspected richness of Japan's flora. Because it had been inpenetrable for so long, even many of the species of its cultivated plants were entirely new to the West: the Sawara and Hinoki cypresses, for instance; the Japanese arbor-vitae which later in the century the Veitch hunter Maries did find growing wild in the mountains of the Central Island; and the amelanchiers which were frequently grown beside the wood and lacquered gateways into shrines and temples.*

The Bavarian botanist lived regally, venerated by the local Japanese and especially those with eye troubles, and respected by the central authorities as a *sensei,* or teacher, because he was so evidently a man of books and culture and care for natural beauty. The Dutch, though, took a very different view of their appointed physician-agent who had failed to do what was expected of him. Expatriates invariably arouse suspicion among their compatriots, especially if they appear to be happy. Moreover, Europeans are often vexed when—as the patronizing expression has it—one of their number "goes native." Philipp Franz van Siebold appears to have done just that and because it was improbable that he would pay much attention to a direct recall from the Dutch East India Company they decided to winkle him out with a trick.

Perhaps his great good fortune in being a totally free plant hunter in a land with so large and interesting a flora reduced Siebold's wariness, or maybe his feeling of well-being made him look kindly and trustingly on men whom he should have remembered were fairly ruthless entrepreneurs uninterested in botany without guilders. Shrewdness, anyway, never has been the hallmark of impetuous men. What-

* Because *Amelanchier asiatica* has been found as a "native" of Hupeh province in China it is called the Chinese service-berry, though W. J. Bean noted that it was originally introduced there from Japan.

ever the Dutch traders promised him was simply a bait which he swallowed entirely and he left the security of his Japanese palace and returned to Holland. There, finding he had been duped, he refused to have anything more to do with the Dutch. His collections of Oriental trees and shrubs at Leyden were secured by Simon-Louis and taken to France, and Siebold himself, unable to face the business of trying to set up again in Japan, went off to his native Bavaria to die of ennui and bad temper, at Würzburg, in 1866.

Though a new era had begun in 1859, only a plant hunter with the prestige of Philipp van Siebold could collect exactly where he wished. John Veitch, who had moved the family firm from Exeter to London, went to Japan himself in 1860 but, being unknown there, his collecting was severely restricted. He was bound to keep within a certain distance of the treaty ports and his movements were under constant surveillance. A vainer man would have found the impositions intolerable; a less cautious one would not have paid attention to the regulations. But Veitch was neither. Like the first Dutchmen on Deshima who, for the sake of trade, had consented to humiliate themselves and spit on the Cross, he saw the value to his firm of submitting to Japanese caprice and he kept to the rules. His plant hunting, therefore, was confined to a small area, and most of his collections were made in Japanese gardens and nurseries, but the enterprise was still highly profitable in terms of commerce. He was the first to introduce the Japanese fir, the tiger's-tail spruce, the Japanese white pine and black pine, and Veitch's silver fir, a Wedgwood-blue beauty of great value to town gardeners because, though a calcifuge, it happily grew in urban surroundings. He also introduced, in quantity, the Japanese umbrella pine,* described by This-

---

* *Sciadopitys verticillata,* the Japanese umbrella pine is so called because the arrangement of the cladodes, or "needles," closely resembles the ribs of an umbrella. It should not be confused with *Pinus pinea,* the umbrella pine of Europe (though this, confusingly, is occasionally listed as stone pine) which has a broad, spreading head on a trunk bereft of branches and so looks like an open umbrella.

telton-Dyer (later the third Director of Kew and, as Sir Joseph Hooker's son-in-law, part of the Hooker botanical dynasty) as unique among conifers and "conjectured to have come down to us from a remote geological past which has obliterated all trace of its immediate ancestors." But the supreme success of John Veitch's short yet productive visit was his introduction of *Lilium auratum*, the golden-ray lily of Japan.

Robert Fortune, a notable collector in the Celestial Empire also was drawn irresistibly to Japan. Most probably he was curious to see as much as he could of a country emerging from obscurity, but humorless men (and Fortune was one) will never admit to the inoffensive and natural practice of "nosey Parkering." And so, in his book *Yedo & Peking* he laid a false paper-chase trail by claiming to have gone there in search of works of art. They turned out to be of the vegetable kind. No plant hunter of Fortune's status could have ignored the fascination of new species and even genera which he saw being cultivated in the gardens of Japan. He paid two short visits: the first for a week in Nagasaki and for a few weeks more in the district near Yedo and Yokohama; the second, in 1861, in the same area. Like John Veitch he was restricted by the Japanese; like Veitch he accepted the restrictions. They were treading where only Siebold had gone before and so much was new and of botanical interest and of commercial value.

Fortune's introductions were of great importance to European gardeners. Hunting out one of them, the magenta-colored *Primula japonica,* involved no effort at all. "I shall never forget," he wrote, "the morning on which a basketful of this charming plant was first brought to my door." As easy to find, because he collected them all from one garden, was the collection of Chrysanthemums which he introduced: "Some extraordinary varieties, most peculiar in form and in coloring, and quite distinct from any kinds at present known in Europe." Two reintroductions were of great importance because the original stock had either failed or had turned valetudinarian: the double-flowered *Deutzia scabra,* and the autumn-flowering and delightfully fragrant osmanthus which, although a hybrid garden species of Japanese origin, was named after him *O. Fortunei.*

It appears odd that, in proportion, Fortune accomplished so much more than Siebold, the doyen of plant hunters in Japan. But, then, he was essentially a professional gardener with an unrivaled technique in packing and shipping plants even in pre-Wardian days, and van Siebold was essentially a naturalist who knew and loved the plants and trees of Japan and whose work, although important, made far less mark upon the gardens of the West. Besides this, they represented the two entirely different types of plant hunter in the nineteenth century, who, in turn, were representative of two different kinds of human being—the accomplishers and the appreciators, those eager to do like Occidental gardeners, and those content to be like their Oriental counterparts. Philipp van Siebold confronted, say, by Fuji made blue at the moment of moonrise would very likely have reflected, Japanese-fashion, on its astonishing beauty and, as a scientist, marveled at its formation. Robert Fortune, confronted by the same inspiring mountain would most probably have endeavored to climb it.

Though the collections of Veitch and Fortune were mainly from plant pedlars, nurseries and the gardens of inns, temples and private houses, and both men were obliged to remain within a restricted area, neither had a guarantee for his personal safety. While Veitch was tracking down pines and spruces and Fortune was writing enthusiastic notes on Chrysanthemums "with petals like long thick hairs, of a red colour, but tipped with yellow," the shogun's well-meaning regent was being butchered not far away at the very gates of his master's castle. In 1861, when England mourned the Prince Consort, and the bloodiest civil war in history blew America's peace to smithereens, and Veitch and Fortune were busy packing up their Wardian cases, the Japanese samurai, indifferent to treaties, were busy chopping foreigners to bits with two-edged swords. A year later the mikado's control tightened, but not before an Englishman named Richardson had been murdered on the Tokaido road between the old and the new imperial capitals. At this enormous affront to British dignity the Royal Navy bombarded, burned and completely reduced the port of Kagoshima. Simultaneously, at the London Flower Show where many of Veitch's treasures were displayed, visitors were so enraptured by the golden-ray lily of Japan that the ladies caught their breath and the gentlemen, as though in church, removed their hats. It was, in fact, a long time before the radical revolution was completed in Japan and European plant hunters could collect there in any degree of security.

John Veitch fretted until it was reasonably safe to send out a collector. Then, in 1875, he chose Charles Maries, one of the firm's nursery foremen to go to Japan. Maries knew his botany well. He had been taught as a boy by Joseph Hooker's father-in-law, Professor Henslow. He was, also, a sound, practical gardener: fit, twenty-four years old, and with no emotional entanglements at home to make him fretful and divert his concentration from the job in hand. John Veitch found that even with all these qualities Maries "lacked staying power"—and he was never able to match his own introductions or Fortune's. But what he did produce was profitable. Veitch knew quite well that though the golden-ray lily was the cake of the firm's trade, the common bread-and-butter would matter as much and maybe more in the end. With this in mind he told his collector to send home seeds from as many different conifers as he could. Maries did, and from this alone he justified Veitch's investment in him, but he made other money-spinning introductions, too.

For three years he was in the Far East and for most of it in Japan. Neither of his two trips to China was happy. On the first he found the *gloriosoides* variety of *Lilium speciosum* beside the Yangtze, but even this triumph hardly made up for the appalling attack of sunstroke he contracted there and which drove him in a madness of pain down to the coast. On the second trip he collected seeds of *Primula obconica*, and again the triumph was spoiled for him when he was caught, robbed and beaten up by bandits. He was happier working in Japan, and was the first plant hunter to collect on the northern island of Hokkaido. There, though he found the climate stern in the winter when bitter winds blew in from the Sea of Okhotsk, there were unquenched fires beneath the frozen ground. For all that the countryside looked like Scotland it was enlivened by the constant threat of earthquakes, volcanic erruptions, gales and tidal waves. It was there that he found so many of the conifers Veitch had asked for, and in addition the Chinese bellflower, *Platycodon mariesii,* and *Lilium splendens,** a lily with dramatic trumpets of light red with livid spots. It was Maries, too, who introduced the witch hazel, a shrub which was to become such a universal favorite that gardeners crowned it as one of the quintet of winter gardens and which, with the ubiquitous daphne, winter jasmine, forsythia and japonica, reigns to this day. Unlike the majority of Veitch's plant hunters who retired to dream of their foreign travels, Maries showed an original streak in settling in India as horticultural adviser to an Indian prince.

In 1872, the foundation of the Arnold Aboretum of Harvard University, and the work done by its director, the sylviculturalist Charles Sprague Sargent, had a large effect upon the collecting of trees. He specialized in the trees of North America, but he collected in Japan, also. He was there not long after Maries, his visit coinciding with the most spectacular of all plant hunters in Japan, Père Urbain Faurie.

Faurie was essentially a botanist and far less interested in the shanghaiing of plants from their native habitats than in identifying and preserving them. He went native in a way that would have warmed van Siebold's heart, taking the trouble to learn what he could of Japanese and generally dressing in the slack and comfortable clothes of a coolie. No foreign botanist had such an intimate knowledge of the flora of Japan; nor, apparently, such energy. Faurie was said to have scaled ninety percent of Japan's hills and mountains,

* Its synonym is *L. thunbergianum sanguineum.*

and he was quite happy to get up two or three times during the night to change the drying papers in his botanical presses. In twenty-four years he collected 22,500 specimens —all carefully dried, preserved, identified, named, labeled and filed—and his influence on local enthusiasts was very great. Far earlier than China, Japan began to produce her own expert plant hunters and send specimens of what they found to botanical gardens in the West. The botanist Shirasawa, for example, discovered the Japanese Douglas fir in 1893 and was responsible for its introduction to Europe and the United States. With their aid, and the careful concern of "Chinese" Wilson, who was sent there to collect by the Arnold Arboretum during World War I, the flora of Japan was systematically cataloged and analyzed. By any standards it was impressive and present-day Western gardens without the plantings originally native to the "Land of the Rising Sun" would appear strikingly incomplete.

NTRODUCTION of Wardian cases and a commercial war entirely revolutionized the export of plants from China. Britain's rôle in what came to be known as the "Opium War" was fairly indefensible. The East India Company's monopoly ended in 1834, but the British government, determined to keep an eye on Chinese trade and affairs, sent out a representative, or Plenipotentiary Minister, to act on its behalf. He was the agent of British gunboat policy rather than an ambassador accredited to the Imperial Court.

The Manchu Emperor Tao-Kuang was favorably disposed to the Europeans and Americans who traded from Canton and Macao. His predecessors on the Dragon Throne, indifferent to Western sophistication, had aloofly called Europe "the Western Ocean" and Europeans either "Franks" or "Red Hairs," but Tao-Kuang was intrigued by the culture, the guns and the astronomy of the Westerners who paid him court at Peking. Yet, though favorably disposed and intrigued, he was not prepared to grant them permission to penetrate into the interior of China. Nor did he hesitate to condemn and forbid their irresponsible introduction of opium as an article of trade. It was having disastrous results. In exchange for the enervating and expensive drug which the British, in particular, were illegally importing from Bengal and England, his country was being drained of silver, tea, silk, porcelain and other profitable products. He complained of this "supervised smuggling" to the British Minister.

Then, as now, dope peddling was a lucrative business.

The Minister paid no attention. To his surprise an imperial commissioner, named Lin, arrived in Canton with great powers and explicit instructions to put a stop to the smuggling at any cost.

Lin happened to be a man of integrity and one of the few imperial servants who did not have a hand in the opium trade. He served his master well, showed he was not open to British persuasion and, to everyone's dismay, he stopped all foreign trade, imprisoned foreign merchants and employees in their factories and presented them with an ultimatum. His sanctions would continue, and forever, if necessary, unless all the British-owned opium lying in the warehouses and in storeships at river moorings was given up. The Minister tried every method to make him change his mind, but he was inflexible. The British had to capitulate and no less than 30,000 fair-sized chests packed to the brim with opium were surrendered to the commissioner. It represented a fortune, and Lin destroyed it. But he was slow to concede old trading rights. There were tales, too, of atrocities committed on prisoners in the trading factories. Claiming that Lin had not kept his part of the bargain, the British government declared war.

A fleet and an army arrived in 1840. The island of Chusan was seized, Canton, Ningpo and Shanghai captured. Warriors and diplomats of the venerable Celestial Empire could not withstand the pressure put on them by professional Western soldiers who, in the days of Victoria, were always spoiling for war. The treaty which followed was of great benefit to Britain, and therefore to Western plant hunters.

By 1842 the ports of Shanghai, Ningpo, Fu-chu and Amoy were open to the trade of the world besides Canton and Macao. Hong Kong was formally ceded to Britain in perpetuity. The Chinese undertook to be less strict in supervising the activities of aliens in the immediate environment of the treaty ports, and journeys of up to fifty miles distant were winked at if not officially permitted or encouraged. This dispensation, and four additional ports, gave collectors more than 1,500 square miles of extra territory in which to hunt plants.

The rocky island of Hong Kong covers less than thirty square miles but it contains notably different terrain varying from the gullies of the north to the bleak, thin lands in the southeast. Its climate encourages growth. Being able to botanize at leisure on British territory, several amateurs, as well as professionals, set about listing the island's flora, and their collections, sketches and notes were used by Bentham (of Bentham and Hooker fame) when he compiled the *Flora HongKongensis.* It turned out to be astoundingly large: almost a thousand species of 550 genera. Officers attached to the invading force and to the British army of occupation provided four of these pioneer plant hunters: a medical officer of the Cameronians, two naval surgeons, and John George Champion, a captain in the 95th Regiment of Foot. Bentham was particularly grateful to Captain Champion because he was a systematic botanist, not simply a collector. Being scrupulously exact, he drew analytical sketches and wrote his descriptions on the spot—not later in the day when his memory might be clouded with tiredness or overeating. Charles Wilford,* a Kew collector of the new generation, made a large contribution to Bentham's *Flora,* as did the land surveyor and deer hunter from Texas, Charles Wright, who took to botany and hunted plants with all the dash and energy he had shown in hunting deer. Bentham was in his debt for a large number of carefully dried and pressed Hong Kong plants. His *Flora* owed a great deal as well to Robert Fortune and Henry Hance, both of such importance in the history of plant hunting in China that they merit separate attention.

Fortune's private plant-hunting expedition in Japan has already been noted. It was, in fact, his only private expedition, and was the last he made in the Far East. His reputation had been established long before.

* When the British government, anxious to sweeten the mikado of Japan, sent him the gift of a steam yacht, the *Emperor,* Wilford was added to the ship's complement from the naval dockyard out to Hong Kong.

By birth he was of Scottish cottage-folk. By habit he was dour, persevering, as unsmiling as David Douglas. By genius he was an excellent descriptive writer with an eye for a "gardener's plant" and a real flair for collecting. By nature he was eccentric, direct, brave and naive. These judgments are speculative, lying within the seemliness of historical probability. His books and numerous articles are straightforward and interesting but curiously impersonal. We see little of Fortune in them, and the diaries and letters he wrote which might have mirrored his personality were destroyed by relatives when he died—a curious procedure, motivated either by caution or censoriousness, but in neither case particularly laudable. Yet, however enigmatic Fortune might have been, his place in the history of plant hunting is a high one.

When details of the Opium War treaty became known, it was not long before the Royal Horticultural Society, brooding on those additional 1,500 square miles of territory, appointed a China Committee. Its progenitor was John Reeves who had retired from his post in Canton and by then lived in London. His knowledge of the Chinese was invaluable, his enthusiasm infectious, his advice that they should pay a collector to go out on the Society's behalf as soon as possible. Fortune was superintendent of the Society's hothouses at Chiswick and eager for the appointment. He was thirty-one, a hard worker, a skilled gardener, and ambitious. Reeves reckoned he would do, and the Scot was provided with a spade and trowels, a life preserver, a fowling piece and pistols, a Chinese dictionary, and long and detailed instruction. His salary was to be £100 a year with an allowance of up to £500 expenses. He must keep a daily journal— to be the Society's property—and write descriptive letters to the Society's secretary: *"This will enable the Society to judge of the progress you are making. All letters must be sent in duplicate, by separate opportunities, so as to guard against accidents."* When sending plants back in Wardian cases he was *"to impress upon the minds of the Captains the indispensable necessity of the glazed boxes being kept in the light, on the poop if possible."* He was to understand and remember that *"to all collections of living plants and seeds the Society lays exclusive claim,"* and he was to prepare for the Society a set of dried specimens of all the plants he came across. He must make inquiries on certain points—why, for example, *"it is a general practice for the Chinese to put up their seeds mixed with burnt bones,"* and *"the circumstances under which the Enkianthi grow at Hong-Kong."* He was required in general to bear in mind that *"the value of the plants diminishes as the heat required to cultivate them is increased. Aquatics, orchidaceae, or plants producing very handsome flowers are the only exception to this rule."* And he was required in particular to collect analyses of soils with twenty-two other items, including *"the plants that yield tea of different qualities,"* *"Peonies with blue flowers, the existence of which is, however, doubtful,"* *"Cocoons of the Atlas Moth,"* *"the Canes of Commerce,"* and *"the plant which furnishes Rice Paper."* A most extraordinary feature of this formidable document was an admission: *"The Society cannot foresee what it may be possible for you to accomplish during your residence in China; which according to their present views they wish to limit to one year."* It showed that even the experienced John Reeves knew very little for certain about China at that time. As it turned out, Fortune was to travel in the East for over nineteen years and, though his introductions were substantial, he took barely one skimming from the cream of China's flora.

He left England on a ship named the *Emu* and, as the Royal Historical Society had directed, he messed with the captain. His first sight of the Celestial Empire was disappointing. Like John Gibson approaching the Ganges Delta he had expected something very different. As it was, he felt let down.

*Although I had often heard of the bare and unproductive hills of this celebrated country, I certainly was not prepared to find them so barren . . . They had everywhere a scorched appearance . . . The trees are few, and stunted in growth, being perfectly useless for anything but firewood.*

Nor did he care for the Chinese:

*From the highest Mandarin down to the meanest beggar they are filled with the most conceited notions of their own importance.*

A little experience and time modified his view of both China and the Chinese. The former he grew to love. The latter he regarded half with affection, but half with vexation because naturally they crowded to see him and they were amused by his eccentric use of smoked spectacles, a trap umbrella, and a hat not unlike the tarboosh of a Turk. He showed a certain gaucherie when a mandarin wanted to make him the gift of a valuable bonsai tree grown in the shape of an animal.

*As it was of no use to me, and my collections of other things were large, I was obliged to decline the present, which he evidently considered of great value, and no doubt wondered at my want of taste.*

Quite likely, too, the mandarin wondered at the Scotsman's lack of affability and courtesy. Foreigner still bit foreigner on the coasts of Cathay.

Though Fortune never went further than thirty miles from any treaty port on his first expedition, his collections justified all the hopeful expectations of the China Committee. Most of the collecting was done by Chinamen "engaged at a small daily remuneration," Fortune himself acting as a plant clearinghouse. But some plants he found in person; a specially prized bag being the "Japanese" anemone, which wasn't Japanese at all and which he found flowering in November in Chinese cemeteries. On this and later expeditions he also introduced weigelia, winter jasmine, bleeding heart, forsythia, tree peonies and many species of plums, primulas, rhododendrons, azaleas and chrysanthemums. He was by no means immune from physical dangers. On returning to Chusan at the conclusion of a short trip into the interior he lay weak with fever on the deck of a junk. His crew were a timid lot who merely screamed with terror when pirates came into sight and bore down on the junk. Fortune could hardly stand. He waited until the pirates were alongside before raking them with a blast from the heavy double-barreled fowling piece provided by the Horticultural Society. They sheered off, considered their chances, and made another attack. Again Fortune blasted as many as he could, and a third time, until they were finally driven off.

With his collections stowed in eighteen Wardian cases on the poop of the Indiaman, *John Cooper,* Fortune made the journey back to England in 1845. His courage and his skill were rewarded with the curatorship of the Chelsea Physic Garden but he held the appointment for only two years. The taste of China was in his mouth and when the East India Company asked him to go out to collect China tea for growing in the highlands of India he accepted at once. The commission was not easy. The Chinese guarded their tea industry with such jealousy that penetrating to the gardens and collecting seeds involved a great deal of personal risk. His "cover" as a botanist was a good one and particularly convincing because there were many wild plants in the Anhwei and Bohea tea districts. And, making so bold as to pretend to be a native from a distant province, he managed to carry it off. For three years running he sent supplies of seeds to Calcutta and the second and third consignments, traveling as germinating seedlings in Wardian cases, were particularly successful.

In the abridged biographies of Fortune he is often described as "the introducer of the Tea plant into India" in 1848. Research by botanists, growers, blenders, plant hunters, geographers and explorers suggests that though the "Tea Ceremony" had been carried on in China for at least three thousand years, and it has long been considered the home of the camellia, whose tips make tea, very probably the first tea drinkers lived in the jungle-covered mountains between Assam and North Burma, especially in the region about the lonely mountain called Dapha Bum; and that far from tea plants traveling from East to West, the contrary is more probably correct. The directors of the East India Company, however, were uninterested in plant ecology. They were principally concerned to congratulate Fortune on his excellent work, because there was a very large chance he would make tea nabobs of them all.

Apart from this achievement Fortune found the barberry, *Berberis bealei* (*Mahonia japonica*), which "far surpassed in beauty all the other known species." Unfortunately there was a belief among the Chinese that the plant had magical properties and he found it difficult to overcome their superstitious dread of parting with any specimens at all. The three little plants which, at last, he wheedled from them were the parents of all the stock now living in Europe and the United States. Another by-product of the tea expedition was his introduction of the seed of the funeral cypress, *Cupressus funebris*. It had been found and described by the botanists attached to Lord Amherst's embassy but not introduced to Europe. Fortune delighted in the tree. Being a Calvinist, and very much a man of his gloomy country and time, he was fascinated by doom and death and all its trappings, and he immediately decided that the conifer would make a fine ornament in Western cemeteries. John Lindley, by then professor of botany in University College, London, agreed wholeheartedly saying the cypress was "perfect for graveyard decoration." Fortune's seeds were grown in England and several cypresses were raised, but in the end it proved to be too tender to grow everywhere and would only mature in the freak regions where fingers of England and Wales are warmed by the Gulf Stream.

Fortune's success as a tea smuggler earned him the East India Company's commission to collect and transport more tea plants and seeds. He found China seized in the Taiping Rebellion, a conflict between the Manchus and mandarins and a revolutionary movement led by a former village schoolmaster who went into ecstasies, flirted with American Methodism, declared himself to be the younger brother of Jesus Christ, and thereafter lived in splendor with thirty wives and one hundred concubines. The internecine struggle was to last twelve years, and in it the government was forced to invite the military intervention of Britain and France, frontier lands were lost to Russia in the north and to Moslems in Yunnan and Turkestan, and the Dragon Throne was several times in real danger of being overthrown. Quite unconcerned with all this, Fortune took advantage of the lack of supervision to hunt plants in areas which were generally forbidden, and take what he wanted from the unguarded tea gardens. His bravery, demonstrated by the way he had dealt with river pirates, was never in doubt; nor was his eccentricity in view of the fact that generally he was armed only with a trap umbrella.

Fortune's fourth trip was under the auspices of the United States Patent Office. This was in 1858. The Taiping Rebellion was still chafing and tearing at the Chinese peoples but Fortune barely seemed to notice it. He was engaged to collect plants and study Chinese horticulture for the American Government, and he did just that; no more. It was his last sponsored plant hunting expedition and it confirmed his standing as a collector.

Fortune had, of course, been lucky to be the first frontranking plantsman on the scene directly after the Opium War. And he had been the first to make extensive use of Wardian cases. But his large success and his fame were mostly due to the fact that he was an instinctive botanical explorer and he was a thorough professional in the handling of seeds and plants.

The fame of Henry Hance, an assistant to the consul at Canton and afterwards vice-consul at Whampoa, rested on different foundations. He, too, collaborated in providing material for Bentham's *Flora HongKongensis* and, though his rank in the consular service was low, his influence in the field of botanical exploration was large and widespread in the south of China. Maybe the two facts were related. Hance was an Englishman with an unusual talent for languages. He spoke French and German as well as he spoke English, and if the classical tongues had been living instead of moribund and confined to scholars and churchmen he could have been as proficient in ancient Greek and Latin. But, though he lived forty-three years in China, and came to love and understand the country as well as any other Englishman of his time, he never managed to learn either Mandarin or Cantonese or even the "coolie talk," which was mangled Mandarin. Because this checked his career in the service some of his contemporaries believed he was simply being stubborn. They overlooked the fact that it was impossible to study Chinese in the same way as any other language; that the written style is undoubtedly the most difficult study in the world; that confronted by five variations of "Mandarin," each requiring as much definite study as a separate language, Hance might well have found the task too time-consuming for his taste. Or, if he did not care for responsibility and promotion, lacking Chinese was an easy way to bar his progress. At any rate, his junior position allowed him sufficient leisure and freedom from worries to concentrate on the matter closest to his heart, the study of plants; and his remarkable administrative powers, lost to the consular service, were used in the service of plant hunters for many years. What Reeves had been in Canton and Wallich in Calcutta, Hance was to be in the humble vice-consulate of Whampoa. If collectors wanted advice, or coolies, or merely someone to talk shop to they went to him. In return he asked no more than that if possible they should send him duplicates of the plants they found. Only occasionally did he hunt plants himself, but he knew and he helped so many collectors in his forty-three years' service that his herbarium became larger and larger. It is now stowed at the British Museum (Natural History) in London—a testament to his knowledge of botany and his talent for administration.

Though he was internationally known and respected,

even Henry Hance could not be at the center of collecting in the whole of China. It is too large a country, stretching over 2,600 miles from Moha in the north to Yaichow in the south; that is the distance from New York to Bogota or from London to Timbuktu. His sphere of influence was primarily in the south and his herbarium represents the flora of that part of China.

The most influential botanist in the north was undoubtedly the Russian, Carl Maximowicz; a man who began with the advantage of having learned his botany at the knee of the great Bunge, and being appointed curator of the St. Petersburg Herbarium at the age of twenty-four. In 1853 he was sent on his first expedition to the Far East, traveling out to China by a frigate in the Russian Navy and back by the overland route. During the next thirteen years he made many other botanical explorations, in Japan as well as Manchuria and the northern provinces, showing a daring and enterprise in looking for plants in out-of-the-way places, which was unique at the time. His most important work, though, was as a type of repository of plants from the north of China, and, unlike Hance who assembled his huge herbarium of southern plants in Whampoa, Maximowicz settled at home in St. Petersburg to collate his own discoveries with those of other people. For years afterward Russian botanists out in the field would send him duplicates of the plants they found, aware that he was in no sense a rival as he was uninterested in the commercially profitable business of introducing plants into cultivation. His principal purpose was to mass together as much information as possible on the flora of North China. Both he and Hance were in positions of great importance in 1860 when, as a result of the second phase of war with the West, China was obliged to open its interior to the Treaty Powers—Great Britain, Russia, France and the United States—and plant hunters could at last follow the rivers to the highlands of the west.

It was an unhappy time for China. The Taiping Rebellion continued right through the war with the West. The war itself was a discreditable affair; a mountain made from a molehill by the West, chiefly with the idea of squeezing concessions from the Chinese government. The Manchus and mandarins, aware that the Empire was disintegrating, shamed by their own stupidity and the gunboat manners of the West, were further humiliated by the necessity to ask their conquerors' help in putting down the Taiping Rebellion. The "Ever Victorious Army," which was badly named but brilliantly commanded by a fireball Scotsman named Gordon, was to achieve this for them, but China had lost something she would never regain.

Yet, if it was a bad time for Chinese statesmen and revolutionaries, there was no time quite like it for botanical explorers. Joseph Hooker's expedition to Sikkim had shown the great promise of the Himalayan Range. His brief plant-hunting trip in Assam where there was warmth and an abundance of rain showed how generative nature could be under those conditions. Plant hunters in Burma, and those in Indochina and Siam had never been in any doubt that an enormous store of hardy flowering plants and trees lay in the forbidden mountain ranges to the north. The botanists on the China coast and those who, with or without leave, had collected in the central plain, had longed to go west for the same reason.

Now they could go.

# Part Four
# The Edge of the World

REATEST of all the collecting districts, for more than a century the most prolific source of flowering plants in all the world, lay at the heart of Asia. Part was in India and part in Burma, more in Tibet, most of all in the three Chinese provinces of Kansu, Szechuan and Yunnan. It was an area drained by the tributaries and main courses of five mighty rivers, the Yangtze-kiang, the Hwang Ho, the Irrawaddy, the Salween, and the Mekong. The size and extent of their headwaters, cataracts, rapids, currents and vortices and the grandeur of the surrounding highlands set the scale for the whole region. The first Westerners to go there found that the immensity of everything made them feel Lilliputian. They were intimidated by these massive rivers, by the extreme variations of climate, the eternal snows, the towering watersheds, the flat, dry plateaus crisscrossed with river beds in chasms over a thousand feet below, the screes over which winds howled and screamed ceaselessly.

The Chinese of the plains had never cared for the mountainous west, and with all the superciliousness of metropolitans they considered themselves a large cut above their provincial fellow-citizens. In fact, the west was a bogy to them and the threat of banishment to the three provinces was regularly used as a means of keeping children well-behaved much as naughty Western children were once threatened with the police, or rag-and-bone men, or Bonaparte. But the banishments were an unhappy reality, not simply a menace in the nursery. At a time when the emperor of

China was not only an autocrat but also the nation's chief priest and mediator, who at each solstice made offerings of silk, roast meats and wine in the Temple of Heaven, it was customary for offending officials and courtiers to be given appointments "South of the Cloud," that is Yunnan, or in "the Land of the Four Rivers," Szechuan. And at the solstice appointments they could even be sent to Kansu where conditions were so primitive that the only form of transport was by wheelbarrow.* These were much-dreaded banishments, though one exile, the renowned poet Po Chü-i, who was sent off to be governor of a remote city in Szechuan, consoled himself by gardening.

*I took money and bought flowering trees*
*And planted them out on the bank to the east of the keep,*
*I simply bought whatever had most blooms,*
*Not caring whether peach, apricot, or plum.*
*A hundred fruits, all mixed up together;*
*A thousand branches, flowering in due rotation.*
*Each has its season coming early or late;*
*But to all alike the fertile soil is kind.*†

Po Chü-i's pleasure was in cultivating fruit trees for their blossom, but the fertile soil of Szechuan was kind to wildings, too; and after the treaty of 1860 it was to become a mecca for botanical explorers.

As reports and dried plants came in from the missionaries and officials who were pioneering the west, both Hance and Maximowicz realized that the rumors and legends of the past certainly were true. The newly opened territory had a flora unequaled by any other region of the world. Moreover, because the climate up in the highlands could be severe, the endemic plants were mostly hardy—which was precisely what Western gardeners were to ask for, for the best part of a century, supply either causing the demand or vice versa.

* It is still the main form of transport today.
† The translation is Arthur Waley's.

It is for this reason that, although front-ranking plant hunters have worked in other parts of the globe during that period, their collections of hardy perennials never have been comparable in quality or quantity with those made in the region which one collector named "the edge of the world"; so the last part of the study is concerned with some of the plant hunters who have collected there. They were legion—moreover, so diverse in nationality, personality, character, approach, collecting methods and degrees of success that the account is necessarily limited and cannot claim to be comprehensive.

EMBERS of the China Committee had shown themselves conspicuously in advance of their time in asking Fortune to search for hardy and half-hardy plants; though, being botanists as well as horticulturalists, they would quite naturally be anxious to secure all types of plants and not merely the commercially viable tropicals which were the chief interest of nurserymen. Bigger and brighter exotic flowers and outlandish curiosities continued to hold the attention and the affections of rich men until the soaring price of glass, fuel and labor drove Croesean gardening out-of-doors again; but the Royal Horticultural Society was anticipating the new gardening public which came into existence in the late Victorian age and which had a purse that could afford only the culture of hardy perennials. Their prophet was an irascible Irishman, William Robinson, and he, with the aid of Gertrude Jekyll, was to revolutionize the style of Western gardening.

Robinson hated glass—most probably because, as a spiteful gardener's boy who could not bear to be rebuked, he had revenged himself on a censorious employer by allowing frost to destroy a handsome collection of stove plants. This led to his permanent exile from Ireland and a loathing for anything in the least artificial in gardening. The curious plants and horror-strikers which gave his contemporaries such thrills of excitement, the heavily scented, iridescent tropicals and the whole regiment of marvelous orchids which they adored, merely made him mad. So did the dense and shady shrubberies of the period, the knickknackery, the wriggly paths, the bedding-out schemes. Strangely enough, though he had a passion for plants he abominated botany and was shrill in his condemnation:

*The subordination of the garden to Botany has been fruitful of the greatest evil to artistic gardening.*

As the apostle of wild gardening and, later, of the herbaceous border—"a child of sun-and color-drenched impressionism"—he was to tyrannize the gardeners of two continents and popularize the sort of hardy and half-hardy trees and shrubs and perennial plants which were to be found in abundance and in great variety in the "furrowed folds beneath the hoary heads of the great mountains of western China." As a result, there was the equivalent of a gold rush to that area, a plant rush which brought enormous satisfaction to amateur botanical collectors, equally enormous profits to the professionals and their sponsors, and thousand upon thousand of new genera and species to the gardens of the Western world.

*three* / *Private Travelers, Consular Officials, Honored Commissioners and Military Plant Hunters*

MONG the first plant hunters in the newly-opened region were the amateurs; that is, they were amateurs in the sense that they were not paid to collect. Some were private travelers such as the distinguished explorer, Henri d'Orleans, and the rich English enthusiast, Antwerp Pratt, who bought a luxurious houseboat on the Yangtze, hired a German assistant collector, Kricheldorf, and went up into Szechuan in the grandest possible style.

Then there were consular officials with a liking for botany. Augustus Margary was one, a brilliant linguist and a somewhat eccentric young man of great promise. Collecting plants was very much his secondary occupation but ultimately one of his chief interests. He was the first Englishman to travel from the Yangtze-kiang to the Irrawaddy. It was a secret mission and formidable because it involved crossing over a thousand miles of totally unknown country. For Margary it was purgatory. He was only twenty-six but all through the journey he suffered simultaneously from toothache, rheumatism, pleurisy and dysentery. And when he had completed his mission and traveled a little beyond Bhamo, he was abruptly and inexplicably murdered. Though a mission was sent to investigate his death, the reason for it never has been satisfactorily explained. One view, expressed later, is that Margary had permitted a dog to be carried in his curtained litter. Such a gross insult—which almost amounted to sacrilege—might easily have caused the litter bearers to murder him. Anyone so rash as to tempt fortune in this manner must have been out of the ordinary. Margary was. Whenever he felt lonely and longed for home, he would stand outside his tent, sing *Clementine, Polly-wolly-doodle, Michael Finnigin,* and *The Lass of Richmond Hill,* and, to the astonishment of his bearers, finish the concert with a thunderous rendering of *God Save the Queen.*

Chungking on the Yangtze, though hundreds of miles from the sea and roughly in the center of Szechuan, was a treaty port and the British kept a consul there. By accident or design three of the consuls in succession happened to be botanists: E. H. Parker, Sir Alexander Hosie, and F. S. A. Bourne. The last should be honored by gourmets for his detailed work on Chinese vegetables, while Hosie is best remembered for his observations on the "Whitewax Industry." This he investigated as an enthusiastic expert in economic plants, and found that as a production process it appeared to belong to the fantasy world of *Alice in Wonderland.* A species of insect, *Coccus pela,* was bred by the million on privets down in the southwest corner of Szechuan, packed in paper parcels of a pound in weight and carried by more than ten thousand coolies (sixty parcels of living insects per coolie) for over two hundred miles through some of the most difficult country in the world to the plains where there were plantations of pollarded Chinese ashtrees, (*Fraxinus chinensis*). There the insects were released onto the trees, and within a hundred days had deposited a layer of wax, a quarter of an inch thick, all over the ash foliage. The branches were then lopped off and the wax removed by heat.

The newly formed Imperial Chinese Maritime Customs Service, staffed mostly by Europeans, also produced "honored commissioners" who hunted plants in the west with great determination. Perhaps the most famous of them was Augustine Henry,* though by inclination he was not a botanist at all. In fact he had been stationed in Ichang by the

---

* He should not be confused with the American missionary, B. C. Henry who was a collector of subtropical and tropical plants in the southern provinces of China, especially Kwantung.

famous Yangtze Gorges for three whole years before he began to collect plants, and at first his collecting was sporadic and designed simply to kill time and relieve ennui.

*Oh, if you knew the weariness of an exile's life. I have become a great collector of plants and after exhausting the neighborhood I thought of going into the mountains.*

The boredom which had driven some exiles to drink had driven Henry to botany. It was hardly less habit forming, and very soon he was a compulsive collector. Because his duties prevented him from going up into the mountains unless he was on long leave he hired and trained Chinese boys to go plant hunting for him. Transferred down to the coast, then by good luck up into Yunnan, he made an enormous herbarium of over five thousand different species. By the time he retired from the service the once reluctant plant hunter was a leading authority on the flora of the Chinese highlands, sufficiently informed to collaborate with Elwes in *The Trees of Great Britain and Ireland,* and lecture as professor of forestry at Dublin for thirteen years.

With the private travelers and explorers, the consular officials and "honored commissioners," there were a number of highly successful military plant hunters. Without exception they were Russian.

Imperial Russia was one of the Treaty Powers of 1860, and made use of the privileges granted by the Chinese to mount expeditions of exploration in Central Asia and Mongolia. They were not entirely scientific. Russia was exceedingly fidgety about British rule in India and she wanted information about the country which lay to the north of India. Her paramilitary expeditions along the frontier were interpreted by the British as a sly attempt to steal away the territories only recently stolen by Lord Dalhousie, "the Annexer." Queen Victoria headed her subjects in expressing alarm and indignation at the csar's effrontery. But poor Alexander II, though of a moribund dynasty and destined to be blown to bloody fragments by a conspiratorial society named the "Will of the People," happened to be one of the few intelligent Romanovs, and he was unmoved by the bogus moral outrage of the "Widow of Windsor." The expeditions continued. Their personnel often included a trained naturalist who was also an officer in the imperial army. And sometimes these naturalists led their own expeditions with the active encouragement of the csar's government. If they were of sufficient standing, large grants were made towards their expenses, and scientific success was rewarded by military promotion, though it often happened that the naturalist had to be content with the promotion and pay for the expenses himself. There was the case of Nikolai Mikhailovich Przewalski, for instance, whose achievements took him literally from being a private soldier to a major-generalship, but who often had to stop and retrace his steps on expeditions because of lack of funds. He was doyen of the Russian collectors in the post-1860 period (distinguished quasi-military plant hunters such as Potanin, Berezovski, Kashkarov and Roborovsi who sent duplicates of all they found to the industrious Maximowicz in St. Petersburg), and like the others he was essentially a naturalist, not a specialist, in botany. In fact his main interest lay in the direction of zoology. Bearing this in mind and remembering, too, that he traveled rapidly and preferably in wintertime, and that most of his collecting was done in an area far less rich in plants than the floriferous south, it is astounding how large his herbarium became. His great aim was to reach Lhasa, and he died of typhoid on the last attempt in 1888, but before then he had collected over fifteen thousand specimens which included over seventeen hundred species. Holy Mother Russia was served well by Major-General Przewalski and his colleagues.

ROMAN Catholic missionaries had been granted special privileges at various times in the history of China, but not until 1860 were they able to proselytize in the mountain provinces of the west. In so rugged a region of weathered, tradition-steeped hilltop people their task was formidable and it is not to deny their zeal as priests to say that in the main they were far more successful in collecting plants than in collecting souls. The first of them, Jean Pierre Armand David was a naturalist *par excellence,* a man of energy and modesty and unfailing amicability, a devoted priest and a candid realist. He soon had the measure of the Chinese hillpeople and he came to love them dearly, but he was not blind to the difficulties. After years of experience he wrote to his godfather:

*Above all do not think China will become Catholic. At the pace things are going now, it will take 40 to 50 thousand years before the whole Empire will become Christian.*

Accepting this unwelcome fact in no way lessened David's attempt to convert the Chinese and prove himself wrong, and his integrity and simplicity of manner as well as his position as archetype of the missionary-botanists mark him worthy of closer attention than this wide study can properly allow. Only a thumbnail sketch is possible.

Armand David was born one of three sons, and in comfortable circumstances at a time and place when and where it mattered; that is, in 1826 in Espelette, a small

Pyrenean town. His father had the delightful Christian name of "Fructueux," and was the local doctor, mayor and magistrate. He inoculated his sons with his own three enthusiasms: passing on to one a love of the practice of medicine; to another, his passion for good food (especially game pie); and to Armand, an abiding interest in natural history. In his free time the boy would collect objects of natural history as acquisitively as a magpie, walking the Navarre foothills for eleven or twelve hours in a day, and eventually he told his delighted parents that he wished to test his vocation as a religious. Fortunately he was not obliged to choose between natural history and the priesthood. It was a simpler, less demanding age before the overspill of knowledge forced specialization onto Western culture. Quite properly, and without any inhibitions that he was betraying either of his vocations, he was ordained and took his vows as a Lazarist in the Order of St. Vincent de Paul. The order then used his skill and made him a teacher of science.

Generally the Lazarist missionaries were sent to South America, Ethiopia, the Levant, Persia, or China. David already had warm feelings for China but his superiors decided to send him to the Italian Riviera, to teach science at the Savona College. Nor was it a merely temporary appointment. He was kept there for ten long years. "All the time I dream of Chinese missions," he wrote; but he did not resent his enforced stay at Savona. It gave him the chance to become acquainted with fellow-naturalists in Europe and perfect his technique as a teacher of science. He was thorough in class, encouraging the able, catching the attention of reluctant pupils by presenting facts in an imaginative and interesting way, being patient with the tortoises and gentle and understanding with those who confessed that natural history was their blind spot. By the time his superiors did choose to send him out to China he was thirty-five years old, and he was already so well-known in Italy and France that when they heard he was going to the Far East five illustrious scientists of the Musée d'Histoire Naturelle asked the order if he might collect for them. David was principally an ornithologist and for his work on birds alone would have won fame, but his comprehensive ability was of more use to science at that time. Permission was given by the superior-general of the Lazarists and David was humble enough to count himself an exceptionally lucky man to be appointed a collector. It never occurred to him that the five illustrious scientists were exceptionally lucky to find a collector who was a first-class geologist, mineralogist, geographer, hydrographer, ethnographer, zoologist and botanist.

It was 1861. The war débris had barely been cleared before the French were building a school in Peking. The headmaster was to be M. Morly; the staff a team of three Lazarists, David to teach science and two fellow-priests to teach mathematics and music. They traveled together from France to Peking and they became fast friends because each one had such an appetite for knowledge and could impart enthusiasm for his own pet subject. M. Morly had a love of anthropology, and David had his natural science, while the priest-mathematician delighted in physics, and the priest-musician in the manufacture of clocks. If Armand David's out-of-school collecting had not been so successful he might have remained on that happy staff for the rest of his life, but the five scientists at the Musée were so flabbergasted by the size and quality of the collections he sent home that they realized he must be properly sponsored for the honor of science and the glory of France.

The Minister of Public Instruction paid a personal call on the superior-general of the Lazarists to ask if Père Armand David could be released from the Peking School of Science in order to lead a collecting expedition into Inner Mongolia. Again permission was granted and the surprised but gratified David set off on the first of his three noted journeys into the interior.

His preparations were sensible. He described the baggage in a diary entry for March 13, 1866:

*It will be cold for another two months in Mongolia, so heavy winter clothes are indispensable, as well as summer*

*clothes for the warm season, which is very hot there. It is*
*imperative, furthermore, to carry bedding . . . Add every-*
*thing that is indispensable for hunting and securing objects*
*of natural history, everything that is required for taxidermy*
*and for herbarium specimens, boxes of all sizes, empty bot-*
*tles, etc., etc. It goes without saying I have not forgotten*
*my ecclesiastical appurtenances.*

The Mongolian expedition was less important botanically than those he made to the Tibetan Marches and
Shensi province. In the second journey, when he was in the
small, almost independent state of Mupim on the Tibetan
frontier, and where the flora was richer than he could possibly have foreseen he made the decision to collect systematically over a particular area. To the meticulously thorough
collectors of later years this would have seemed an obvious
thing to do but Armand David was, in fact, the first of Far
Eastern plant hunters to be so methodical and painstaking.
Maybe the first, niggling restrictions of mandarins had put
his predecessors in the habit of collecting haphazardly wherever and whenever they could, and this they continued to do
when, on the edge of the world, they were unnerved by the
sheer immensity of China's flora. Like pigs in a rich truffle
ground they rushed hither and thither, hunting plants un-
systematically. David must have been strongly tempted to
do the same, and, as the opportunities before him on the
Tibetan border were so large, it speaks highly for his ideas
of scientific discipline that he did not collect at random.

The same scientific approach made him a discoverer
rather than an introducer of plants, and he was far more
interested in the scholar's herbarium than the pleasure garden. His bag was substantial, specimens of more than two
thousand species of plants. It did not compare with the
collections of other missionary-botanists who worked after
him in the Tibetan Marches—Jean Marie Delavay, for instance, has been credited with personally collecting, drying
and pressing more than two hundred thousand specimens,
and the collections of Farges, Soulié, Bourdonnec, Monbeig,

Dubernard, Geraldi and Boudiner were considerable as well
—but David's was by far the largest herbarium to be sent to
Europe in his own time and he made a point of remarking
that his collection was simply a token of the Asian flora yet
to be discovered. Moreover, he was simultaneously making
no less than six other collections, of insects, mollusks, fishes,
reptiles, birds and mammals.

In zoology he is famed for his introduction to Europe of
the David Deer, *Elaphurus davidianus,* an odd creature
which brays like a donkey, has the gait of a mule, and
splayed feet as though its natural habitat must be in
marshy ground. The Chinese showed their appreciation of
the deer's assymetry by calling it "Ssu-pu-hsiang" or "the-
four-characters-which-do-not-match." It had been extinct
in the wild for a century or more and in David's time only
existed in the imperial park in Peking. How, precisely, he
wheedled some living specimens from the park keepers is
not known, but it could not have been easy though he
himself made light of the matter. The deer he sent to Europe became the parents of all zoo specimens and the large
herd kept at Woburn Abbey by the Duke of Bedford.

David celebrated his forty-third birthday up in Mupim
and he continued his boyhood habit of collecting for eleven
or twelve hours at a stretch. And often, at this time, he was
walking more than thirty miles a day over mountains. It
was punishing to his body and he began to feel the strain.
Moreover, his whole existence was lived on a knife-edge. He
used to say with a chuckle that the Frenchmen's beards,
quite as much as their muskets, kept off the almost hairless
Chinese brigands. Anyone with less confidence in the essential goodness of mankind would not have turned his back so
often on people who for generations had been taught to
mistrust and even hate the "Red Hairs" and the "Franks."
Peking's enforced change of policy which allowed the
Chinese to meet Westerners for the first time was too abrupt to be taken in and understood by provincials in the
mountains. But, either David was lucky, or—and this is
more likely—his sense of humor and his unruffled trust were

marked, for he and his property were respected in a way which surprised even the Chinese themselves. His attitude towards food was characteristic, and no doubt won him friends among the hillpeople. He confided in his diary:

*As for food, I depend on the Chinese, and I believe that with a little goodwill, one man can live wherever another can. I do not burden myself, therefore, with carrying food, except a bottle of cognac for emergencies.*

Nevertheless, it was always a strain in being among people whose ways and language were largely unknown. The terrain so dramatically beautiful was also remarkably dangerous. Collecting in the rarified air was bad enough but there were regular and wearing dangers to be faced in the form of dacoits, avalanches, spider's web rope bridges across chasms so deep that the noise of water torrents far below was only an indistinct murmur, and river travel. Like Douglas in America, David was almost killed when his boat was smashed to pieces on a rocketing mountain river, and he lost a large part of the herbarium material he had been collecting.

All these strains piled one on top of another proved to be too much for him and he fell ill. He was still unwell when he returned to the plains and, though he waited and rested for some time before making his third expedition through the central provinces to Shensi, his health broke down on the journey and he only just managed to get back to Shanghai. It was the end of collecting in China for Armand David and, in 1874, he returned to the mother house of his order to teach, and write up his notes, and tell traveler's tales with his accustomed modesty and charm.

He was well and affectionately remembered after his death in 1900: by his pupils as "a handsome old man with a quick step, his face framed in longish white hair, with deep-set, keen eyes under a broad and high forehead"; by gardeners for his discovery of a multitude of first-rate garden plants; by the naturalists of France for his distinguished contributions to their sciences; by his order as one of the most famous of all Lazarists. But in his home town of Espelette, where he was still "old Fructueux' boy," they remembered him best because on his last visit he had shown them all a spider, "as big as his fist, which was trained to retrieve and answer a summons."

URING the twenty-five years following Armand David's departure from China the manner of plant hunting on the edge of the world underwent some change. It was unnoticed by the vast majority who, in that time, had more important affairs to think about. Fresh ideas were literally altering the face of the world. Nine more states were admitted to the Union and the United States was becoming a powerful reality. It fought and won a war against Spain and occupied the Hawaiian Islands and the Philippines. In its domestic and social life the spots and pangs of adolescence were disappearing. True, the assassination of James Garfield by a demented tuft-hunter made him the second president to be murdered, and the romanticized cowherds in the West and the flatboat bullies who manhandled their arks and broadhorns downriver to New Orleans were unspeakably wild, but it was forging an independent culture of its own.

As the New World shook down the Old World was threatening to blow up. The fossilized monarchies of Europe were almost at their last gasp. And so, though they did not perhaps realize it, were the Manchus on the Dragon Throne of China. The Taiping Rebellion was eventually put down but—humiliatingly—only through the assistance of a former enemy, General Charles Gordon. He was a Scot, farouche, undoubtedly a little mad (putting up notices which forbade the peasants to drown unwanted children in his water supplies); but because he was a brilliant tactician and leader they had to honor him with the yellow jacket and the peacock's feather, and give him command of the Ever Victorious Army. Since then the Manchus had fought and lost a war against Japan and, in a further series of humiliations, had been obliged to grant privileges, rights and territories to the empires of Japan, Russia, Germany, France and England. Even before Armand David died the old Empress Dowager—whose private life was sensationally depraved and, of more moment to the history of China, whose passion for ponds and peonies led her to misappropriate naval funds for the enlargement of her pleasure grounds—was driven out of her own capital by a Western force of Americans, Germans, Russians, French and Englishmen, and kept out for a year.

Against such dramatic events any changes in the mode of botanical exploration were barely perceptible. But they occurred.

The amateur, with one or two notable exceptions, no longer led the field. The academic botanist was becoming equally rare. In fact, among the plant hunters who have collected on the edge of the world only the self-taught Augustine Henry, the Swedish scholar, Doctor Harry Smith, the Austrians, Camillo Schneider and Handel Mazzetti, and the American professor, Liberty Hyde Bailey of Ithaca, could be classed in this rare category. The remainder were primarily plantsmen. They collected herbarium material for botanical study but this was of less importance than the collecting of seeds and living stocks for introduction into cultivation. Plant-hunting methods also underwent a change. Haphazardly skimming the cream off the milk would no longer do. Clearly it was more practical and profitable in the end to be systematic and either make an exhaustive search for anything new over a defined area, as Armand David had done, or set out for a single objective armed with information as to its most likely whereabouts.

*Fin de siècle* plant hunters were more scientific than any of their predecessors and more lavishly rewarded for the pains they took. Unfortunately, though their adventures were well documented by written journals and published accounts, their portraits seldom came through. And so the introverts in their number gave an unreal appearance to the world of being strong, silent, lean, bronzed, dedicated, fearless, and with all their tendencies, regrettable or otherwise, kept strictly under control—in effect, the Hornblowers of plant hunting; while the few extroverts gave an equally unreal appearance of being sparkling and romantically eccentric. Their true characters were hidden, deliberately or otherwise, because of "good form" before death and the principle *"de mortuis nil nisi bonum"* after it. Yet by a careful pruning of inessentials, and with regard for the lack of interest or otherwise of those who have reported on their manner and their careers, it is just possible to see something of the real men who undertook the great plant hunting enterprises in Central Asia after Armand David. There were many of them, and all played some part in the establishment and stocking of wildernesses, herbacious borders and alpine gardens in the West, but a few stand out for the size or the nature of their contribution.

RRIVING in China on a June day in 1899, the doyen of modern collectors had been sent from England to the edge of the world with the specific task of tracking down and collecting David's dove tree, *Davidia involucrata*. In this, and on many expeditions afterwards he was to prove so able that in the public mind his name, like that of General Gordon, was quickly associated with the country where he made such successes, and he was popularly known as "Chinese" Wilson. He never cared for the name.

He had been born Ernest Henry Wilson in the Gloucestershire country town of Chipping Campden and the cultivating of plants interested him from an early age. His first job was as apprentice gardener's boy to a nursery firm at Stratford from which he went on to the Birmingham Botanic Gardens. He did well enough to graduate, as it were, to Kew, but his prospects there were not bright and he was obliged to think of getting himself trained as a teacher of botany. He did not like the idea, caring less for the schoolroom than the laboratory, less for the laboratory than fieldwork. Already he was the open-air man of the day—with clipped moustache and pipe to match. But without that slice of luck which has been vital to many great plant hunters he would certainly have gone on to teaching. As it was, Kew's Director, Sir William Thiselton-Dyer, was asked to recommend a plant hunter to the firm of Veitch and his eye fell on the twenty-three-year-old Wilson. From that day the young man's future was assured.

Veitch's instructed him for six months in the practical side of things: in the principles of plant recognition; the taking, stowing and transport of herbarium material, seeds and propagating stocks; in the use of collecting equipment and a camera. The last had already become an important article in the kit of a plant hunter and Wilson was to prove an excellent photographer, but he had the strangest fad to use always a full-plate camera. Hawking such a weighty and awkward article through the wilder parts of Asia can hardly have been easy, nor for that matter was the taking of photographs. Present-day users of the matchbox-size marvels which produce equally good results would find his insistence on whole-plate machine, complete with tripod in brass and mahogany and large, black headcloth, particularly mad.

When Wilson had finished the course—and not before —Veitch's sent him off on his first expedition to China. He was given three instructions. First he was to travel by America, and not by the eastern route, so that he could call at the Arnold Arboretum in Boston, Massachusetts. The keeper, Professor Charles Sprague Sargent, had introduced many Japanese trees and shrubs to the United States and would be able to help Wilson with general advice on collecting in the Orient. Perhaps, later, Veitch's came to regret this part of their instructions because Sargent and Wilson got on so well together that acquaintance quickly ripened to a lasting friendship and Wilson ended up collecting for the Arboretum. Veitch's, though, were to have his services for two expeditions. Their second, clear instruction was that on arriving in China he should make for southwest Yunnan where Doctor Augustine Henry was living and ask his advice on collecting in Central Asia. This would be of particular assistance to him in carrying out their third instruction: to find and introduce *Davidia involucrata*.

Wilson enjoyed his visit to Doctor Henry in Yunnan. He was there two months, botanizing with his host and learning a great deal from him about local conditions. Then, at Henry's suggestion, he set off for the area round the gorges at Ichang on the Yangtze in search of the elusive dove tree.

That the first quarry of the first modern collector should be the davidia or dove tree showed how systematic plant hunting had become. Armand David had first found the tree up in Mupim and had described it enthusiastically both because it was beautiful and because he guessed rightly that it stood on its own in the vegetable kingdom, its nearest ally being the nyssa, and was, therefore, a scientific curiosity. He had made up herbarium specimens of some of its parts but being a scientific collector this was sufficient for him and he did not even try to introduce the tree to France. Paul Farges, another missionary-botanist who was in China after David, also found the tree, and in 1897 he sent a packet of thirty-seven seeds to M. Maurice L. de Vilmorin who had made a huge botanical collection of Chinese trees and plants in his pleasure grounds at Les Barres. Whether the directors of Veitch's and Ernest Wilson knew of this is uncertain. They could not have known that out of Père Farge's thirty-seven seeds only one germinated and that it actually put out its shoot on the June day when Wilson landed at Hong Kong.

The davidia was a tree worth looking for. Since that time it has been called a number of names—the dove tree, pocket-handkerchief tree, and ghost tree—all on account of the pairs of white, hood-shaped bracts of uneven size which in Maytime are shown off to perfection by the tree's aromatic leaves of a vivid green. They could be said to resemble doves gone to perch or, at a pinch, pocket-handkerchiefs on a linen line; and as they flutter down from the branches the bracts do give a ghostly effect.

Wilson scoured the countryside around Ichang, moving slowly west and into the Land of the Four Rivers which was to become his special collecting territory, and eventually he found what he had been sent to collect. Wilson's luck was proverbial. On this occasion he not only found a colony of davidias but beside them some tetracentrons, a genus which had been discovered and described by Augustine

Henry but yet had to be introduced to the West. *T. sinensis* was added to the expedition's bag. The davidia, though, commanded all his interest for the moment.

He had been brought up to be thorough and trained in exactness by a Veitch foreman. The first essential at that exciting moment was to establish that the small colony of small trees in front of him really were davidias. In all particulars save two they corresponded with Armand David's notes: but whereas he had described the underside of the leaves as whitish and felted, the underside of the leaves before Wilson were a yellow-green frog color and perfectly smooth. Clearly, though, they were davidias whatever the species.

In a diary entry dated May 31, 1900, Wilson wrote:

*. . . Ascending a precipice with difficulty, we soon reached the Davidia trees. There are over a score of them growing on a steep rocky declivity; they vary from 35 to 60 feet in height, and the largest is 6 feet in girth. Being in a dense wood they are bare of branches for half their height, but their presence is readily detected by the numerous white bracts which have fallen and lie strewn on the ground . . .*

Later he would come back for seed, a hard, winged nut contained in a pear-shaped fruit the color of a damson. Meanwhile he proposed to make a permanent record of the discovery. We are reminded with a jolt he actually had that massive, full-plate camera with him in the wilderness. He decided to photograph the davidias in their full May glory. On a steep slope in a dense wood, and with a camera as unwieldy as an orange box on legs, the task was formidable. But Wilson was a practical man and a great improvisor. He noted that one of the tetracentrons was growing on the edge of a cliff overlooking the davidias. Two of the party joined him in scaling the tree and chopping away branches to make a clear space so that he could photograph the nearest davidia. Pulling up a woodsman's axe on ropes, and afterwards the unmanageable camera, was difficult enough. Perching behind that camera with head shrouded in a black cloth while focusing on an upsidedown davidia was even worse. Worst of all, as Wilson found in climbing the tree, the wood of a tetracentron is exceedingly brittle and he commented in his diary:

> . . . this does not add to one's peace of mind when sitting astride a branch about 4 inches thick with a sheer drop of a couple of hundred feet beneath.

It was disconcerting, too, not to be absolutely sure whether or not he had found David's tree, and years would pass before he could know. In fact M. Vilmorin's single seedling grew to flower as a tree at Les Barres in 1906, and this differed from the others in that the underside of its leaves were hairless but a glaucous colour. It was listed as *Davidia vilmoriniana*. The seed Wilson sent home in quantity from his first expedition, that is from the trees with frog-green, hairless leaves, grew into trees which were named *D. laeta,* and on a later journey in China he took seeds of Armand David's original discovery, *D. involucrata.*

Typically, Wilson had eyes and interest for nothing save his quarry. At the very time he was taking photographs from a high and insecure perch in Szechuan, the antimissionary (and certainly antiforeigner) Boxer tong was murdering and looting in Shantung and other northern provinces. The demands of the Treaty Powers had become excessive; their open contempt for all things Chinese particularly offensive. In the Shanghai park, for instance, which was largely ruled by British interests, an insulting notice declared "Dogs and Chinese not allowed." Inevitably there was a reaction from those Chinese who found the constant humiliations unbearable. The Empress Dowager and the mandarins at first mildly opposed the Boxers but then openly supported them. The German minister at Peking was knifed, several of the foreign legations were ransacked and burned, and upwards of two hundred foreigners took refuge in the British Legation where they withstood a siege until a Western expedition arrived by ship, blew the Chinese forts to bits, and advanced steadily to their relief.

It was less than safe to be a "Red Hair" or a "Frank" anywhere in China at that time, but there was Ernest Wilson, obsessed with plants, apparently indifferent to menacing tongs, and vexed because the political situation obliged him to keep within a certain distance of Ichang.

Having found a davidia, if not "the" davidia, he filled in the time while waiting to return for seed by searching for other plants. He also got himself shipwrecked on the Yangtze-kiang when his river sampan—mixture of barge and houseboat—was snagged on a boulder and turned turtle. A good many of his belongings, including the full-plate camera and hundreds of exposed and unexposed plates, went to the bottom. Wilson cursed, got himself ashore, replaced the camera as soon as he could, and regarded the disaster as a good Puritan should; that is, as a sort of divine chastisement to balance against his undoubted good fortune while hunting plants. Though English, he had many of the characteristics of Scottish collectors, being Puritan and suspicious of pleasure and prizing hard work and being provident as spiritual virtues. He shared, as well, their dourness and their thoroughness. The methodical fashion in which he hunted plants almost always brought him success; and his thoroughness applied to an area where a large variety of temperate plants grew in great abundance was bound to have a startling effect.

From his first expedition alone when hemmed in by Boxers he produced not only what he and everyone else thought was David's dove tree but also the seed of 305 other plant species, thirty-five Wardian cases of tubers, corms, bulbs, rhizomes and rootstocks and the dried and pressed herbarium material of 906 plant species.

Needless to say he had hardly been in England for six months before Veitch's sent him out again: on this occasion to aim principally at the yellow Chinese poppy or lampshade Poppy, a meconopsis (*M. inteqrifolia*) with Claudetint yellow, cup-shaped flowers a handspan in diameter and topping three feet in height. Antwerp Pratt had discovered the plant and promised that it was one of the most striking in all the Chinese-Tibetan frontier lands. For this trip he based himself at Kaiting-fu, which lies much further west than Ichang and is in the heart of Szechuan. Nearby is precipitous Mount Omei, one of the three holiest Buddhist mountains in China, peppered with shrines and temples, and this with two other mountains makes a triangle on the map of an area which is so wild that the Chinese call it the Laolin. It is limestone country, pocked with crags and gullies, and it is drenched for the greater part of the year; Wilson discovered it was an Aladdin's cave to a plant hunter. There he found Antwerp Pratt's lampshade poppy, and another meconopsis, *M. punicea*, smaller and scarlet, but no less a beauty; the famous rhubarb, *Rheum Alexandrae;* several unknown primulas and rhododendrons (despite the fact that their feet were in limestone); two favorite species of roses, *Rr. moyesii* and *willmottiae*, and a poplar, *Populus lasiocarpa* which though it is not often seen today has one of the most handsome of all foliages. For the poplar alone all Wilson's efforts would have been worthwhile. His Puritan sense was gratified by the fact that he had to "pay," so to speak, for his successes with fatigue, discomfort, the perpetual threat of being deserted by his coolies and, on a never-to-be-forgotten occasion, even with starvation. He was far away from Kaiting-fu and took an unknown and almost disused track through difficult country in appalling weather. The party had insufficient food and the few people they met were themselves dying with hunger because the harvest had failed. Wilson and his men only just escaped with their lives.

After two expeditions on behalf of Veitch, Wilson bound himself to Professor Sargent and the Arnold Arboretum. It was a sensible move. The firm of Veitch was running down. Its financial resources were evidently limited. Its directors were coming to the ostrich conclusion that almost everything worthwhile had already been collected in China. As a result, their instructions to Wilson were precise and his activities hedged about with financial restrictions. Working on behalf of an American university gave him larger scope and a greater freedom than he had known previously for, although he was naturally expected to hunt out ligneous plants, he could do so wherever his knowledge and instinct told him to go.

The outstanding success "paid for" with hardships was a pattern that was to repeat itself throughout most of his collecting career. Except on his last and most leisurely trip to the Far East when he introduced the 'Taiwania' from Formosa and saw, for the first time, Kure azaleas in Japan, Wilson regularly met with taxing adventures. His very near escape from death under an avalanche when he gained his "lily limp" has been described. There were other episodes as well which would have worn away a less robust man. In his published writings Wilson was either too technical and remote or too chatty to show himself very clearly, but it seems that he met, accepted, and then shrugged off the difficulties and dangers as part of the job. In compensation no one ever collected so many fine plants—both woody and herbaceous,* and when his plant-hunting days were finished, he continued to enjoy good fortune and attract disaster right to the end. He was made assistant director at Arnold Arboretum and then his friend Sargent's successor as keeper. The enjoyment of so superlatively suitable a post was cut short when he and his wife were killed in a motoring accident in 1930, on a highway near Worcester in Massachusetts.

* Professor Sargent proved the extent of Wilson's accomplishments by writing an account of his introduction of woody plants to the Arnold Arboretum. It was entitled *Plantae Wilsonianae,* and was published in nine parts forming three large volumes.

NSTITUTIONAL collectors was the name given by E. H. M. Cox to those who hunted plants for a botanic garden or government. Clearly they were mainly restricted to the particular interest of the institution they represented but, as "Chinese" Wilson found when he changed from a firm of professional nurserymen to work for the Arnold Arboretum, they enjoyed a certain amount of liberty. Indeed they were expected to be enterprising. Wilson's contemporary, the American Frank Meyer who worked for the United States Department of Agriculture was one of the most enterprising and original institutional collectors of his day.

By birth Meyer was a Dutchman, and had been an assistant to Hugo de Vries. But he was no laboratory botanist and he was a hobo at heart. He not only adored traveling but he preferred to do so on foot, and even at a time when walking was a possible and pleasurable exercise, and when, by inclination, there were many hikers in the States, Meyer's energy and gusto as a walking explorer-botanist became well known. He was actually striding through the southern states and Mexico when the department heads selected him to be their economic plant hunter in Eastern Asia.

The post was entirely new; created to meet a demand at home for greater varieties of grain, fruits and vegetables. These were surprisingly limited considering that North America contained four floristic regions and eight climatic provinces. Reports from the opened-up interior of China suggested that its agriculture, though primitive, was robust. And in far away Russian and Chinese Turkestan there might well be many hardy strains of seed best suited to the colder parts of the United States. As for the rest, the department's collector was required to use his initiative or, as they put it then, his head.

No appointment could have pleased Meyer more. Like Joseph Hooker he enjoyed romance as well as the practice of science, and, being so passionately devoted to detail that he would spend hours investigating and describing the habitat of a single plant, his awareness of its other attributes could easily move him to hail it in an ode. In Eastern Asia he could indulge himself in both romance and science, and walk and walk and walk. Furthermore, he would be in one of the largest and most dramatic regions on earth, and would be paid for it in the bargain.

Meyer made four expeditions for the department going as far west as Russian and Chinese Turkestan and traveling extensively in the east: right through the great Chinese plains, Manchuria and Korea, up by Lanchow on the Great Wall and into Kansu. Unlike Caesar, he did not keep to winter quarters but spent the time inspecting grain and, as their sap was down, taking fruit tree scions. He found new varieties of rice, beans and fodder plants as well as fruit and vegetables, and his total work for the department was enormously important to husbandry in the United States. Farmers from Cape Flattery to Florida and from the Bay of Fundy to San Diego ought to keep an annual Meyer feast in grateful remembrance of his work in Asia. Gardeners, on the other hand, have scarcely heard of him. In the main his introductions were economic plants, concerned far more with the pot than with pleasure grounds, though this is not to say economic plants have no esthetic appeal. On the contrary. Some of Meyer's soya and other beans, and certainly his fruit trees, had a distinctive attraction and beauty of their own. And as Meyer tramped from place to place and from clue to clue in trying to trace a particular strain to the center of its distribution, though he always had one-and-a-half-eyes open for other economic plants, half an eye was spared for solely decorative species.

He refound and introduced the single yellow rose canary-bird, *R. xanthina,* a discovery of Armand David's more than thirty years before; *Actinidia kolomikta,* a fragrant, white-flowered climber, and varieties of wild plums, peaches and almonds, viburnum, juniper and lilac. Three of the shrubs he introduced, the Chinese spindle tree, *Euonymus bungeanus, Syringa villosa* and *Kolkwitzia amabilis,\** only did well in the States in areas where the seasons are well-defined. In England, sharp and unseasonal frosts cut them back and they never could reach their full size or show off their full beauty. The list is by no means complete and for a plant collector who could spare but half an eye for ornamental plants and who often traveled during wintertime, when identifying sleeping trees and shrubs was difficult, it was something of an achievement. No doubt, as well, it would have been more impressive still if his collecting career had not been cut short.

His last expedition took him over the frontiers of Wilson's country. After wintering near Peking, making forays deep into the surrounding countryside, he went south across the Great Plain of China to the old treaty port of Hankow on the Yangtze-kiang. It was an important trade center and ideal as the headquarters of an economic plant hunter because among its main exports were tea, silk, a grass cloth made from *Boehmeria nivea* fibers, sesame seeds, beans, tobacco, timber, vegetable oils and Chinese herbal medicines. In the vegetable market alone there would be a large number of species differing in characteristics from those grown

* The syringa and the euonymus had in fact been introduced to Kew in a consignment of seeds sent there by Dr. Bretschneider where they grew to be half-pint specimens; and the kolkwitzia was introduced to England by Wilson in 1901 though it never became popular. With many of his other introductions cultivated at Veitch's Coombe Wood nurseries, the *Kolkwitzia* came under the auctioneer's hammer just as it was about to flower for the first time and no effort was made to propagate it. Meyer's introduction of all three plants was on a large scale and permanently effective.

in the States: Chinese peppers, for instance; that is the pulverized fruits of *Zanthoxylum bungei,* were grown on everyone's cabbage patch but were grown only for export in the Min Valley far away upstream from Hankow. And from the same area, especially the plain of Chengtu, came capsicums and chillies and salted shoots of the bamboo *Sinarundinaria nitida.* From the warm south came supplies of dried bamboos. From overseas, for distribution to other markets in the provinces, came junkloads of an unusual vegetable, the seaweed *Porphyra vulgaris.* There would be mounds of roots and flowerheads and stem vegetables and seeds and leaves, dried and fresh and salted, all mostly unfamiliar but not unpleasing to Meyer's "Western" palate.

Once he was on the scent of an economic plant which might be of value in the States no bloodhound could have been more determined in following it. On this occasion his nose took him upstream from Hankow to Ichang. He established a base and made a thorough survey in surrounding Hupeh for the large part of twelve months. Then something happened, but to this day the facts are hidden.

At the beginning of June, in 1918, his swollen corpse was found floating in the sluggish waters of the Yangtze below the port of Anking. Perhaps he had been on his way downstream making for Shanghai and then America. But no one could be certain.

The Yangtze was sometimes the plant collectors' friend. It had carried professionals, missionary-botanists, consular officials, and "honoured commissioners of Customs" up into the high western provinces. Upon it Antwerp Pratt had sailed in state with his German assistant, Kricheldorff. But it was not always gentle, claiming Wilson's equipment and almost Wilson himself. Now it had swallowed up Frank Meyer.

IENNA—for five hundred years a center of botanical interest—was the birthplace of Joseph J. Rock who may be accounted the most distinguished of America's institutional collectors. He was something of a prodigy, being well-schooled in science and many languages at a stage when most boys still have their interest focused on the football field, and in every way he was suited for the rather quaint chair of Chinese and botany to which he was appointed at the University of Hawaii in 1907. In 1913 he became an American citizen and, in 1920, economic plant collector of the Department of Agriculture.

Rock's first mission was to track down *Taraktogenos kurzii*, a tree called the kalaw by native tribesmen and of large medical importance. The adventure was invested with fantasy right from its beginning.

Imaginary cures for leprosy often featured in Eastern folklore, and the administrators of British India were understandably cynical when miracles were accredited to a tree which grew high in the wet forests of Central Asia. The account was too whimsical altogether. It even began like a fairy story: "Once upon a time there lived a king of Benares called Rana, and Rana was a leper . . ." The tale followed a romantic and fantastic theme. Rana, bound by his own laws, honorably cast himself out and, not wanting to be seen, hid himself in the wet forests. There he lived in a hollowed-out tree called the "Kalaw" and he ate the tree's fruit. Soon he found that the hated white patches on his skin were disappearing. Within a month he was entirely cured. To add a relish, the story continued that in a nearby cave lived a princess who also had leprosy, and that Rana cured her with kalaw fruits, married her, gave her sixteen pairs of twin sons, and not one of the thirty-two had leprosy. Everyone lived happily ever after.

It seemed to be against reason to suppose the story had any basis in fact. But in Indian markets a foul-smelling, dark-colored oil called "chaulmoogra" was sold at dizzy prices because it was claimed to cure leprosy. And this oil, said the vendors, had been brought down from the high forests of Central Asia where it had been pressed from kalaw fruits. Though it appeared mad, medical officers could not afford to ignore any means of trying to cure leprosy and they made tests. To their astonishment they found a drug in the oil which, though it hardly worked miracles, did stay the disease and was particularly useful in its treatment. The administration and world medicine were impressed. The discovery made it imperative to start kalaw plantations without delay because, clearly, eight or ten years would have to pass before the trees were sufficiently mature to produce oil.

The largest snag in proceeding with the plan was that no one in the plains had the least idea what a kalaw looked like. Bazaar merchants produced seeds which they said were of the kalaws but ten years later, when the seeds had germinated, grown into trees, matured and given their first lot of oil, they were found to be no such thing. If they were kalaws they belonged to a different species from the kalaw which produced chaulmoogra oil. The true kalaw remained undetected until 1890 when a botanist sent in seeds to the director of a botanical survey in India and they were identified as the bearers of genuine chaulmoogra. But the absurd frustrations continued. The seeds had been sent from Chittagong but no one had troubled to note their place of origin.

On the basis of this single clue, various attempts were made to trace the kalaw but met with no success. Yet expensive chaulmoogra oil still found its way through the jungles to the bazaars of Calcutta and from there was distributed to Western drug dealers.

In 1920, officials of the United States Department of Agriculture reassessed the chances of tracking down the tree. It was in that year, too, that Professor Rock resigned his chair of Chinese and botany and took his exceptional gifts into their service. He was instructed to find the kalaws and succeed where for so long others had failed.

He aimed first for Siam, determining to move north from there as far as the trail might lead him. His only consolation was the undoubted fact that the tree existed and did produce chaulmoogra; otherwise, so fantastic was the hunt, he would have been tempted to give up. In Bangkok all his inquiries met with the same reply. Yes, everyone knew about the kalaw. Everyone. But, no, no one knew where it could be located. No one. A clue—merely the girlhood memory of a viceroy's wife—took him to Korat. There he was told that his quarry would be somewhere deep in the jungle. Fruiting trees had to be a long way from trails or villages because the saplings made fine firewood and kalaws near villages never survived to mature. Further clues took him on a 350-mile trek across Siam to the hill city of Chiengmai. It was a false trail, but the next, by houseboat downriver to Rahang was much more promising. When this turned out to be another disappointment, Rock almost turned back. Anyone less dogged would have done so, but a short rest and an interesting piece of bazaar gossip put new life into him. He followed the trail right over the mountains between Siam and Burma, having his first taste of leopards, tigers, and a local and particularly virulent brand of snake. But, in compensation, he at last found a species of kalaw. A few. But either they were mules or the season had been a bad one, for none of them carried any fruit. Rock went on to Moulmein in the Gulf of Mataban and then up north into the hills. He came across a single fruiting tree. Neither was this the *Taraktogenos kurzii* he had been commissioned to find but a closely related species, and though he managed to collect 170 seeds he found himself in strong competition with monkeys who ate the fruits and threw the seeds away and with porcupines below who went for the seeds as crazily as a hound will follow aniseed. He pressed on northwards, following clues, rumors and speculations until near a filthy village on the upper Chindwin River he found a colony of the true kalaws. It left a good deal to be desired. Many of the trees had been lopped for kindling and the villagers had ringbarked others to make an infusion with flakes of the strippings. He could collect only a very few seeds. But he was obviously on the tree's trail. In the very next village he found more kalaws, and finally his small party was "loaded with seeds and could carry no more." At this point a man-eating tiger began visiting the village where they had their headquarters, to seize a villager a day. Then a storm and a rogue elephant finished off the village altogether. Rock and his men were lucky, escaping the depredations of tiger, tempest, and elephant, and they had sufficient seeds for plantations of kalaws to be established in American possessions in the Pacific and so assure constant supplies of pure chaulmoogra. It was a dramatic end to one of the most arduous of all plant hunts when the quarry seemed to belong more to the realm of myth and magic than to scientific fact.

The pattern of Rock's collecting career thereafter was much wider than that of other modern plant hunters. His principal collections were of plants, but he also hunted birds and animals, and in addition to working for the United States Department of Agriculture he collected for the Arnold Arboretum and the Harvard Museum of Comparative Zoology. He twice made expeditions under the auspices of the National Geographical Society of Washington. The seeds and plants he collected on the last expeditions were syndicated to private gardeners and commercial nurserymen both on the Pacific coast of North America and in Great Britain.

He traveled widely; in Yunnan where his collecting crossed that of George Forrest and Frank Kingdon-Ward;

in the small and partly independent state of Muli where he
found few plants but made great friends with the king; and
in the land of the Ngoloks, a belligerent tribe of Tibetans
who lived by the Amne Machin. This range of high peaks,
separated from the Min Shan by the most turbulent and
untamable of all rivers, the Hwang Ho, was on the roof of
the world, and with its nine-month winter and three-month
summer it had little of value for Rock in the way of plants;
but he called it "one great zoological garden . . . wild animals grazing contentedly . . . deer, wapiti, and many
others." He enjoyed himself most, though, in what he called
Tebbu land; that is, the country peopled by the Tepos
south of the Min Shan which is divided into two by the
Satani Alps.

Between Vienna and the land of the Ngoloks, Rock
managed to see more of the world than most men. It was
Tebbu land which fired his imagination.

*I have never in all my life seen such magnificent scenery. If*
*the writer of Genesis had seen the Tebbu Country he would*
*have made it the birthplace of Adam and Eve.*

Finally Rock made an expedition which in some ways
was as fantastic as his first in search of the kalaw. This was
in a wild area to the west of Muli in Szechuan which had
once been under the control of the Tibetan prince of Litang.
Since the Chinese-Tibetan frontier quarrels the region had
become wilder and wilder and by 1928, when Rock wanted
to collect there, it was entirely lawless and in the hands of a
rogue, Drashetsongpen, who had turned from the holy life
of a lama to the excitement of being a bold robber chieftain.
Fortunately for Rock, this larger-than-life bandit was a
friend of his old friend, the king of Muli, and he was given
special permission to botanize throughout his wild domain.
He enjoyed his visits and planned to go back there to collect
seed, but when bad conditions ruined the grain and poppy
harvest the peasants were on the lookout for someone to
blame. A white stranger wandering in the hills, picking

flowers and irritating the gods would do. A polite message was sent from the robber's stronghold to the royal court at Muli to suggest that, in view of the circumstances, it would be imprudent for Mr. Rock to return. And Mr. Rock did not.

EGINALD Farrer and Henry John Elwes were amateur modern plant hunters among a large number of professionals. And both had colorful personalities. No more than Banks in the seventeenth century could either of them settle to enjoy the privileges of their birth as Edwardian country gentlemen. Elwes was from Gloucestershire, Farrer from Yorkshire. Their common taste for collecting was motivated by very different reasons.

Elwes retired from a Guards regiment at the age of twenty-four because he considered peacetime soldiering too cozy and moribund for a man of spirit. To slake his thirst for adventure he took to field studies of zoology, ornithology and botany. Being very rich he was able to travel extensively and he would, literally, leave at a moment's notice if he had news of a rare plant to collect or a rare bird or beast to shoot and stuff. On the trail he collected in China and Japan, Siberia and Russia, Tibet, India, Turkey and the Americas. He was not, though, simply a slaughterer and bagger of rarities. He became learned in the sciences which interested him, especially botany. His collaboration with Augustine Henry in the seven-volume work, *The Trees of Great Britain and Ireland,* and his illustrated *Monograph of the Genus Lilium* were evidence of his scholarship.

Reginald Farrer was equally learned in his own department, and a plant hunter of larger importance. He was not especially interested in adventures; nor, being short and portly, was he the sort of man to give vent to his high spirits by taking violent and dangerous exercises. On the contrary, his interest in botany began because as a boy he was delicate. He had to be tutored at home and an inevitable part of such an informal education would be nature rambles in the nearby limestone hills and dales. Farrer's imagination was stirred by the thought of finding a plant there which no one had ever listed before. In the 1890's, even in Yorkshire, this was aiming high. But he was successful, discovering a new species to Great Britain, *Arenaria gothica.*

At the age of fourteen he had a rock garden of his own and had begun to serve that apprenticeship which one day was to make him the prince of all alpine gardeners. Discovering that an impoverished mixture of stone chippings plus a modicum of loam or leaf mold were best suited to alpines, he found that he could grow plants from high altitudes with much greater success than those who indulged them with composts and stimulating chemicals. His method of constructing rock gardens also guaranteed that the plants had the light, air, food and water which they needed.

To begin with, then, he was a practical gardener and a collector; but after traveling widely—in Japan where, like many before and since, he lost his heart to the Japanese and their way of life,* and in the European Alps which he turned inside out in his search for plants—he became well known as a writer. Had he never made any plant introductions at all his name as a writer on plants would have been assured a place among gardening *cognoscenti,* and his views on alpine gardening very soon commanded high respect. He fulminated against the average Edwardian rockery, and he poked fun at the prime showpiece of the day which had been constructed at Henley by a solicitor whose recreations were listed as "company law, horticulture and microscopy." This monster rockery was studded with caves and had an imitation Matterhorn done in slate and concrete complete with herds of tin chamois. Farrer's influence in altering the

---

* Not, though, to their cuisine. He had a word of praise for a farthing bun—"light and misty in composition and her flavour is of toffee, strangely subtilised"—but he disliked raw fish with gills pullulating on the plate to prove the freshness, and he particularly resented the loss of a favorite kitten which was served up to him at dinner in a species of béchamel.

style of rockeries was considerable and his classic, *The English Rock Garden,* remains a perfect bedside book and is much sought after.

During his preliminary researches for the book he came across references to Prezewalski's collecting in the north of Kansu and to Potanin's in the south, and because the province seemed to be typically alpine, it was a natural magnet to him. He set off for China and arrived in 1914.

Farrer's expedition in Kansu, where wheelbarrows were the main form of transport, was made with William Purdom, a professional collector who had worked for Veitch and the Arnold Arboretum. He enjoyed it immensely. As an alpinist he found the flora absorbing. As an imaginative writer he was delighted to find that one of their camps happened to be in the territory of a mad bandit called "White Wolf." As a plantsman he was much interested in the diversity of crops caused by the variations in climate throughout Kansu. He saw wheat growing, and dates, beans and tobacco, grapes, onions, and rhubarb in great quantities. Finally, as a man of keen sensibility, he found the countryside spellbinding. The province contained hundreds and hundreds of miles of the Great Wall, and, like Gaul, was divided into three parts: the southern river valley, the eastern plateau of loess crisscrossed by ravines, and the northwestern section hemmed in between mountains and desert. The separating ranges were awe inspiring. He described the mountains as "stretching across the world from easterly to westerly in one unbroken rank of impregnable, eighteen-thousand-foot dolomite needles, crags, castles, and pinnacles."

The outbreak of World War I in August completely upset the expedition. Though he knew that he was medically unfit for active service Farrer wanted to hurry home and offer to help in any way he could. The expedition was cut short and a rush made back to Europe. As a result many of his plants were lost in transit and the few which did get through had to endure the neglect imposed on gardening affairs in time of war. Not many survived. Among those which did were the nippy threepenny-bit rose, *R. far-reri*, the sweet-scented edelweiss, *Leontopodium haplophyl-loides*, the silver geranium, *G. farreri*, and *Buddleia alterni-folia* which Farrer described in its native habitat as sweeping "in long streaming cascades from all the loess cliffs like a gracious, small-leaved weeping-willow when it is not in flower, and a sheer waterfall of soft purple when it is."

Farrer's war was spent by day at the Ministry of Infor-mation, and by night, writing. He added to and corrected *The English Rock-Garden* and wrote two books about Kansu, *On the Eaves of the World* and *Rainbow Bridge*. And as soon as peace came he was off again to the Far East to carry on collecting. This time he had as his companion E. H. M. Cox who clearly respected his skill as a plantsman and was gentle with his whims.

Their destination was the result of elimination. Farrer did not want to return to Kansu. He longed, instead, to go to Nepal, but the political situation ruled that out. Sze-chuan and west Hupeh were exclusively Wilson's country and he wasn't generously disposed towards poachers. Like-wise, Yunnan was being methodically picked over by a Scotsman, George Forrest. The only region which offered a whole scalp in 1918–19 was Upper Burma, and there Farrer went with Cox.

The expedition brought in pelf, no more. After a pre-liminary trip Cox had to return to England, taking with him a vivid recollection of Farrer in the field:

*. . . his stocky figure clad in khaki shorts and shirt, tieless and collarless, a faded topee on his head, old boots, and stockings that gradually slipped down and clung about his ankles as the day wore on. The bustle of the early start; the constant use of the field glasses which always hung round his neck . . . his intense satisfaction when a plant was once in the collecting tin and was found worthy; his grunt of disapproval when it was worthless; the luncheon interval with its cold goat rissole and slab chocolate; his enjoyment of our evening tot of rum, a necessity in the*

*rains; and, above all, his indomitable energy that never spared a frame which was hardly built for long days of searching and climbing.*\*

Farrer was altogether an improbable character. There has never been an alpine gardener like him, nor a plant hunter so dashing and individualistic. Though indifferent, as Cox wrote, to appearances out in the field, in London society he was something of a dandy and not a little vain of the drooping black moustaches which gave him the look of a Mexican generalissimo. His manner of pronouncing proper nouns in his own way anticipated Churchill's idionsyncrasy and, as Chinese is not easy to catch precisely, he made it much more difficult for himself and everyone else by marking his maps and writing names in his books as they sounded phonetically to him. With all this, he was a kindly and cultivated man, a reader of metaphysical poetry and never without a complete set of Jane Austen, even in the trackless regions where wild flowers grow.

Though Cox had had to leave him, Farrer decided to continue collecting in Upper Burma, and set out on his plump pony (improbably called "Spotted Fat") accompanied by a faithful servant (improbably called "the Dragon"). His days were much the same as before; hunting out plants and taking seed whenever it was possible and worthwhile. He had a habit of disregarding plants which, in his expert opinion, would not tolerate transportation to an alien soil, or were not worth the trouble. As a result his herbarium, though put together with meticulous care, was a plantsman's not a botanist's. The dried plants were records of species from which later he intended to take seeds or propagative parts. Trying to dry them in the sodden Burmese jungles was an unenviable, next to impossible task.

Farrer did his best. He invariably did. But, although he was only forty, the climate caught at his chest and wrung out his strength. He could do less and less each day, and faded before his coolies' eyes. Unable to eat anything, he

\* *The Plant Introductions of Reginald Farrer: E. H. M. Cox* was reduced to a diet of whisky and soda. At length, eight thousand miles from home, in the unrelenting rain of the Chinese-Burmese borderlands he died; "without"—as "the Dragon" wrote to Mr. Cox—"giving any pain or trouble to us."

ESERVING a Roman triumph from gardeners all over the world for the number, quality and character of their introductions from Central Asia were two twentieth-century professional collectors. One, Frank Kingdon-Ward, typified the widely roving explorer who collected wherever he happened to be traveling or who, on occasion, set out to search for a particular plant. The second, George Forrest, typified the systematic plant hunter who combed district after district with such thoroughness that it soon became known as his.

Frank Kingdon-Ward shared with Joseph Hooker the inestimable benefit of being born into botanical circles. His father was professor of botany at Cambridge and many friends of the family were academic and field botanists who stimulated the boy's inquisitiveness by talking shop. Very quickly he showed an insatiable appetite for exploring, and would go to great lengths to gratify it. Simply to get to the Far East he took a schoolmaster's job out in Shanghai, and there broke his three-year contract because he had a chance of going up into west China with the American zoologist, Malcolm P. Anderson. He afterwards described this memorable journey by junk and on foot as an adventure across the breadth of China "from the coast to the edge of the world," and it inspired him to set up as a professional explorer-writer-photographer-botanical collector. Like Frank Meyer, thereafter he led a full and happy life doing precisely what he wanted and being paid for it in the bargain. His journeys provided him with material for travel books and articles, photographs, herbarium material for botanical institutions,* and—most profitable of all—with seeds and plants for gardeners. At first working for a nursery firm, and afterwards for private patrons or syndicates of gardeners, and once for the New York Botanic Garden, he hunted plants in parts of Yunnan, Szechuan, Upper Burma, French Indochina and southeast Tibet, as well as gleaning after Hooker in the Assam Himalaya, and between 1909 and 1957 he introduced hundreds of new species into cultivation. His largest bag was in Rhododendrons and primulas, but he also hunted down trees for coffin timber ("to the Chinese the best thing to look forward to in life is a first-class funeral"), some remarkable lilies and gentians, pitcher plants, tea plants, and the famous blue poppy of Tibet. He added new names and contours to unmapped regions and taxonomists have testified to their high regard for his work by using his own name for two genera, *Kingdon-Wardia* and *Wardaster,* and for no less than forty-two specific names. It is not surprising that with Shackleton and Scott, Teddy and Kermit Roosevelt, Whymper, Sven Hedin and General Pereira, Kingdon-Ward was very much a schoolboy's hero of exploration before World War II. At the age of seventy-two, he was still working and actually planning two more plant-hunting expeditions, one to North Persia and the other to Vietnam, when suddenly and unexpectedly he died. It seemed unbelievable for he had that weathered, sinewy quality which gives a man the appearance of being immortal.

Confident, competent and bold, Kingdon-Ward had a distinguished and rewarding career. Because no man accustomed to command could show forever the self-effacement of an Oriental, he was sometimes charged with vanity, and because success breeds envy he must have had his enemies. But any strains and stresses he experienced he decently kept under, which made him appear a very uncomplicated, friendly man. The botanical explorer's cap he chose to wear fitted him very comfortably.

---

* His dried specimens are now in Cambridge, Edinburgh, London, Chicago, New York and Gothenburg.

George Forrest, the methodical comber of districts, was different; a solitary made brusque by his lack of confidence, and as self-punishing as all stubbornly independent people. In the course of twenty-eight years he sent home from the high province of Yunnan no less than 31,000 herbarium sheets and an equal number of separate parcels of seeds; a demanding undertaking in which the physical and mental dangers and discomforts, with the intolerable tediousness of so much that had to be done, showed what the trained human frame and spirit could withstand. Forrest's were well trained. His personality had been forged a good deal by the bleakness of his background, by the loneliness and the un-happinesses of his youth, and by the hard business of ma-turing on a shoestring. For this reason his character seems to be more interesting than Kingdon-Ward's and his career is chosen to conclude this short account of modern plant hunting.

With David Douglas, Robert Fortune and many of the greatest collectors Forrest was a Scot of humble birth. He came from Falkirk in Stirlingshire though he went to school on the other side of the Lowlands, in the Ayrshire town of Kilmarnock. His first job in apprenticeship to a pharma-ceutical chemist was not to his liking though his meager knowledge of medicine and drugs and his willingness to practice a primitive form of surgery was very useful to him later in Central Asia. As a part of his training he had to study botany and collect local plants. But this, too, was not to his liking. He was another reluctant botanist with no more inclination to hunt plants than Augustine Henry. His twofold aim was to better himself and, if he could, work out of doors. Pharmacy could not hold him. He went off as a lad to Australia to work as a rouseabout in the bush, and he remained there several years. The work was out of doors but within the narrow standards of his class and background the life of fossickers and rouseabouts "down under" was scarcely respectable. He, with characteristic phlegm, said nothing about it at all. It is doubtful if he collected plants or took

any interest in botany out in Australia but when he returned to Scotland in 1902 his half-apprenticeship in pharmacy was useful to him. He applied for work in the Edinburgh Botanic Garden. Professor Sir Isaac Bayley Balfour
interviewed the stocky little man whose weatherbeaten, unsmiling face was rather daunting, and the professor apolo-
gized. He was very sorry, but the only available job was a
humble, clerky one in the herbarium, with poor pay and no
prospects, and was hardly suitable for a man of thirty. He
was surprised and not a little impressed when Forrest took
it.

Forrest was always a keen shot and fisherman and he
loved walking. Because he could not abide towns he walked
six miles into Edinburgh each morning and back again at
night. From nine to five he stood at a desk, scrutinizing and
arranging dried and pressed plants sent in from all over the
world. It would have been drudgery as tedious as a factory
hand's job on a conveyor belt, if Forrest, with Scottish
determination, had not determined to learn about and master the plants which at first he hated and which he came to
love. Within two years he was the botanic garden's expert
identifier and arranger of dried material; and then, by
chance—that precious ingredient so necessary to ninety percent of plant hunters—Sir Isaac was asked by a rich Cheshire industrialist to recommend a man who could undertake a
botanical exploration in western China. Cinderella's fairy
godmother could not have done more for George Forrest. Sir
Isaac highly valued his work in the herbarium but he would
not keep him from such an opportunity. The Cheshire industrialist accepted the recommendation.

In 1904 Forrest left for Yunnan, the Chinese province
"South of the Cloud" which was to become his special territory. Augustine Henry had collected there before him, and
other, less important plant hunters had collected sporadi-
cally and spasmodically in the area, but, after 1904, Northwest Yunnan was Forrest's preserve and he guarded it tena-
ciously. He was biting with those who considered that a

plant hunter could flit like a moth from place to place and
that no single collector had rights over an area, and he was
thunderously menacing with poachers and claim jumpers.

Right from the beginning he was enchanted by the
province which was to become his home. North Yunnan
wore a dramatic face; windswept downs, all at an altitude
higher than any mountain in his native Scotland, between
low ranges of mountain peaks and intersected by deep
gorges. The rivers, which tumbled and stormed below, occasionally disappeared into subterranean courses. Cart traffic
on the potholed tracks was possible, but only just. In the
west Forrest found that the mountain ranges were so high
and the rivers so deep that crossing either was a gargantuan
task. In the south and east, where Augustine Henry had
lived and where Forrest went to rest between seasons and
between expeditions, he found green country where large
lakes were common and fine crops of rice and maize and
buckwheat and opium poppies were grown.* He also liked
the Yunnanese who resembled the Scots in that they were
hill people and wore homewoven cloth marked with special
identifying patterns, in the manner of Highland tartans.
Their mode of life, if a Western parallel could be made, was
more French than anything; and this, again, was much to
Forrest's taste. He never cared for going into society, nor for
entertaining, but when he was tricked into it he found
Yunnanese society less formidable than similar gatherings
in Scotland, and once he had become used to the order of
dishes, he found the food more palatable than the tasteless
and boring diet he had been brought up on. A meal in
Yunnan began, Scandinavian fashion, with salty fish bits,
moved on to rice with vegetables especially the ubiquitous
radish and turnip, then to eggs, duck or pork, and finished
with a clear and delicately flavored broth of chicken and
mushroom which cleaned the palate. In his twenty-eight
years there Forrest learned to appreciate this classic order

* Opium was being produced in large quantities when Forrest first
went to Yunnan, though the antiopium edict of 1906 brought the industry
officially to a halt.

and, in the end, far preferred it to what he called "dropping hunks of steak into a pond of brown Windsor."

Everything, then, was to be nearly perfect for George Forrest in Yunnan except that, when first he arrived there, the political situation was boiling up into an eruption. The unpoliced and uncontrollable marches had never been in a settled state of order, and the ordinary hostilities had been exacerbated by a British expedition to Lhasa under the command of Francis Younghusband, former political agent of Tonk. His idea was to negotiate a settlement with China and to settle relations between India and Tibet. In neither was he successful, and he made the great mistake of forcing his way into the Tibetans' holy city at the head of troops. They resented this so bitterly that after his withdrawal every white man in the frontierlands was automatically classed as a "White Devil." It was at this unpropitious moment that George Forrest arrived in Yunnan. But with Scottish obstinacy, British sangfroid, and the average plant hunter's indifference to outside concerns, he refused to be worried by the threat of Tibetan guerillas (who were generally Buddhist monks) and he set about the business of collecting.

There was no holding Forrest in such a delectable paradise for plant hunters. He established a permanent base at Teng-yueh and with a party of seventeen servants and collectors he set off north, moving up the river valleys of the Shweli and Salween, then across the divide to the river Mekong. Eventually he reached the French Mission Station at Tseku where in 1905 he set up a temporary headquarters as the guest of the old missionary-botanist Père Dubernard.

At Yaregong, on the Tibetan border some distance away, was one of the most remarkable of the French missionary-botanists, Jean André Soulié; a skilled physician, much loved by the local people, fluent in all the frontier dialects, and an inveterate collector who sent more than seven thousand dried specimens to Paris from the Tibetan marches. He was assisted there by yet another missionary-botanist Père Bourdonnec. In the spring of 1905 they were warned by friendly lamas that a frontier dispute was developing between the Tibetans and Chinese in which "White Devils" would stand very little chance of survival. The lamas had a long-standing affection for Soulié and begged him to leave instantly, but his year's botanical collections had not yet been sorted and packed for despatch and Soulié temporized.

A few weeks later Père Bourdonnec crawled into Tseku. He was half-starved, half-naked, in a terrible condition. He told Père Dubernard and Forrest of the warning they had been given at Yaregong, and that, true to prophecy, the mission had been attacked by Tibetan monks. He himself had managed to escape but Père Soulié had been taken prisoner. Dubernard had lived in the province many years and he found it difficult to believe they stood in any danger at Tseku, but then more news came from Yaregong. Poor Soulié had been tortured with increasing cruelty for fifteen long days and nights and then, mercifully, shot. Moreover, the same Tibetan monks who had murdered him were about to descend upon Tseku.

Père Dubernard ordered an immediate evacuation. Forrest's party added to the mission staff made the total up to eighty. They fled. Twenty-four hours later the menace which at Tseku was so chilling seemed, somehow, to lose part of its reality. They caught an easy air of confidence from one another. Their pace slackened. There was even talk of turning back. It was at this point, bunched together in a river valley, that the Tibetan monks caught up with them.

Sixty-eight out of eighty were killed; among them all of Forrest's personal following save one. Soulié's assistant, Père Bourdonnec, having escaped from one massacre, was now shot through with poisonous arrows and while shrieking and writhing in agony was chopped to bits by double-handed swords. Old Père Dubernard was seized and tortured, quite literally, to death.

Forrest, new to the country, managed to escape. He hid up by day and tried to move south at night. The Tibetan monks hired women scouts to track the few who had escaped the massacre, and on the second day of his run Forrest discarded his boots because they made distinctive tracks. In forty-eight hours all he had to eat was a handful of parched peas and a few ears of wheat. The female scouts came so close to tracking him that he took to an icy stream wading down its course with the water up to his chest. Despite this he was spotted and had occasion to thank God that he was little for his hat was shot through with two poisoned arrows. By making a violent effort he outdistanced his pursuers, but they kept hard at his heels. He wrote later:

*At the end of eight days I had ceased to care whether I lived or died; my feet were swollen out of all shape, my hands and face torn with thorns, and my whole person caked with mire.*

Starvation drove him to risk approaching a village. There, happily, the people were friendly towards him; but, unhappily, they gave him parched barley to stay his hunger and this swelled up inside him causing him agony for hours.

Clutching at his belly he ran on, through canebrakes and along river torrents. Then it began to rain. The Tibetans were still on his trail. He saw them, and their torches at nighttime. Slightly changing his direction he made a way for six days over glaciers, snow and ice and tip-tilted, jagged, limestone strata which ribboned his feet. At last he reached what he thought must be a safe region, and there, in a path on the edge of a maize field, he stepped on a farmer's *panji*—a bamboo stake, sharpened and firehardened, stuck into the soil as a booby trap.

*The spike, fully an inch in breadth, passed straight between the bones of my foot, and protruded a couple of inches from the upper surface.*

He tore his foot free, stumbled on, and eventually found refuge in a mission house in a town where Chinese troops were garrisoned. Another famous French missionary, Père Monbeig,* was also there, having escaped from his station in the north.

It took many months before Forrest's pierced foot was properly cured, and quite as long for him to trust the sight of a Tibetan. But from this harrowing honeymoon his relationship with Yunnan ripened into a fine and highly romantic marriage.

His success as a plant hunter and as a specialist in rhododendrons was quite phenomenal. Indeed there were complaints that he was too efficient, too thorough, and sent home far too many seeds. Gardeners, however keen they were to raise new species, simply could not cope with the influx of seeds from Yunnan especially as Kingdon-Ward and Joseph Rock were also sending huge quantities to Europe and America. His superb ability to delegate and organize was responsible for the size of his collections. Whereas most modern plant hunters preferred to take seed and plants for drying with their own hands, Forrest adopted and developed Augustine Henry's idea of training and sending out collectors. He did it on a massive scale—as the executive, the chief of staff who received reports of discoveries, sent scouts to look over likely areas, and delegated seed gatherers at harvest time. His most enviable talent was for training his men; choosing them all from the same village so that they were related to one another and had a common loyalty to him; instructing them in what to look out for, how to cover ground systematically, how to take specimens for drying, and to memorize precise and detailed information about plant habitats. When they brought in seed at harvest time he superintended its drying, and he selected the best for sending to England. He also wrote up all the field notes in his own hand. As he was a trained botanist rather than a practical gardener some of his introductions were of small use to horticulture, but there was no denying his conscientiousness nor his ability to organize men and

* Nine years later Père Monbeig was chopped to bits by frenzied Tibetan monks in the station where Soulié had been murdered.

hold their loyalty. And it would be a mistake to think of him simply as a tented staff officer sending waves of private soldiers into the front line without doing any of the collecting himself. Far from it. He covered huge areas of ground, noting plants and their sites so that gatherers could be sent out at seeding time. The machine he created worked so smoothly that it went on operating when he was on leave in England, and even after his death it took some time to run down. His friend at Teng-yueh, Rolla Rowse, continued sending home packets of seed as they were brought in by the trained collectors.

Forrest's long and happy career in Yunnan could have met with no more satisfactory end than it did. His men had been collecting over a very large area and the season had been good. He wrote a letter home from Teng-yueh towards the end of 1931:

*When all are dealt with and packed I expect to have nearly, if not more than two mule-loads of good clean seed, representing some 4–5,000 species, and a mule load means 130–150 lbs. That is something like 300 lbs. of seed . . . If all goes well I shall have made a rather glorious and satisfactory finish to all my past years of labour.*

While the last parcels were being packed he went snipe shooting. Because he had had pains in his chest he was carried out to the paddy fields in a chair and he sat on a low wall between the drowned fields while his bearers walked some distance away to flush the birds towards him. A noise made him look up. A snipe was drumming overhead, toppling at an immense speed and with that extraordinary throbbing sound of vibrating wing tips. Forrest leapt to his feet and fired. The snipe fell, and so did he. Both, when they were picked up, were dead.

# ❧ Appendices

PLANT FRONTIERS are not easy to account for, nor are they easy to map. The world's divisions into climatic and physical regions, and the artificial boundaries imposed by difference of race, language, modes of living and thinking hardly correspond at all to the frontiers of plant distribution. North America, for example, has been divided into four floristic regions: Arctic, Atlantic North American (divided into Northern and Southern), Pacific North American, and Caribbean. Yet climatically it includes twice that number of provinces. And no system of geobotany can successfully account for the eccentricities of plant distribution when one alpine meadow needs sometimes to be considered in separation from its neighbor, or one section of a Burmese rain forest regarded as different from the rest, because each alone is endowed with unique botanical riches. There is the noted example of a line of division between the Arctic flora of America and the Arctic flora of Greenland. And, on a much smaller scale, there are tiny regions with unique floras which command the attention of serious plantsmen. There is the Great Orme for instance; no more than a hill, attached as if by accident to the Welsh seaside town of Llandudno which has a fascinating flora; and the small, mountainous area of Gargano on the Adriatic coast of southern Italy which is a positive Cinderella's ball for botanists. Most fantastic of all is the rocky plateau above the Kaieteur Falls in Guyana described by A. Hyatt Verrill in his *Wonder Plants and Plant Wonders,* where he claims many strange plants are forced to a gigantic size by the warm, moist conditions. Among them are stout, lily-like plants which collect water at the base of their eight-feet leaves, and in these vegetable pools live "golden frogs and tiny silvery fish which have never been found anywhere else on earth."

Three other points have to be kept in mind.

First, there is a curious and unaccountable similarity in floras between certain, far-flung regions. Astoundingly, for example, there is a close connection between the floras of the eastern seaboards of the United States and those of eastern continental Asia and Japan.

Second, it is important to recall that floristic maps which inadequately express altitude are of little use. As all collectors have discovered on hills of any size, the vegetation and flora vary considerably at different heights up to the summit.

Third and last, however firm a plant frontier appears to be it must always be open to invasion. Seed dispersal by many ingenious methods from the explosion of released spring coils to burrs caught on clothing make all plant frontiers fluid, open to attack in force when a strong wind blows thistle, bullrush and dandelion down, or by "fifth column" penetration through the alimentary canal of a single finch. If a similar habitat exists elsewhere and a seed can be transported there naturally without damage, the plant's original frontier is broken. It is on account of this that anomalies occur making mongrels of most floristic regions and national floras. Plants from the Americas have been discovered in Ireland. Arctic plants have been found growing in the bland English west country. Others, endemic to the Basque country have popped up unexpectedly in Wexford, Cork and Clare. Wall pennywort, a plant highly esteemed by the Japanese and truly native to the Orient, accommodates itself on the Mediterranean littoral and the moist English west country. White bryony is a great favorite of English people, unknown to Americans, and hails originally from the tropics. In all these cases frontiers have fallen and boundaries altered shape. Plant life has evolved.

Unhappily, plant territories are sometimes artificially tampered with by speculators and exploiters. Inevitably there was a strong spirit of competitiveness when plant hunting was so profitable, and some very disagreeable things were done in the name of profit.

One particularly horrid illustration will do.

In 1870, when the Prussians showed they were determined to extend their influence in Europe far, far beyond the Pomeranian bog from which they had originated, one of their number, a professional plant hunter, bought from a tea planter in high India a variety of the Slipper Orchid which grew in a small and limited area, and which—so far as he could see—was entirely unknown. It had a tinge of jade in its cream and violet blossoms, and was certainly worth buying. He took a number of specimens and nurtured them. Generously he named the orchid after Spicer, the tea planter, *Cypripedium spicerianum;* then, with unbelievable malignity, this thorough son of Prussia ruthlessly destroyed the whole wild colony so that he alone would enjoy the distinction of introducing a unique orchid into the markets of the West.

Inexcusable depredations such as this have never been common but they have added to the fluid state of all plant frontiers. Yet, in type, and bearing each of their weaknesses and limitations in mind, plant frontiers do exist, and it is this, and not the readily understood fact that grass is greener on the other side of every hedge, that has accounted for man's need to travel far and often under dangerous circumstances in pursuit of valued plants. When he has found them, noted a description, the exact location, the altitude, their associates, the nature of the soil and surroundings, he is faced with the problem of transporting his plants home, wherever that might be, and of recreating as far as possible the original habitat.

At its simplest, an original habitat is recreated when an apricot is grown in England sheltered by a south garden wall; and at its grandest when such a modern masterpiece as the Climatron in the Missouri Botanical Garden is made to house over a thousand tropical plants in addition to a collection of orchids. This is the most advanced of all attempts to create an artificial substitute for original habitats —a large geodesic dome made of light metal arranged in hexagonal patterns and, as well as plants, stuffed with mechanical apparatus programmed by a supervisory data center. Before a panel studded with buttons, switches and dials, a supervisor sits—like God at the nerve-center of creation— producing at will dry tropics, mist forest, tropical lowland jungle, and a bland oceanic climate; bounding, in fact, over a good many plant frontiers in one magnificent leap.

two / *Plant Names*

IN ITS TIME, plant naming has aroused as much controversy as any other scientific subject.

Although Latin is internationally understood, a good many gardeners refuse to use botanical names under any circumstances. They regard it as both unnecessary and vexing to those who might otherwise be drawn in to share their pleasures. The more recherché among them would "English" even the best known botanic names such as fuchsia, dahlia, hydrangea, chrysanthemum and pyrethrum, though whether the "Englished" or the Latinized version is easier to memorize is a matter of conjecture.

The disadvantages of using vernacular names make themselves especially obvious to anyone who talks or writes about a plant. English and American names for the same plant are dissimilar quite often. The English fathen is pigweed in the States, lesser periwinkle turns into myrtle, wall pepper is love-entangle, the rare, lacelike orchid, creeping ladies' tresses, makes the startling change to dwarf rattlesnake-plantain. Then, in different American states and different English counties local names vary quite as much as local customs. Duckweed, for example, the ordinary *Lemna minor,* is less rich in equivalents than most English natives, but it still has ten, among them boggart creed, jenny green-teeth, duck's meat and toad spit.*

All these difficulties exist in the one vernacular language. They are multiplied many times for the amateur botanist who collects in foreign lands when changes of

* *An Englishman's Flora:* Geoffrey Grigson (Phoenix House, 1958) gives the fullest list yet printed of English vernacular names.

language, dialect and accent are frequent. That beautiful if noisome iris, *I. foetidissima,* the gladdon or roast beef plant, has many extraordinary European names: Xyris Puant in France, Giglio dei Morti and Flamma Fetida in Italy, Korallenschwertel in Germany, and its Turkish name has the ring of a bitter curse—Fena Kokulu Kuzgun Kilici.

There are, though, equal disadvantages in Latin. Possibly the most surprising is the exasperating fashion in which botanical names are altered with or without authority. Critics of the use of Latin have something to say when what they call marsh yellow cress, named in Latin by Dr. Candolle *Nasturtium palustre,* is renamed *Rorippa islandica* on the authority of two later botanists Thellung and Schinz; when the melancholy thistle, called *Carduus heterophyllus* on the authority of no less a man than Linnaeus himself, has its name changed by Scopoli, an Italian, to *Cirsium helenionides.* And what did the great Reichenbach think he was up to when he changed his own nomination *Habenaria chloroleuca* to *Platanthera chlorantha?*

Such alterations are inevitable as the science of botany matures and is more subject to accurate classifying; in other words, as it becomes altogether clearer to real botanists it becomes more and more opaque to the rest of us, and this is a pity because so many who might well enjoy collecting are too easily frightened away by the apparent labor of studying elementary botany and nomenclature. They may be reassured by a note on the purpose of using botanical names.

From the time of the early Greeks, plants were named with a short description of their chief characteristics. The aim was to be brief, apposite and provide an easily identifiable word-picture for other people to recognize. It was too clumsy a device to succeed if only because descriptions of colors, scents, and even of form, are largely subjective, but in particular because the economic use of words appeared to be beyond most botanists. Their names were tediously long and, as a means of identification, a spectacular failure.

Since then, chiefly because of Bauhin and Linnaeus, the vegetable kingdom has been divided and subdivided again and again into an orderly pattern.

At its simplest, it breaks down like this:

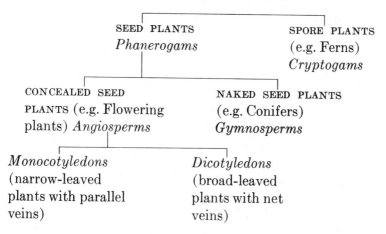

ALL VEGETATION

SEED PLANTS
*Phanerogams*

SPORE PLANTS
(e.g. Ferns)
*Cryptogams*

CONCEALED SEED PLANTS (e.g. Flowering plants) *Angiosperms*

NAKED SEED PLANTS (e.g. Conifers) *Gymnosperms*

*Monocotyledons* (narrow-leaved plants with parallel veins)

*Dicotyledons* (broad-leaved plants with net veins)

All monocotyledons and dicotyledons are divided into:

ORDERS
FAMILIES (once called "Natural Orders")
GENERA
SPECIES

Bauhin managed to impose on most of his contemporaries the excellent idea of economizing in words and giving each plant no more than two names, but it was Linnaeus who formalized the plan, and the two-word system was permanently established. The first corresponds to our surname; the second, the equivalent of our Christian name, is used to describe the species within that genus. The comparison is more meaningful than whimsical. A human family has one surname, and each member his own distinguishing Christian name. So it is with a genus and, really, it is only necessary to know two names of any plant. The overfastidious would say this is insufficient. Species are as splittable as genera, and they add a third or even a fourth name to show the distinction. These are the varietal names which should follow the abbreviation "var."; e.g. the Jew's mallow with double flowers is *Kerria japonica* var. *flore-pleno*. Enthusiasts for this precise classification occasionally go to extraordinary lengths and are called "splitters"; the rest of us, content with only two names, are called "lumpers."

Unlike plant names which are generally printed in italics (and, nowadays, with no capitals for specific or varietal names), the abbreviation "var." is printed in ordinary Roman type. So is the abbreviation "syn." for synonym (the renamers still cause sufficient chaos for it to be necessary to put alternative names) and the names of cultivars should also be enclosed in single quotes; e.g. from among the large number of lily hybrids, *Lilium longiflorum* 'White Queen,' and *L. philippinense formosanum* 'White Superior.'

Hybrids are sometimes natural. That is, they have occurred spontaneously through clandestine love matches rather than arranged marriages. The fruit of one such liaison in 1797 was to produce an illegitimate but exceedingly beautiful magnolia. In the garden of a M. Soulange-Bodin not far from Paris two species of magnolia grew: a wine-violet *M. liliflora* and *M. conspicua* which has flowers of an uncertain white color—almost that of dressed tripe. Between them they produced one seedling—the parent of all stocks of *M. soulangeana*.

But more often than not hybrids are the fruit of laboratory work, research and careful breeding by private enthusiasts or commercial nurserymen. Amazing garden flowers like the sweet peas of Unwin and the lupins of Russell commemorate the hybridizers with their names. Other garden hybrids are named from their place of origin, e.g. *Cystisus kewensis*, a Tom Thumb broom which occurred unexpectedly at Kew, or from the chief area of their distribution, such as the French and African marigolds of today. Both the last are, in fact, Mexican but one was mainly introduced to

Europe through North Africa and the other through France. Many of the actual names used for cultivars show a strange taste for the commonplace or downright ugly. Whereas wild flowers and many garden plants enjoy beautiful and memorable names, some of the grandest achievements of the hybridizer's art have been saddled with the opposite. Can the French marigold, 'Miniature Lemon Drop' compare with Snapdragon, or the African Marigold, 'Chrysanthemum-flowered Super Glitters' with Scarlet Pimpernel? An exquisite and unusual lily deserves a better name than 'Corsage'; a clematis with lavender flowers and slate-blue anthers suffers forever as 'W. E. Gladstone'; three of the finest geraniums ever produced are doomed as 'Fifth Avenue', 'Foxtrot' and 'Grand Slam'; and no one can begin to imagine what possessed the rosemen when they named their triumphs 'Cafe', 'United Nations', 'Rumba', 'My Fair Lady', 'Honeymoon' and 'Lilibet'. It seems unfair to flowers.

Linnaeus hardly ever made this mistake. He and his followers were "lumpers"; they had two primary objectives, to give a distinctive name to each genus, and an accurately descriptive specific name. With the former, Linnaeus honored the pantheon of Greece and Rome, the great men and heroes of the past, his friends and fellow-botanists—though not all. With a salty sense of humor he named an American plant *Milleri* after his rival botanist, Miller, because the flower had a calyx which was "close, short and completely enclosing the seeds." The description suited Miller to a nicety. He, too, was short, plump, and notoriously tight-fisted with information and with seeds.

With the specific name it was a question of describing the plant's outstanding characteristic, generally in Latin or in Latinized Greek. So *Stapelia bufonia* is named after the Dutchman, J. van Stapel, and it does look "toad-like," and another species in the same genus is hairy, *S. hirsuta*.

A casual acquaintance with such words as *glaucescens* (bluish-green), *sylvestris* (of woods), *trichocarpa* (hairy-fruited), *officinalis* (literally, 'of the shop' i.e. the apothecary's, and therefore, the type of herb he would naturally have in stock), *scutatus* (shield-like), *festalis* (gay), *ligulate* (tongue-shaped); in fact, any one of the more than seven hundred * from *abbreviatus* (shortened) to *zeylanicus* (from Ceylon), does make botany as international as music and disease, and does add to a clearer understanding of the subject, and, in the long run, to the pleasures of collecting.

Botanical Latin is odd; that is, to anyone whose acquaintance with the language has been strictly orthodox. Yet once it is appreciated, like Katisha's right elbow, it has a fascination that few can resist. Whole books have been written about its history, grammar, syntax, terminology and vocabulary, and they contain gems of information. The Latin for certain names of places is revealing: New Jersey turns out as Nova Caesarea; Pembroke as Transwallia; Ipswich is made declinable as Gippeswicum, and the Paiken Islands are honored as Crocodilorum Insula. Much can be learned about watery habitats from these books, that an ordinary marsh (uligosa) is by no means the same as a peat bog (turfosa), or even a water-meadow which is periodically flooded (inundata), or a swamp which dries up like a sponge in summer (paludes). Then, if it gives pleasure to decline nouns with strange endings nothing could be more pleasurable than manipulating *bostryx* (*m.*). It has a musical ablative in the singular. By, with, or from a *bostryx* is simply *bostryche*.

Today it is sometimes necessary to decline botanical substantives; that is, on those dodo-like occasions when a new plant is found and named. When the discoverer or introducer has his name Latinized to make a specific it is expressed either in the possessive-genitive case, e.g. *Clematis davidi* (David's clematis) or as an adjective, e.g. *Prunus davidiana* (Davidian peach.) There is no strict rule about which use is correct, and following one or other practice has, in its time, caused trouble in botanical circles. No greater or more bizarre affair has ever occurred than in the struggle

---

* C. O. Booth has compiled a very useful list which appears on pp. 453–459 of his *Encyclopaedia of Annual and Biennial Garden Plants* (Faber and Faber, 1957).

between supporters of *Victoria regia* and the supporters of *Victoria regina* in the naming of the Amazon water lily which took place over a hundred years ago. It involved eminent botanists of all nations, two learned societies, half the drawing rooms of Potsdam, Paris and London, a collection of explorers, two dukes, and Queen Victoria herself.

*three / Plant Collecting*

ANYONE with sufficient interest to go out and collect generally knows what he is doing. He will not gather a single
specimen or one of a small colony if the species is rare. He is
aware that plants are stimulated to more vigorous growth
by being thinned, and—though a collector—he has the interests of the species much in mind and will never do a
hundredth of the harm done to wild life by "legitimate"
despoilers such as farmers, roadmen, roadmakers, and urban
developers.

This is the answer to those cranky conservators who
maintain that the only proper method of "collecting" plants
at the present time is with a camera. Besides, as has been
noted on page 110, neither photographs nor even sketches
can be considered as accurate a representation as a dried
and pressed plant.

Collections can be arranged according to a variety of
systems. The most usual is to classify them under each
genus: or, if this is too large a number (there are over five
hundred genera in Britain alone), they may be arranged in
families (see p. 259). Physiological botanists will arrange
their collections to show the functions of plant parts, and
morphological botanists arrange theirs to show distinctive
forms. And some will prefer to make collections of special
types of plant; climbers, for example, or parasites or insecti-
vorous plants. But some of the most interesting are made
according to habitat; that is, arrangements of plants taken
from both natural environments such as rock screes or river
banks or heaths or wild woods or marsh saltings or sand

dunes, and from man-made habitats like cattle pastures, stone walls and roofs, railway sidings, wharf banks and sewage farms, motorway verges and rubbish dumps. These divisions may be subdivided again into those which are wet and those which are dry, those which have acid soils and those which have alkali, and so forth.

EQUIPMENT IN THE FIELD

The modern amateur botanist will need to consider using some or all of the following:

1. A collecting box—either a proper botanist's vasculum, japanned green or black, and with a snap lid like that of a snuff box; or simply a rigid, plastic container slung on a piece of string.

2. If plants are to be pressed on the spot—either a portable press containing drying papers and tied with straps; or an old paperback book held fast both lengthways and sideways by thick rubber bands.

3. A supply of plastic bags for carrying aquatics and marsh plants, and specimens which are to be transplanted into the garden at home.
   It is also important to have lengths of thin, paper-covered wire to nip the necks shut.

4. A trowel and pocket knife, the smallest possible pair of shears and a pair of scissors; or a type of Bowie knife which can serve both as a cutter and digger.

5. A watchmaker's lens for examining minute identifying marks.

6. Some tiny, numbered labels for attaching to plants. Notes on each plant's habitat and precise location can be written against the corresponding number in a small, pocket book, because it is important to know a plant's location if, later, seeds have to be gathered from it.

PREPARATION FOR DRYING

1. *Cleaning:*
   Dust off mud and insects and the soil from roots with a
   pastry brush.
   Remove dead, diseased, unshapely or surplus parts.
   If the plant is too large, trim it down to size.
2. *Treatment of fleshy plants:*
   Plants like euphorbias, brassicas and seaside species
   have to be treated like lobsters and thrown into boiling water. Otherwise they will continue growing in
   the press.
3. *Aquatics:*
   Limp water plants cannot be taken directly from a pool
   or they collapse and lose their form. Float them from
   the pool into a saucer. Then lift them out on a strip
   of thin paper to dry.
4. *Preserving color:*
   (a) Some plants have a tendency to go black when
   dried; e.g. mints and figworts. Iron them when fresh
   under a layer of brown paper with a hot iron.
   (b) The color of orchids can most effectively be preserved by smoking them for ten minutes with a sulphur candle in a closed box. They look pallid when
   freshly smoked but the colors soon return and remain
   fixed for a long time.
   (c) With all other plants, change the drying papers as
   often as possible. This helps, though it does not guarantee, to preserve colors.

DRYING & PRESSING

*Materials:*
1. Drying paper: use commercial filter paper or unglazed
   tissue paper—but, if possible, not blotting paper or
   newspaper.
2. Cotton buds and tweezers for arranging specimens; and

Spencer-Wells forceps which click into a fixed position until released for dealing with brambles, etc.
3. Thin pieces of glass to weigh down plants while arranging their parts.
4. Ventilators—wooden slats or lengths of heavy-gauge
wire—to place crosswise between layers of drying
plants.
5. A press—either a botanical press with boards and straps,
or an improvisation made of two plywood boards
pressed down by scale weights or books or bricks.
6. Thin cotton wool or lint for laying under thick flower
heads so that they will be under equal pressure and
remain unshriveled.

*Method:*
1. Cut off delicate flowers and dry them separately. They
can be reattached later to the stem.
2. Drying takes from a few days to a fortnight.
Change the drying papers as frequently as possible.
The first change should be made within twenty-four
hours.
3. As soon as papers are removed from the press, dry them
out in an oven or in the sun.
4. When all the specimens are dry, put them aside between
store sheets of newspaper.


MOUNTING & STORING

*Materials:*
1. Strips of music binding paper to stick down the plants,
and a pure gum to attach small parts. It is wise not
to use sticking tape which is too strong, easily discol-
ors, collects dust round the edges, and contracts dras-
tically within a year or two.
2. Reasonably heavy paper of a uniform size, quarto or
folio.
3. Snap-back folders or, better still, box files closed with
tapes, for mounted specimens.

*Method:*

1. Try to resist the temptation to make an attractive arrangement of mixed species on one page. It is easier in the end to mount one species only on a single sheet because it allows them to be arranged systematically.
2. Label each species as carefully as possible with its botanic and local names, habitat, exact location, and the date it was collected.

   The information may be written on the sheet, or against a reference number in a separate notebook.
3. Store the plants in a dustproof file or made-up cabinet and in a dry place.

   Keep the collection free from insects with napthalene pads or mothballs.

# ❧ A List of Selected Books

*Not all the works referred to in the text, notes and appendices are listed in this bibliography. Those of particular interest which do appear are marked with an asterisk.*

Allan, M. *The Tradescants*. London: 1964.
———. *The Hookers of Kew*. London: 1967.
Anderson, A. W. *The Coming of the Flowers*. London: 1950.
Arber, A. *Herbals, Their Origin and Evolution, a Chapter in the History of Botany, 1470–1670*. Cambridge: 1912.
Bean, W. J. *Trees and Shrubs Hardy in the British Isles*. 1st ed., 2 vols. London: 1914.
Bentham, G. *Flora HongKongensis*. London: 1861.*
Booth, C. O. *Encyclopaedia of Annual and Biennial Garden Plants*. London: 1957.*
*Botanical Mercury, The* (Thomas Johnson); Vol. I (1634); Vol. II (1641)*
Boyle, F. *About Orchids*. London: 1893.*
Bretschneider, E. *History of European Botanical Discoveries in China*. London: 1898.*
Carpenter, E. F. *The Protestant Bishop: being the life of Henry Compton, 1632–1713, Bishop of London*. London: 1956.
Cox, E. H. M. *Farrer's Last Journey*. London: 1926.
———. *The Plant Introductions of Reginald Farrer*. London: 1930.*
———. *Plant Hunting in China*. London: 1945.
Dampier, W. *A New Voyage Round the World*, ed. A. Gray. London: 1927.*
Darwin, C. *Journal of researches into the Natural History and Geology of the countries visited during the voyages of H.M.S. Beagle*. 2nd ed., London: 1845.*

————. On the Origin of Species. London: 1859.*

Darwin, E. Botanic Garden. London, Litchfield: 1789–91.*

David, A. Diary 1866–1869, ed. and trans. H. M. Fox. Cambridge, Mass.: 1949.

Dodge, B. S. Plants that have changed the World. London: 1962.

Douglas, J. Journal kept by David Douglas during his travels in North America, 1823–1827. London: 1914.

Elwes, J. H. J., and Henry, A.: The Trees of Great Britain and Ireland. 7 vols. London: 1906–1913.*

Elwes, H. J. Monograph of the Genus Lilium. London: 1880.*

Evelyn, J. Kalendarium Hortense. 6th ed. 8° London: 1676.*

Farrer, R. The Garden of Asia. London: 1904.

————. On the Eaves of the World. 1st ed. London: 1917.*

————. The English Rock Garden. London: 1919.*

————. Rainbow Bridge. London: 1921.*

Fletcher, H. R. The Story of the Royal Horticultural Society, 1804–1968. London: 1969.

Fortune, R. A Residence among the Chinese; inland, on the coast, and at Sea. London: 1857.

————. Three Years' Wanderings in the North Provinces of China. London: 1847.

————. Yedo and Peking. London: 1863.*

Gardener's Magazine, The (ed. John Claudius Loudon), 1833 and 1839.

Gerard, J. The Herball. F°, London: 1597.*

Good, R. The Geography of the Flowering Plants. London: 1947.*

Goodspeed, T. Plant Hunters in the Andes. London: 1961.

Gourlie, N. The Prince of Botanists, Carl Linnaeus. London: 1953.

Gray, A. Observations upon the Relationship of the Japanese Flora to that of North America. Mem. Amer. Acad. Arts and Sci.: New Ser.: 1859.

Green, J. R. A History of Botany in the United Kingdom. London: 1914.

Grigson, G. The Englishman's Flora. London: 1955.*

Hadfield, M. Pioneers in Gardening. London: 1955.

Hagberg, K. Carl Linnaeus. London: 1952.

Hagen, V. von. South America Called Them. London: 1949.

Harvey, A. G. Douglas of the Fir. Cambridge, Mass.: 1947.

Henry, A. and Elwes, H. J. The Trees of Great Britain and Ireland. 7 vols. London: 1906–1913.

Herbst, J. F. *New Green World, A Life of John Bartram*. London: 1954.

Hooker, J. D. *The Botany of the Antarctic Voyage*. Pts. 1–3. London: 1844–60.

———. *Himalayan Journals*, 2 vols. London: 1854.*

———. *Outline of the Distribution of Arctic Plants*. Trans. Linnaeus Society, London: 1861.

Kämpfer, E. *History of Japan*. 3 vols. London: 1906.*

Kew, H. W. and Powell, H. E. *Thomas Johnson, M.D. of Selby*. London: 1932.

Kingdon-Ward, F. *The Romance of Plant Hunting*. London: 1924.

———. *Pilgrimage for Plants*. London: 1960.

Lemmon, K. *The Golden Age of Plant Hunters*. London: 1968.

Linnaeus, C. *Flora Japponica*. 8° Amsklaedami: 1737.*

———. *Species Plantarum*. Holmiae: 1753.*

Livingstone, J. *Observations on the Difficulties which have existed in the Transference of Plants from China*. Hort. trans., vol. III: 1820.*

Lloyd, C. *William Dampier*. London: 1966.

McClintock, D. *Companion to Flowers*. London: 1966.

Millican, A. *The Travels and Adventures of an Orchid Hunter*. London: 1891.*

Ohwi, J. *Flora of Japan*. Washington, D. C.: 1965.

Oliver, F. W. *Makers of British Botany*. Cambridge: 1913.

Oliver, S. P. *The Life of Philibert Commerson*, ed. G. F. Scott Elliott. London: 1909.*

Parkinson, J. *Paradisi in sole Paradisus terrestris*. London: 1629.*

———. *Theatre of Plants*. London: 1640.*

Porter, C. L. *Taxonomy of Flowering Plants*. San Francisco: 1959.

Raven, C. E. *John Ray, Naturalist, his life and works*. Cambridge: 1942.

Ray, J.: *Catalogus plantarum Angliae, et insularum adjacentium*. 8° Londini: 1670.

———. *Synopsis methodica stirpium Britannicarum*. 8° Londini: 1690.

Robinson, W. *The Wild Garden*. London: 1870.

Sargent, C. S. *Plantae Wilsonianae*. Cambridge, Mass.: 1913–17.*

Siebold, P. F. van. *Manners and Customs of the Japanese*. London: 1841.

Sighart, J. *Albert the Great, of the order of Friar-preachers, his life and scholastic labours.* From original documents by J. S., trans. from the French by T. A. Dixon. London: 1876.

Smith, E. *The Life of Sir Joseph Banks.* London: 1912.

Spruce, R. *Notes of a Botanist on the Amazon and the Andes.* London: 1908.

Standish & Noble. *Practical Hints on Ornamental Plants and Planting.* London: 1852.

Stearn, W. T. *Botanical Latin.* London: 1966.

Taylor, G. *Some Nineteenth Century Gardeners.* London: 1951.

Tergit, G. *Flowers through the Ages.* London: 1961.

Turner, W. *A New Herball.* F° London: 1551.*

Turrill, W. B. *The Royal Botanic Gardens at Kew.* London: 1959.

——. *Joseph Dalton Hooker.* London: 1964.

Veitch, J. H. *Hortus Veitchii.* London: 1906.

Verrill, A. H. *Wonder Plants and Plant Wonders.* New York: 1939.*

Wallich, N. *Upon the Preparation and Management of Plants during a voyage from India.* Hort. trans., Vol. I, 2nd Series: 1835.

Ward, N. B. *On the Growth of Plants in Closely Glazed Cases.* London: 1842.

Wilson, E. H. *A Naturalist in China with Vasculum, Camera and Gun.* Intro. C. S. Sargent. London: 1913.

# ❧ Index